ANTIMICROBIAL THERAPY FOR NEWBORNS

SECOND EDITION

GEORGE H. McCRACKEN, JR., M.D.

JOHN D. NELSON, M.D.

Department of Pediatrics
University of Texas Health Science Center at Dallas
Southwestern Medical School
Dallas, Texas

GRUNE & STRATTON
A Subsidiary of Harcourt Brace Jovanovich, Publishers
New York   London
Paris   San Diego   San Francisco   São Paulo
Sydney   Tokyo   Toronto

Library of Congress Cataloging in Publication Data

McCracken, George H.
   Antimicrobial therapy for newborns.

   Includes bibliographical references and index.
   1. Infection in children—Chemotherapy.   2. Infants
(Newborn)—Diseases—Chemotherapy.   3. Anti-infective
agents.   I. Nelson, John D.   II. Title.   [DNLM:
1. Anti-infective agents—Therapeutic use.   2. Infant,
Newborn, Diseases—Drug therapy.   QV 250 M132a]
RJ275.M3   1983   618.9'201   83-12617
ISBN 0-8089-1565-7

Grune & Stratton
111 Fifth Avenue
New York, New York 10003

Distributed in the United Kingdom by
Grune & Stratton Inc. (London) Ltd.
24/28 Oval Road, London NW 1

Library of Congress Catalog Number 83-12617
International Standard Book Number 0-8089-1565-7
Printed in the United States of America

Contents

Preface

While revising this book, we read what we had written five years ago in the preface to the first edition. We were bemused by the apologetic tone of the words in that preface. We talked about "therapeutic orphans," we bemoaned the lack of pharmacokinetic data for many drugs given to neonates, and we expressed the hope that well-designed studies of antimicrobial drugs would be conducted in newborns.

The magnitude of the revision we have done is an index of how far the field has progressed in five years. We have not just updated chapters by adding a few references. New antibiotics have appeared, and we have learned a great deal more about the old drugs. Thus this is not merely a revision, it is a new book.

The section on antimicrobial agents (Chapter 2) contains detailed information on the clinical pharmacology and dosage schedules of both the old and the new drugs. This is designed as a reference source for physicians. By contrast, the emphasis in the clinical section is on decision making concerning the use of antimicrobial drugs in newborns. The clinical chapters are not intended to be encyclopedic. They are, rather, a backdrop to the scenario of infectious diseases of neonates. You will have to seek elsewhere for detailed clinical information.

We hope that our pragmatic approach will help physicians with rational, safe, and effective use of antimicrobial drugs for newborns.

GEORGE H. MCCRACKEN, JR.
JOHN D. NELSON

PART I

Pharmacologic Aspects

1
Pharmacologic Concepts in the Newborn

PHYSIOLOGIC FACTORS AFFECTING PHARMACOLOGY

The rapidly changing physiologic processes that are characteristic of the neonatal period may profoundly affect the pharmacokinetic properties of antimicrobial agents. Dosage must be considered in relation to infant maturity as reflected by gestational and chronological ages. Dosage recommendations for 1-day-old infants do not necessarily apply to infants who are 10 days or 30 days old. Data derived from studies of normal adults cannot be applied to infants without risking either ineffective or toxic drug dosages.

Absorption, distribution, metabolism, and excretion of drugs are constantly changing during the neonatal period. Many physiologic and metabolic processes, acting either singly or in concert, influence the pharmacokinetics of antibiotics in neonates. These processes include, among others, drug biotransformation, extracellular fluid volume, protein binding, and renal immaturity.

A number of enzyme systems are deficient or absent during early neonatal life. As a result the metabolism of antibiotics may be profoundly altered. For example, immaturity of hepatic glucoronyl transferase in neonates results in diminished conjugation of chloramphenicol to the inactive acid glucuronide. This, coupled with diminished glomerular and tubular function, produces elevated serum concentrations of both free and conjugated chloramphenicol. Accumulation of the free, antimicrobially active drug in serum is associated with cardiovascular collapse and death (gray syndrome) in some infants treated with excessive dosages of this drug.

3

Drugs may directly inhibit enzyme action, resulting in accumulation of metabolic products that are toxic to the infant. A good example of this phenomenon is hyperbilirubinemia associated with administration of novobiocin to neonates. This macrolide drug is a potent inhibitor of hepatic glucuronyl transferse the substance that catalyzes bilirubin conjugation. Sulfonamides or nitrofurantoin may induce hemolysis in infants with erythrocyte glucose-6-phosphate-dehydrogenase deficiency.

The extracellular fluid volume of the newborn is approximately 35 percent of body weight, which is considerably larger than that of children and adults. Although there is a rapid loss of excess fluid during the first days of life, the extracellular fluid volume does not decrease to adult proportions until late infancy. The volume of distribution of drug is different for each class of antibiotics, and peak serum concentrations of a drug generally correlate inversely with the distribution volume. For example, after being given identical doses, preterm infants have larger peak serum concentrations of kanamycin than full-term infants, which is due in part to a smaller volume of kanamycin distribution in the premature baby. An additional consideration is that the excretion of drugs distributed in the expanded extracellular volume of preterm infants usually is delayed. This may explain the observation of shorter serum gentamicin half-life values in older infants than in neonates, even when the rates of creatinine clearance are similar.

The clinical significance of antibiotic protein binding is unknown. As a general rule, a protein-bound drug has little or no antibacterial activity. Because protein—drug complexes tend to be retained in the intravascular space, distribution into tissues may be limited. Excretion of a protein-bound drug is primarily by renal tubular mechanisms. Generically similar drugs with lower protein binding potential may have enhanced antimicrobial activity and greater tissue distribution. With one possible exception, however, there are no clinical data to confirm this assumption. In the early 1940s penicillin K, a preparation that is highly protein-bound, was found to be less effective in the treatment of syphilis than were other penicillins with less protein binding.[1] By contrast, methicillin and dicloxacillin appear to have comparable clinical efficacy in the treatment of staphylococcal disease despite greater protein binding of the latter drug (98 percent versus 37 percent). However, a well-designed prospective study comparing these two drugs in staphylococcal disease has not been performed.

The affinity of a drug for serum protein may have important clinical consequences. For example, sulfisoxazole is known to compete with bilirubin for binding sites on albumin. This greater affinity of the sulfonamides for albumin releases bound bilirubin into the circulation, which may then deposit into extravascular sites such as the geniculate ganglia, producing kernicterus in some neonates. Novobiocin may also displace substances from protein binding sites, but the clinical significance of this displacement in neonates is unknown.

The penicillins and aminoglycosidic drugs are excreted primarily by glomerular filtration in newborn and young infants. Diminished glomerular filtration rates during the neonatal period result in sustained serum concentrations of drug and prolonged half-life values. Because renal function is constantly changing in the first month of life, pharmacokinetic data must be obtained at various times during this period in order to determine the proper dose and frequency of administration for each antibiotic. The two pharmacologic functions used to evaluate diminished glomerular and renal tubular function in neonates are the serum half-life and clearance of drug from plasma. These two pharmacokinetic properties are used to calculate dose intervals of a drug. Improper dosage schedules have resulted in administration of excessive antibiotic dosages, leading to accumulation of drug in serum to potentially toxic concentrations. Permanent ototoxicity in some neonates caused by streptomycin and kanamycin is explained in part on this basis.

PHARMACOLOGIC EVALUATION OF
ANTIMICROBIAL AGENTS IN NEONATES

Because of the ethical prohibitons against testing drugs in healthy babies, basic pharmacokinetic data must be obtained from studies of sick neonates. The antimicrobial agent to be tested must first have undergone Phase I studies in adults. Phase I studies, as defined by the Federal Drug Administration (FDA), usually involve administration of drugs to healthy adult volunteers in order to obtain data regarding absorption, metabolism, excretion, and acute safety. These data serve as guidelines for initial dosage and safety precautions in neonates.

The first step in evaluating an antibiotic for use in neonates is to determine the drug's *in vitro* effectiveness against commonly encountered bacterial pathogens of this age group. Organisms that are resistant to the currently available drugs of the same class should be susceptible to a new antimicrobial agent. For example, a new aminoglycosidic drug should be effective *in vitro* against kanamycin- and gentamicin-resistant coliforms and ideally against *Pseudomonas* strains also.

The next step in evaluation of an antibiotic is to obtain pharmacokinetic data by substituting a single dose of the new drug for a prescribed drug of the same class. The decision to treat an infant with antimicrobial agents is made by the physician caring for the infant and not by the investigators. Substitution of only one dose does not expose the infant to the jeopardy of a prolonged period of either possibly ineffective therapy or toxic concentrations that might occur if an untested new drug were administered repeatedly. Multiple serum samples are obtained by the heel-stick technique and assayed by a micromethod that is capable of measuring antimicrobial activity in 0.02-ml specimens. Urine is also collected in 4-hour fractions over the 12-hour or 24-hour test period in order to determine rate and amount of antibiotic excretion.

From the serum concentration time curve constructed from these data, the regression line for the disappearance rate is calculated by least mean squares analysis and used to estimate the serum half-life, volume of distribution, and plasma clearance of the drug. Alternatively, computer programs such as the NONLIN least square regression program can be utilized to determine the pharmacokinetics and adaptation of the data to a one- or two-compartment model. These basic pharmacokinetic data are analyzed with regard to gestational and chronological ages and used to formulate dosage schedules and intervals between doses in newborn infants. The dosage regimen is then tested in a larger number of neonates, and concentrations of the antibiotic in serum are monitored after repeated administration. Thus amplification of clinical pharmacologic data is obtained at the same time that efficacy and safety are being evaluated. Studies of safety must involve the following minimum number of tests obtained at the start and completion of therapy: complete blood count, urinalysis, and tests to determine levels of serum creatinine, serum glutamic oxalic transaminase, and serum bilirubin (direct and indirect fractions). Safety studies of antimicrobial agents in neonates are not complete when drug therapy is stopped. Long-term prospective studies of infants who are treated with new antimicrobial agents must be undertaken to rule out possible adverse effects such as ototoxicity, renal dysfunction, or impairment of physical or mental development.

We have found that this method of dosage information and antibiotic evaluation assures safe and effective use of new drugs in newborns.

REFERENCES

1. Committee on Medical Research: The United States Health Service and the Food and Drug Administration. JAMA 131:271–275, 1946.

2
Clinical Pharmacology and Dosage

BETA-LACTAM ANTIBIOTICS

The penicillins have been used for many years in the treatment of neonatal bacterial infections. In general, these drugs are safe and effective for therapy of streptococcal, pneumococcal, and susceptible staphylococcal diseases. The broader spectrum of antimicrobial activity possessed by ampicillin and carbenicillin has led to greater use of these drugs against such pathogens as *Listeria monocytogenes,* enterococci, *Proteus mirabilis,* some *Escherichia coli* strains, and, in the case of carbenicillin, against *Pseudomonas aeruginosa.*

Adverse reactions to the penicillins are rare in the newborn. A significant clinical problem is erythema and induration that may occur at the site of repeated intramuscular injections. We have documented diminished absorption of penicillin and ampicillin injected into such indurated areas. Immune-mediated reactions such as urticaria, serum sickness, or anaphylaxis rarely occur during the early months of life. Further, administration of a penicillin to an infant of a known hypersensitive mother has not been a clinical problem, presumably because of the privileged immunologic sanctuary that the placenta provides for the fetus. It is theoretically possible that an adverse reaction could develop in an infant who is breast feeding from a hypersensitive mother, because of the gastrointestinal absorption of sensitized lymphocytes present in colostrum and milk.

Although the older cephalosporins have been used extensively in children and adults, there are few pharmacologic data and little clinical experience with these drugs in newborns and young infants. These agents have limited usefulness for neonates because of the greater efficacy and safety record of the penicillins and new generation cephalosporins in this age group. Furthermore, the older cephalosporins should not be used for systemic therapy of neonatal bacterial infections unless meningitis has been definitely excluded. The older cephalosporins do not penetrate into cerebrospinal fluid (CSF) in sufficient concentrations to inhibit the bacterial pathogens of neonatal meningitis.

Some newer beta-lactam antibiotics have been approved by the Food and Drug Administration (FDA) for use in newborn infants (moxalactam, cefotaxime, and mezlocillin) while others (cefoperazone, ceftriaxone, ceftazidime, and piperacillin) are likely to be so by the mid-1980s or sooner. Where available, information on these new drugs will be given in the appropriate sections below.

Penicillin G

Penicillin has been used since the early 1950s for treatment of neonatal bacterial disease. Although it is universally accepted as a standard for therapy in newborns, there have been few studies of its clinical pharmacology during the neonatal period.

The penicillins act by interfering with biosynthesis of bacterial cell wall mucopeptides. For the past 30 years many *Staphylococcus aureus* and coliform strains have shown increased resistance to penicillin G by virtue of R factor mediated penicillinase production. In most hospitals over 50 percent of *S. aureus* strains are resistant (MIC greater than 1 μg/ml) to penicillin G. Most pneumococci and group A streptococci are inhibited by 0.01 μg/ml penicillin G. A penicillin-resistant pneumococcal strain (MIC greater than 1.0 μg/ml) has been isolated from blood or CSF of 2 infants in the United States,[1,2] and it is estimated that 5–10 percent of strains are relatively resistant or "insensitive" (MIC 0.1–1.0 μg/ml) to penicillin.[2-3] The MIC values for group B streptococci are approximately 10 times greater than those for group A organisms, 90 percent of group B strains being inhibited by 0.06 μg/ml or less. Several GBS strains have minimal bactericidal concentrations (MBC) that exceed the MIC by 32 or more times.[4] These GBS strains are referred to as *tolerant* strains. Their clinical significance is uncertain; clinical and bacteriologic failure of penicillin therapy has been attributed to this phenomenon.[4]

Mean peak serum concentrations of 22–25 μg/ml (range 8–41 μg/ml) are observed 0.5–1.0 hour after a 25,000-u/kg (15.5 mg/kg-) dose of penicillin G is given intramuscularly (see Table 2-1).[5] Serum concentrations 12 hours after the dose is administered are dependent on the plasma clearance rates and vary from 4 μg/ml in infants weighing less than 2000 g at birth and 0–7 days old to 0.4 μg/ml in infants weighing 2000 g or more at birth and older than 7 days.

Table 2-1

Pharmacokinetic Properties of Penicillin G in Newborns

Birthweight/Age Groups	Peak Serum Concentration § (µg/ml)	Serum Half-life (h)	Volume of Distribution (ml/kg)	Plasma Clearance (ml/min/1.73 M^2)
*Crystalline penicillin G**				
≤ 2000 g				
≤ 7 days	24.0	4.9	668	30
8–14 days	23.6	2.6	650	48
> 2000 g				
≤ 7 days	22.3	2.6	511	52
8–14 days	21.0	2.1	603	75
Procaine penicillin G†				
≤ 7 days‡	8.9	6.1	1702	50
8–14 days	6.2	5.4	2755	93

* Dose: 25,000 u/kg (15.5 mg/kg)
† Dose: 50,000 u/kg (31 mg/kg)
‡ Average weight = 3100 g
§ Mean values

When doses of 50,000 u/kg (31 mg/kg) are administered to newborn infants, mean peak serum concentrations of approximately 40 μg/ml are observed.[5] Grossman and Ticknov[6] administered 1 million units of penicillin G intramuscularly to 19 infants (average dose 330,000 u/kg). A mean serum level of 140 μg/ml was observed 2 to 4 hours after injection, and concentrations of approximately 7 μg/ml were present 24 hours later.

The half-life of penicillin in serum is inversely correlated with birthweight and postnatal age. During the first week of life, a mean half-life value of 4.9 hours is seen in infants weighing less than 2000 g at birth, and a mean half-life value of 2.6 hours is seen in those weighing 2000 g or more at birth. These values are shortened to 2.6 hours in the low birthweight babies, and 2.1 hours in the larger infants who are 7 days of age and older.[5]

The calculated volumes of penicillin distribution in the newborn are slightly larger in the lower birthweight infants than in larger babies, but the differences are small enough so that there is no substantial effect on peak concentrations of penicillin in serum.

The clearance of penicillin from plasma is directly correlated with birthweight and postnatal age. As the clearance rates increase, the half-life values of penicillin in serum decrease.

The concentrations of penicillin in urine vary considerably. The highest concentrations are noted during the first 4 hours after a 25,000-u/kg dose of penicillin G and range from 31–2000 μg/ml.[4] Approximately 30 percent of the adminstered dose is excreted in the urine over a 12-hour period. Excretion of penicillin in newborns is correlated directly with clearance of creatinine.[5,7]

Compared to other beta-lactam antibiotics, penicillin G does not penetrate well into CSF. Peak concentrations of approximately 1–2 μg/ml are observed 0.5–1.0 hour after 50,000-u/kg doses of penicillin G are given intramuscularly.[8] These concentrations are maintained for approximately 4 hours during the first days of treatment for meningitis, but by day 5 of illness the concentrations of penicillin in CSF 4 hours after the dose is administered are approximately 0.1 μg/ml. By the 10th day of illness, it is often impossible to detect penicillin in CSF 2 hours after the dose is given.

The dosage recommendations for penicillin G are shown in Table 2-2. For bacterial diseases other than meningitis, 25,000 u/kg (15.5 mg/kg) are administered every 12 hours for infants 0–7 days old, and every 8 hours for infants older than 7 days. For patients with suspected or confirmed meningitis, the individual dose is 50,000–75,000 u/kg (31–47 mg/kg) administered every 12 hours for infants during the first week of life and every 6 hours thereafter. Recent reports of relapse of group B streptococcal meningitis in some infants emphasize the importance of either increasing the total daily dose of penicillin G to 150,000–250,000 u/kg, depending on the birthweight and age of the infant or adding an amino-

Table 2-2
Dosage Recommendations for Penicillin G

Individual dose	25,000 u/kg (15.5 mg/kg); 50,000–75,000 u/kg (31–47 mg/kg) for meningitis
Intervals	Every 12 h for infants < 2000 g and 0–7 days; every 8 h for infants < 2000 g and > 7 days and for those ≥ 2000 g and 0–7 days; every 6 h for infants ≥ 2000 g and > 7 days
Route	IV (preferred) as 15–30-min infusion; IM
Total daily dose	50,000 u/kg for infants < 2000 g and 0–7 days; 75,000 u/kg for infants < 2000 g and > 7 days and ≥ 2000 g and 0–7 days; 100,000 u/kg for infants ≥ 2000 g and > 7 days (dose is doubled for meningitis)
Comments/cautions	Larger dosages recommended for treatment of group B streptococcal meningitis than for pneumococcal meningitis; excessive dosage (> 250,000 u/kg/day) should be avoided because of possible CNS toxicity
Trade names	Potassium or sodium penicillin G for injection (Squibb)
Supplied as	Potassium penicillin G for injection, 1-million u vials for reconstitution; sodium penicillin G for injection, 5-million u vial for reconstitution

glycoside to the regime for treatment of this disease.[4,9] Intravenous administration is preferred, and penicillin G should be infused over a 15–30-minute period. Bolus injection of penicillin G, particularly in the dosages required for meningitis, may result in seizure activity caused by central nervous system toxicity.

Procaine Penicillin G

Procaine penicillin G in a single daily dose of 50,000 u/kg (31 mg/kg) produces peak serum concentrations of approximately 9 μg/ml in infants 0–7 days old and of 6–7 μg/ml in older neonates (see Table 2-1).[5] Serum concentrations of 1 μg/ml or greater are maintained for 24 hours during the first week of life and for approximately 12–16 hours in older neonates. There is no accumulation of penicillin in serum after 7–10 days of daily doses of procaine penicillin G, and the drug is well tolerated without evidence of local reaction at the site of injection or of systemic reaction.

The half-life of penicillin G in serum after administration of the procaine preparation is approximately 5.5–6.0 hours during the neonatal period. These values are longer than those observed after administration of the crystalline penicillin G preparation, primarily because absorption from

Table 2-3
Dosage Recommendation for Procaine Penicillin G

Individual dose	50,000 u/kg (31 mg/kg) for all neonates
Intervals	Every 24 hours for all neonates
Route	IM
Total daily dose	50,000 u/kg (31 mg/kg)
Comments/cautions	Used for congenital syphilis and minor cutaneous infections caused by susceptible organisms
Trade names	Crysticillin A.S. (Squibb), Wycillin (Wyeth)
Supplied as	300,000 u/cc and 600,000 u/cc

the injection site continues over a longer time period. The clearance of pencillin G from plasma following procaine penicillin administration is comparable to that following administration of the crystalline preparation. The volumes of drug distribution are 3- to 5-fold greater than those of crystalline penicillin G, reflecting the deposition of drug in the muscle mass.

Procaine penicillin G should be used only for therapy of congenital syphilis and minor cutaneous infections caused by highly suspectible bacteria such as group A streptococci. A dose of 50,000 u/kg (31 mg/kg) administered intramuscularly once daily is appropriate for all neonates (see Table 2-3)

Benzathine Penicillin G

A 50,000-u/kg (31 mg/kg-) dose of benzathine penicillin G given intramuscularly to newborns results in detectable antimicrobial activity for at least 12 days.[10-11] Peak serum concentrations of 0.4-2.6 μg/ml (mean, 1.2 μg/ml) are reached 12-24 hours after the dose is given, and concentrations of 0.07–0.09 μg/ml are still detectable 12 days later. Urinary concentrations of penicillin after a 50,000 u/kg dose of benzathine penicillin G range from 4–170 μg/ml for 7 days, and 0.3–25 μg/ml for 8–12 days after the dose is given. The benzathine preparation appears to be well tolerated by neonates (see Table 2-4).

The principal indication for benzathine penicillin G is treatment of congenital syphilis when central nervous system involvement has been excluded.[12] A single 50,000-u/kg dose is currently recommended by the US Public Health Service Committee on Venereal Disease for asymptomatic infants with congenital syphilis. Benzathine penicillin has also been used as prophylaxis for group A streptococcal infection during nosocomial outbreaks.

Table 2-4
Dosage Recommendations for Benzathine Penicillin G

Individual dose	50,000 u/kg (31 mg/kg)
Intervals	Single dose
Route	IM
Total Daily Dose	Total dose 50,000 u/kg
Comments/cautions	Used primarily for congenital syphilis (if CNS syphilis is ruled out) and rarely for minor group A streptococcal infections
Trade names	Bicillin L-A (Wyeth)
Supplied as	Bicillin L-A injection, 300,000 u/cc

Orally Administered Penicillins G and V

There is rarely an indication for orally administered penicillin in new-borns. Huang and High[13] gave potassium penicillin G orally to newborns. Serum concentrations of 1.3 µg/ml at 1 hour and of 0.6 µg/ml at 6 hours were measured in premature infants after a 22,000-u/kg (14 mg/kg-) dose was given. The serum concentrations in full-term babies were 2.1 µg/ml at 0.5 hours and 0.2 µg/ml at 6 hours after the dose was given.

We are unaware of pharmacologic data about serum concentrations following administration of penicillin V to newborns. Our work has shown that a 12,500-u/kg (8 mg/kg-) dose of penicillin V given to infants aged 1–8 months results in peak serum concentrations of 1–2 µg/ml at 0.5 1.0 hour after the dose is given.[14] The peak concentrations after administration of penicillin V to fasting infants are approximately twice those attained after administration of the drug with milk. Serum concentrations at 2, 4, and 6 hours after the dose is given are not significantly different for the two modes of administration.

Ampicillin

Ampicillin is commonly used in combination with an aminoglycoside as initial treatment for suspected or confirmed bacterial infections in new-born infants. Ampicillin is not as effective *in vitro* as is penicillin against pneumococci, streptococci, and susceptible staphylococci; the spectrum of antimicrobial activity of ampicillin, however, is broader than that of peni-cillin. Approximately 90 percent of group B streptococci and *L. monocy-togenes* are inhibited by concentrations of 0.06 µg/ml or less of ampicillin. Virtually all enterococci are inhibited and killed by 2.5 µg/ml or less of

Table 2-5
Pharmacokinetic Properties of Ampicillin (Dose, 50 mg/kg) in Newborns

Birthweight/Age Groups	Peak Serum Concentration* (μg/ml)	Serum Half-life (h)	Volume of Distribution (ml/kg)	Plasma Clearance (ml/min/1.73 M^2)
≤ 2000 g				
≤ 7 days	104	6.4	516	21
8–14 days	130	2.2	296	30
> 2000 g				
≤ 7 days	81	4.9	623	42
8–14 days	84	2.3	442	63

* Mean values

ampicillin. Almost all *P. mirabilis* and 50 percent of *E. coli* are inhibited by ampicillin. Approximately 60 percent of the gram-negative enteric bacilli isolated from CSF cultures of infants enrolled in the second Neonatal Meningitis Cooperative Study (1976–1978) were inhibited and killed by 10 μg/ml or less of ampicillin.[15] *Klebsiella, Enterobacter,* and *Pseudomonas* species are resistant.

Mean peak serum concentrations of approximately 40–60 μg/ml are noted 0.5–1.0 hour after 20–25-mg/kg doses of ampicillin sodium are administered intramuscularly.[16-17] The serum concentrations at 12 hours range from 1–15 μg/ml, with a mean of 5 μg/ml.

When a dose of 50 mg/kg ampicillin sodium is given, the ensuing peak serum concentrations are 100–130 μg/ml in infants weighing less than 2000 g at birth and 80–85 μg/ml in infants weighing 2000 g or more at birth.[18] The mean serum concentrations 12 hours after 50-mg/kg doses are 20–30 μg/ml in infants less than 7 days old and 3–5 μg/ml in older neonates (Table 2-5).

The half-life of ampicillin in serum correlates inversely with birthweight and postnatal age. Half-life values of 5.0–6.5 hours are demonstrated in infants less than 7 days old, and values of approximately 2 hours are demonstrated in those 7 days of age or older. The volume of drug distribution is greatest during the first week of life. Peak serum concentrations are inversely related to the volumes of ampicillin distribution.

The rate of ampicillin clearance from plasma is directly correlated to birthweight and postnatal age. In general, the half-life values of ampicillin are inversely correlated with the plasma clearance values during the newborn period.

Concentrations of ampicillin in CSF vary considerably and are dependent on the dosage, type of administration, and time after administration of the dose.[19] In young infants with *Haemophilus influenzae* meningitis, peak CSF concentrations of from 5–10 μg/ml and 2–5 μg/ml are observed at 0.5 hours after 50–mg/kg doses are given intravenously and intramuscularly, respectively.[19] Values of approximately 1 μg/ml or greater are maintained for about 4 days of therapy but decline thereafter to 0.1–1.0 μg/ml on the 10th day. The peak CSF concentrations exceed the MIC$_{90}$ values for group B streptococci and *Listeria* 20- to 100-fold and are equal to or several times greater than the MIC values for many susceptible *E. coli* strains.

Grossman and Ticknor[20] gave from 5 mg/kg to 50 mg/kg ampicillin trihydrate orally to fasting newborns. Peak serum concentrations occurred at 2–4 hours after the dose. A 20-mg/kg dose gave peak serum levels of 10–20 μg/ml, while a 30-mg/kg dose produced peak values of 20–30 μg/ml. These serum concentrations are approximately 25–30 percent of those observed after similar doses were given intramuscularly. Silverio and

Poole[21] demonstrated that the more soluble anhydrous preparation of ampicillin is absorbed more completely after oral administration to newborns, resulting in serum concentrations greater than those obtained with ampicillin trihydrate.

Studies in our own clinics have revealed that ampicillin trihydrate is absorbed as well in fasting infants as in those given milk with the drug. Peak serum concentrations of approximately 5 μg/ml occurred at 0.5–1.0 hour after 25-mg/kg doses.[14]

Ampicillin is a safe drug when administered parenterally to newborns. Nonspecific rashes and urticaria are rarely observed. Alteration of the gastrointestinal bacterial flora may occur after parenteral administration, but overgrowth with *Pseudomonas* or *Candida albicans* is unusual, as is diarrhea. Significant changes in the bowel flora and diarrhea are common with the oral preparations. Elevation of serum glutamic oxaloacetic transaminase (SGOT) and creatinine phosphokinase values may occur following intramuscular administration and most likely represents local tissue destruction at the injection site.

Extensive clinical experience indicates that ampicillin is safe and effective for therapy of neonatal bacterial infections. Because of its broad antimicrobial activity against many gram-positive bacteria, including group B streptococci, *L. monocytogenes,* and enterococci, and against certain gram-negative organisms such as *P. mirabilis* and many *E. coli,* ampicillin combined with an aminoglycoside is rational initial treatment for many types of suspected bacterial disease in neonates. Ampicillin and gentamicin, or one of the other aminoglycosides, continues to represent the most appropriate initial therapy of neonatal meningitis. Alternative regimens include ampicillin and moxalactam, or ampicillin and cefotaxime. Limited experience suggests that these combinations are comparable in efficacy and safety to ampicillin and an aminoglycose. Neither of these new beta-lactams should be used alone for initial therapy because they are ineffective against *Listeria* and enterococci. Ampicillin is the drug of choice, either alone or in combination with an aminoglycoside, for therapy of infections caused by *Listeria* or enterococci.

For bacterial infections other than meningitis, the individual dose should be 25 mg/kg administered every 12 hours for all infants 0–7 days old, and every 8 hours for infants 8 days or older. The dosage is increased to 50 mg/kg for therapy of meningitis and administered every 12 hours during the first week of life, and every 6 hours in infants 1–4 weeks old. A 15–30-minute intravenous infusion is the preferred administration route (Table 2-6).

In infants with otitis media or urinary tract infections who are to be treated with an orally administered antibiotic, we prefer amoxicillin to ampicillin because the former agent is more completely absorbed from the

Table 2-6

Dosage Recommendations for Ampicillin Sodium Trihydrate

Individual Dose	25 mg/kg; 50 mg/kg for meningitis
Intervals	Every 12 h for infants < 2000 g and 0–7 days; every 8 h for infants > 7 days and < 2000 g and for infants > 2000 g and 0–7 days; every 6 h for infants > 2000 g and > 7 days
Route	IV (preferred) as 15–30-min infusion; IM
Total daily dose	50 mg/kg for infants ≤ 7 days; 75 mg/kg for infants ≤ 7 days and ≥ 2000 g or for infants < 2000 g and > 7 days; 100 mg/kg for infants > 7 days and ≥ 2000 g (dose is doubled for meningitis)
Comments/cautions	Few or no indications for oral administration in the newborn
Trade names	Omnipen-N (Wyeth), Polycillin-N (Bristol)
Supplied as	All preparations available as 125-mg, 250-mg, and 500-mg vials for reconstitution

gastrointestinal tract, resulting in larger serum concentrations. Peak serum concentrations and bioavailability of amoxicillin are approximately twice those of ampicillin after comparable doses.[22] The dosage of amoxicillin for otitis media is 50 mg/kg/day in 3 divided doses and that for urinary tract infection is 30 mg/kg/day in 2 divided doses. It should be emphasized that newborns with urinary tract infections should initially receive parenteral antimicrobial therapy until bloodstream infection has been ruled out and the susceptibility of the urinary pathogen has been determined.

Carbenicillin

Carbenicillin was the first penicillin analog possessing activity against *Pseudomonas* and indole-positive *Proteus* strains. There has been only one comparative efficacy trial in which carbenicillin and gentamicin were compared with ampicillin and gentamicin for therapy of neonatal bacterial infections.[23] These two regimens were equally efficacious and safe in this relatively small clinical study.

Carbenicillin has bactericidal activity against many gram-positive and gram-negative bacterial pathogens. Like ampicillin, carbenicillin is effective *in vitro* against the two most common pathogens of neonatal septicemia and meningitis—*E. coli* and group B streptococci. *L. monocytogenes* and enterococci are relatively less susceptible *in vitro* to carbenicillin than to ampicillin.[24] *Klebsiella* and *Enterobacter* species and some *Pseudomonas* species other than *P. aeruginosa* are resistant to carbenicillin. *In vitro* studies

Table 2-7
Pharmacokinetic Properties of Carbenicillin (Dose, 100 mg/kg) in Newborns

Birthweight/Age Groups	Peak Serum Concentration* (μg/ml)	Serum Half-life (h)	Volume of Distribution (ml/kg)	Plasma Clearance (ml/min/1.73 M^2)
≤ 2000 g				
≤ 7 days	180	5.7	722	25
8–14 days	186	3.6	630	35
> 2000 g				
≤ 7 days	185	4.2	692	45
8–14 days	143	2.1	597	77

* Mean values

have demonstrated that gentamicin and carbenicillin combinations are synergistic against *P. aeruginosa* and many enterococci and *Listeria* strains.[24]

Carbenicillin-resistant *Pseudomonas* strains have been reported from areas such as burn units where the drug is used extensively. Constituitive beta-lactamases appear to be the primary mechanism of carbenicillin resistance.

The pharmacokinetics of carbenicillin are similar to those of ampicillin in newborns. A 100-mg/kg carbenicillin dose results in peak serum concentrations of approximately 180 μg/ml 1–2 hours after the dose is given in all neonates except those more than 2000 g at birth and older than 7 days, in whom peak serum concentrations of 140–150 μg/ml are observed.[25] Serum concentrations of 50μg/ml or greater are found 12 hours after the dose is given in all neonates 7 days or younger, after approximately 8 hours in low birthweight infants older than 7 days, and after 4–5 hours in larger and older babies (Table 2-7)

Serum half-life values for carbenicillin correlate inversely with birthweight and postnatal age. Mean half-life values of 4–6 hours are observed during the first week of life, and 2–3.5 hours in infants 1–4 weeks old. These values correlate inversely with the clearance of carbenicillin from plasma. As with ampicillin, clearances of 20–30 ml/min/$1.73M^2$ are observed in the low birthweight infants (less than 2000 g) during the neonatal period, while average values of 45–80 ml/min/$1.73M^2$ are observed in the larger babies. Yoshioka and coworkers[26] report similar pharmacokinetic data in newborn infants after intramuscular administration.

Because carbenicillin is eliminated by renal mechanisms, extremely large concentrations are present in the urine.[25] After a dose of 25–50 mg/kg is given, urine concentrations of 1000 μg/ml or greater are detectable. These concentrations are 10–50 times greater than the MIC values for most *Pseudomonas* and *Proteus* species. Excretion of carbenicillin, expressed as a percentage of the administered dose, is significantly correlated with clearance of creatinine in neonates.

Carbenicillin appears to be well tolerated and safe in newborns. Thrombocytopenia, hypokalemia, and allergic manifestations observed in older patients have not been reported in neonates. Some infants who receive carbenicillin intramuscularly will show mild elevation of the SGOT, which most likely represents destruction of muscle at the local injection site.

In summary, because of its broad antimicrobial activity, including activity against *Pseudomonas* and indole-positive *Proteus* strains, carbenicillin combined with either gentamicin or another aminoglycoside is a suitable regimen for initial therapy of neonatal bacterial disease, particularly in nurseries encountering *Pseudomonas* or *Proteus* infections.

Table 2-8
Dosage Recommendations for Carbenicillin Disodium

		Alternative Schedule
Individual dose	100 mg/kg	100 mg/kg "loading" dose; 75 mg/kg for infants ≤ 2000 grams; 100 mg/kg for infants > 2000 grams
Intervals	Every 12 h in infants, every 8 h for infants ≤ 2000 grams and > 7 days or ≥ 2000 g and 0–7 days; every 6 h for infants > 7 days and > 2000 g	Every 8 hours for infants < 2000 g and 0–7 days; every 6 hours for others
Route	IV (preferred) as 15–30 min infusion; IM acceptable if volume not too large	
Total daily dose	200 mg/kg for infants 0–7 days and < 2000 g; 300 mg/kg for infants < 2000 grams and > 7 days and ≥ 2000 g and 0–7 days; 400 mg/kg for infants > 2000 grams and > 7 days	
Comments/cautions	Observe for bleeding disorder in patients with renal failure; may produce hypokalemia; "ampicillin-like" skin rashes seen in older patients have not been observed in neonates	
Trade names	Geopen (Roerjig), Pyopen (Beecham)	
Supplied as	Geopen, Pyopen for injection, 1-g vials for reconstitution	

Dosage recommendations per carbenicillin in neonates are presented in Table 2-8. A dose of 100 mg/kg is recommended, given every 12 hours to infants 0–7 days and weighing under 2000 g, every 8 hours to those weighing under 2000 g and greater than 7 days old or 2000 g or more and 0–7 days old, and every 6 hours to infants weighing 2000 g or more and older than 7 days.

A 15–30-minute intravenous infusion is the preferred administration route. Carbenicillin (or ticarcillin) and an aminoglycoside should not be mixed in the infusion bottle before administration nor should they be given at the same times in patients with renal failure.[27] Aminoglycosidic activity is inhibited under these conditions, and the effect is greatest when carbenicillin and gentamicin or tobramycin are used together.[28]

Ticarcillin

Ticarcillin has pharmacologic and toxic properties that are virtually identical to those of carbenicillin. It is more active *in vitro* against *P. aeruginosa* than is carbenicillin. The pharmacokinetics of ticarcillin in neonates have been determined, but there are no studies in this age group that compare the efficacy and safety of this agent with those of carbenicillin.

Mean-peak serum concentrations of ticarcillin of 189 μg/ml and 159 μg/ml were detected at 1 hour after a 75 mg/kg dose was given intramuscularly to infants 1–7 days of age who weighed 2000 g or less, or more than 2000 g, respectively (Table 2-9).[29] A 100-mg/kg dose given to infants over 2000 g and an average age of 34 days produced a mean peak serum level of 125 μg/ml.

The half-life of ticarcillin in serum correlated inversely with age and ranged from 2.5 hours to 8 or more hours in the first week of life and from 1 to 3 hours during the remainder of the neonatal period.[29] As with carbenicillin, the plasma clearance of ticarcillin increased with increasing postnatal age and correlated inversely with the serum half-life (Table 2-9).

Because of the theoretical advantage of the increased *in vitro* activity against *P. aeruginosa*, we prefer ticarcillin to carbenicillin for therapy of suspected *Pseudomonas* infection. Initial therapy in this situation is usually with ticarcillin and an aminoglycoside, either gentamicin or tobramycin. A simplified dosage schedule, similar to that of carbenicillin, is 75 mg/kg administered every 12 hours to infants under 2000 g and 0–7 days old, every 8 hours to those 2000 g or more and 0–7 days old or under 2000 g and more than 7 days old, and every 6 hours to infants 2000 g or more and over 7 days old (Table 2-10). An intravenous infusion of 15–30 minutes is preferred. As with carbenicillin, ticarcillin should not be mixed with an aminoglycoside before administration nor given to patients with renal insufficiency.[28]

Antistaphylococcal Antibiotics

Antistaphylococcal antibiotics were used frequently in neonates in the late 1950s and early 1960s. When phage group 1 *S. aureus* strains became resistant to penicillin, the only drugs available to treat staphylococcal disease were novobiocin, vancomycin, and bacitracin. In 1963 methicillin was introduced in the United States as the first antistaphylococcal penicillin. This agent has been used extensively in neonates in spite of the relative paucity of data concerning its pharmacology and safety in this age group. Other antistaphylococcal drugs such as nafcillin and oxacillin have been used in some nurseries, while the newer antibiotics such as cloxacillin and

Table 2-9

Pharmacokinetic Properties of Ticarcillin in Newborns

Weight/Age Groups*	Peak Serum Concentration § (μg/ml)	Serum Half-life (h)	Volume of Distribution (ml/kg)	Plasma Clearance (ml/min/1.73 M^2)
≤ 2000 g* and ≤ 7 days	189	5.6	663	31
> 2000 g† and ≤ 7 days†	159	4.9	715	54
1–8 weeks‡ (average, 34 days)	125	2.2	761	118

* Dose: 75 mg/kg IM
† Dose: 75 mg/kg IM
‡ Dose: 100 mg/kg IM
§ Mean values

22

Table 2-10
Dosage Recommendations for Ticarcillin Disodium

Individual dose	75 mg/kg
Intervals	Every 12 h in infants < 2000 g and 0–7 days; every 8 h for infants < 2000 g and > 7 days and for those ≥ 2000 g and 0–7 days; every 6 hours for infants > 2000 g and > 7 days
Route	IV (preferred) as 15–30-min infusion; IM acceptable if volume not too large
Total daily dose	150 mg/kg for infants < 2000 g and 0–7 days; 225 mg/kg for infants < 2000 g and > 7 days and for those ≥ 2000 g and 0–7 days; 300 mg/kg for infants > 2000 g and > 7 days
Comments/cautions	Well tolerated in neonates. Hematologic abnormalities (thrombocytopenia, neutropenia, anemia) and rash possible but unusual in neonates.
Trade name	Ticar (Beecham)
Supplied as	Ticar for injection, 1-g vials for reconstitution

dicloxacillin have not been approved for use in newborns because of insufficient pharmacologic and clinical data.

The antistaphylococcal penicillins are resistant to beta-lactamase (penicillinase) by virtue of a substituted side chain that acts by steric hindrance at the site of enzyme attachment. Most penicillin-resistant staphylococci are inhibited by 2.5 µg/ml or less of methicillin, by 0.4 µg/ml or less of nafcillin, and by 1–2 µg/ml or less of vancomycin. Methicillin-resistant *S. aureus* strains account for less than 5 percent of infections in most areas of the United States. There have been several nursery outbreaks of infection caused by methicillin-resistant *S. aureus*. In 1977 Sabath and associates[30] called attention to the *in vitro* phenomenon of tolerance among *S. aureus* strains to the antistaphylococcal agents. *Tolerance* is the ability of an antibiotic to inhibit but not kill a microorganism. By definition, tolerance exists when the MBC of an antibiotic is at least 32-times larger than the MIC. The prevalance of tolerant *S. aureus* strains is unknown, and the clinical implications of this laboratory finding are unclear. We request our clinical laboratory to determine the MIC and MBC values for all *S. aureus* strains isolated from infected body fluids. Because of the cross-tolerance among the antistaphylococcal drugs, several agents should be tested, including methicillin, nafcillin, and vancomycin.

The advantage of some of the antistaphylococcal penicillins of greater *in vitro* activity than methicillin is possibly offset by the fact that these drugs are protein-bound to a greater extent than is methicillin. For example, the degree of protein binding of cloxacillin (93–95 percent) and of dicloxacillin (95–97 percent) diminishes *in vitro* antimicrobial activity when tests are performed in serum. The clinical significance of protein binding is unknown.

Methicillin

Mean peak serum concentrations of 55–60 μg/ml occur 0.5–1.0 hour after a 25-mg/kg dose in infants 2000 g or less at birth, and concentrations of 45–50 μg/ml in infants more than 2000 g at birth, during the first 2 weeks of life.[16-17, 31] Peak concentrations of approximately 40 μg/ml are found in older neonates. The mean serum concentrations 12 hours after the dose is given are 3–5 μg/ml in low birthweight babies 0–14 days old, and 0.5–1.5 μg/ml in all other neonates, with the exception of infants who are more than 2000 g at birth and 15 days or older; in this last group, serum concentrations of approximately 1 μg/ml are observed 6 hours after the dose is given (see Table 2-11).

The half-life of methicillin in serum is inversely correlated with birthweight and postnatal age. The mean half-life value is approximately 3 hours in low birthweight infants during the first 2 weeks of life, and 2 hours in the larger babies of the same age. The mean values are 1–2 hours in neonates who are 3–4 weeks old.

The volume of methicillin distribution correlates inversely with peak serum concentrations. Distribution volumes of approximately 400–500 ml/kg are observed during the neonatal period. The clearance of methicillin from plasma increases throughout the neonatal period and correlates inversely with half-life values.

Like the other penicillins, methicillin appears to be well tolerated and safe in newborns. Methicillin appears to be associated with urologic toxic effects in 5 percent or less of children treated with methicillin. Of 117 methicillin-treated children in our institution, 4 (3.4 percent) developed hematuria and other manifestitations consistent with either interstitial nephritis or cystitis.[32] These abnormalities occurred exclusively in those who were older than 5 years and received daily doses of 200 mg/kg or more of methicillin. In a prospective randomized study that compared the safety of methicillin with that of nafcillin in infants and children, Kitzing and associates[33] demonstrated definite urologic toxic effects in 5.3 percent of methicillin-treated subjects and in none of the nafcillin-treated subjects. The frequencies of fever, rash, eosinophilia, neutropenia, anemia, and abnormal hepatic enzymes were the same in the two treatment groups. In a retrospective review of 124 children treated with methicillin, Yow and coworkers[34] found microscopic hematuria in 8 percent and gross hematuria in 4 percent. In 1 patient cystitis was documented by cystoscopy. Urologic toxic effects of methicillin have not been observed in the newborn.

Table 2-11

Pharmacokinetic Properties of Methicillin (Dose, 25 mg/kg) in Newborns

Birthweight/Age Groups	Peak Serum Concentration* (µg/ml)	Serum Half-life (h)	Volume of Distribution (ml/kg)	Plasma Clearance (ml/min/1.73 M^2)
≤ 2000 g				
0–7 days	58	2.8	388	32
8–14 days	58	3.1	366	27
≥ 15 days	39	1.8	513	79
> 2000 g				
0–7 days	49	2.2	404	62
8–14 days	45	1.8	452	102
≥ 15 days	41	1.1	470	128

* Mean values

Table 2-12
Dosage Recommendations for Methicillin Sodium

Individual dose	25 mg/kg except for meningitis (50 mg/kg)
Intervals	Every 12 h for infants ≤ 2000 g and 0–7 days; every 8 hours for infants ≤ 2000 g and > 7 days or those > 2000 g and 0–7 days; every 6 h for infants > 2000 g and > 7 days
Route	IM; IV as 15–30-min infusion
Tota daily dose	50 mg/kg in infants < 2000 g and 0–7 days; 75 mg/kg in infants ≤ 2000 g and > 7 days or those > 2000 g and 0–7 days; 100 mg/kg in infants > 2000 g and > 7 days (dose is doubled for meningitis)
Comments/cautions	The nephrotoxocity occasionally seen in older children has not been reported in neonates, but monitoring is advisable.
Trade names	Celbenin (Beecham), Staphcillin (Bristol)
Supplied as	Celbenin or Staphcillin for injection, buffered, 1-g vials for reconstitution

The only indication for using methicillin in newborns is in treatment of suspected or proved staphyloccal disease. If an *S. aureus* isolate from a patient with staphyloccal infection is shown by *in vitro* testing to be susceptible to penicillin, penicillin G is preferred. The standard dose of methicillin for neonates is 25 mg/kg; the frequency of administration is determined principally by the infant's chronological age (Table 2-12). In very low birthweight premature infants (under 1500 g) methicillin is given every 12 hours in the first week of life and every 8 hours thereafter. In full-term babies the every 8- and 6-hour regimens are appropriate. For the rare cases of staphylococcal meningitis, the dose should be doubled. If the putative *S. aureus* isolate is tolerant (MBC 32 or more times MIC) to methicillin, the susceptibilities to nafcillin and vancomycin should be determined to be certain that the strain is not cross-tolerant. The addition of an aminoglycoside to the regimen usually overcomes the tolerance to the antistaphylococcal agent.

Oxacillin

The concentrations of oxacillin in serum of newborns are similar to those of methicillin. Mean peak serum concentrations are approximately 50 μg/ml after 20-mg/kg doses are given, and 100 μg/ml after 50-mg/kg doses.[17,35] Antimicrobial activity is detectable in serum for 12 hours in infants younger than 7 days old and for 6 hours in older neonates who are treated with the larger doses. The half-life of oxacillin in serum of premature infants is approximately 3 hours during the first week of life and 1.5 hours thereafter.

Table 2-13
Dosage Recommendations for Oxacillin Sodium

Individual dose	25 mg/kg
Intervals	Every 12 h for infants ≤ 2000 g and 0–7 days; every 8 h for those > 2000 g and 0–7 days or for those ≤ 2000 g and > 7 days; every 6 hours for infants > 2000 g and > 7 days
Route	IV preferred as 15–30-min infusion; IM
Total daily dose	Same as for methicillin
Comments/cautions	Limited pharmacology and efficacy data for the recommended dosages
Trade name	Bactocill (Beecham), Prostaphilin (Bristol)
Supplied as	Bactophil for injection, 500-mg vial for reconstitution; Prostaphilin for injection, 250-mg and 500-mg vials for reconstitution

Urinary concentrations of oxacillin after a 20-mg/kg dose range from 174 to 510 µg/ml in the first 2 hours after administration; 17 percent of the administered dose is excreted within 6 hours during the second week of life, and 34 percent during the third and fourth weeks of life.[17]

Because of limited experience with this drug in newborns and the similar pharmacokinetics of oxacillin and methicillin, the dosage schedules for oxacillin are identical to those for methicillin (see Table 2-13).

Nafcillin

Compared with methicillin, nafcillin is more active *in vitro* against *S. aureus*. It is metabolized and eliminated by hepatic mechanisms. Until recently there was little information on the pharmacology of this drug in newborn infants. Studies performed in the 1960s showed mean serum concentrations of 22 µg/ml and 36 µg/ml at 1–2 hours after 10-mg/kg and 20-mg/kg doses, respectively.[20,36] The half-life was approximately 4 hours for infants less than 5 days old.

Sarff[37] presented data indicating mean serum concentrations of 73 µg/ml and 40 µg/ml at 1 hour and 6 hours after a 25-mg/kg dose given intravenously to infants less than 7 days old. The other mean pharmacokinetic values in these infants were half-life of 5.9 hours, distribution volume of 297 ml/kg, and plasma clearance of 16 ml/min/1.73M^2. He found that gestational age, birthweight, and chronologic age were less important variables in determining dosage schedules for nafcillin than for the other beta-lactams in neonates.

Banner and associates[38] gave 50-mg/kg doses of nafcillin to infants less than 7 days old and observed mean peak concentrations at 0.5 hours

Table 2-14
Dosage Recommendations for Nafcillin Sodium

Individual dose	25 mg/kg
Intervals	Every 12 h for all infants 0–7 days and every 8 h for infants > 7 days
Route	IV as 15–30-min infusion; IM
Total daily dose	50 mg/kg for infants 0–7 days; 75 mg/kg for infants > 7 days (dosage is doubled for meningitis)
Comments/cautions	The manufacturer recommends 10 mg/kg every 12 h IM for neonates and makes no claims for the IV route of administration; limited efficacy data
Trade name	Unipen (Wyeth); Nafcil (Bristol)
Supplied as	Unipen for injection, 500 mg

of approximately 160 μg/ml. The mean half-life was 4.1 hours in those infants. The mean half-life in infants who were 8–28 days old was 3.2 hours.

Limited experience with nafcillin in the newborn prevents our making definitive dosage recommendations. The schedule presented in Table 2-14 should provide satisfactory and safe serum concentrations in most infants. The half-life of nafcillin may be prolonged in jaundiced infants. As with methicillin, the susceptibility (MIC and MBC values) of *S. aureus* isolated from the patient to the drug should be defined to be certain that the strain is not tolerant (MBC 32 times or more the MIC).

Vancomycin

Vancomycin is not a beta-lactam but is placed in this section because its primary indication is for therapy of staphylococcal disease. With the emergence of methicillin-resistant and tolerant *S. aureus* strains, interest in vancomycin has been renewed. The agent is bactericidal against most gram-positive cocci and rods and ineffective against gram-negative bacteria. It is not metabolized and is excreted primarily in the urine. The MIC of 90 percent of *S. aureus* and *Staphylococcus epidermidis* strains is 1.25 μg/ml. Tolerance to vancomycin is uncommon, and we have encountered only one organism (*S. epidermidis*) that showed cross-tolerance with methicillin and nafcillin.

After a 15-mg/kg dose of vancomycin, peak serum concentrations of from 17–34 μg/ml are observed at completion of the 30–60 minute infusion (Table 2-15).[39] The levels decline over 6 hours to 7–14 μg/ml. Mean half-life values are 6–7 hours in the first week of life and 4.1 hours at a mean age of 3 months. The values are inversely correlated with the plasma clearance of vancomycin.

Table 2-15
Pharmacokinetic Properties of Vancomycin (Dose, 15 mg/kg) in Newborns

Age/Weight Groups	Peak Serum Concentration* (µg/ml)	Serum Half-life (h)	Volume of Distribution (ml/kg)	Plasma Clearance (ml/min/1.73 M^2)
< 7 days				
Mean weights				
1.6 kg	25	5.9	706	27
3.1 kg	30	6.7	690	30
> 30 days (mean, 3 mos)	26	4.1	595	50

* Mean values

Table 2-16
Dosage Recommendations for Vancomycin Hydrochloride

Individual dose	15 mg/kg
Intervals	Every 12 h in all infants 0–7 days and every 8 h in infants > 7 days
Route	IV as 60-min or longer infusion
Total daily dose	30 mg/kg for infants 0–7 days and 45 mg/kg for infants > 7 days
Comments/cautions	An erythematous, pruritic rash over the upper body and face may develop if infusion is < 60 min
Trade name	Vancocin (Lilly)
Supplied as	Vancocin, intravenous, 500 mg

Concentrations of from 1 to 12.3 µg/ml (mean, 3.9 µg/ml) were measured in 23 ventricular fluid specimens from infants with ventriculoperitoneal shunt infections.[40] The average ventricular fluid white blood cell count and protein content in these specimens were 433/mm and 261 mg/dl, respectively.

The principal indication for vancomycin is for therapy of *S. aureus* or *S. epidermidis* infections that are resistant or unresponsive to therapy with methicillin or vancomycin. Staphylococcal central nervous system infections or disseminated disease is also best treated with vancomycin alone or in combination with an aminoglycoside until results of susceptibility studies (MIC and MBC values) are available. Vancomycin administered orally in a daily dosage of 45 mg/kg in three divided doses is effective for treatment of antibiotic-associated pseudomembranous colitis caused by *Clostridium difficile*. This condition occurs rarely in newborn and young infants.

Vancomycin is administered intravenously over a 60-minute or longer period. More rapid infusions may be associated with a erythema multiforme–like reaction with intense pruritis that occurs on the upper body, neck, face, and upper arms and lasts 3–5 hours.[39] Systemic manifestations are not seen, and administration of antihistamines relieves the pruritis but has little effect on the rash. We have also observed this in infants who received vancomycin before surgery for shunt replacement or revision. The role of perioperative sedatives or anesthesia in this reaction is unknown.

The dosage of vancomycin in newborn infants is 15 mg/kg administered every 12 hours in the first week of life and every 8 hours thereafter (Table 2-16).

The drug is well tolerated, and we have not observed hematologic, renal, or auditory toxicity with this regimen. The half-life is prolonged in patients with diminished renal function.[40] Dosage schedules in these patients should be based on determination of serum concentrations and calculation of half-life values.

Cephalosporins

The older first generation cephalosporin derivatives had limited use for therapy of neonatal infections. Their activity against gram-negative enteric bacilli is inconsistent, and they do not penetrate well into the central nervous system. There are consequently few pharmacologic or efficacy data for these drugs in neonates. In the mid-1970s the second generation cephalosporins became available for use in pediatrics. These agents possess greater activity against aerobic and anaerobic gram-negative bacilli, including *H. influenzae, E. coli, Klebsiella,* and most *Proteus* species. There is limited information about the pharmacokinetics of these drugs in newborn infants. Further modification of the cephalosporanic acid nucleus of these drugs resulted in a new series of beta-lactams referred to as the third generation cephalosporins. These drugs have even greater *in vitro* activity against most gram-negative enteric bacilli, except *P. aeruginosa* and *Acinetobacter,* than the second generation cephalosporins. They are generally less active than cephalothin against gram-positive cocci. By mid-1982 two new generation beta-lactams had been approved by the FDA for use in newborn infants. Additional agents in this series will be approved in the next several years.

First Generation Cephalosporins

The prototype of these agents is cephalothin, an agent with *in vitro* activity against most gram-positive and some gram-negative bacteria. As with the antistaphylococcal penicillins, the antimicrobial activity of these drugs is approximately one-tenth that of penicillin G. The mean MIC values of cephalothin for commonly encountered pathogens are illustrative of the group: *S. aureus* (penicillin-sensitive), 0.25 μg/ml; *S. aureus* (penicillin-resistant), 0.25 μg/ml; group B streptococcus, 0.1 μg/ml: *Diplococcus pneumoniae,* 0.06–0.12 μg/ml: *E. coli,* 2–8 μg/ml; and *Klebsiella* species, 2–32 μg/ml. *Enterobacter,* enterococci, indole-positive *Proteus,* and *Pseudomonas* species are resistant to the cephalosporins.

Resistance to the cephalosporins is based on cephalosporinase production. Methicillin-resistant staphylococci are also usually resistant to the cephalosporins.

A 10-mg/kg dose of cephalothin given to full-term infants who are 1–5 days old results in 1-hour serum concentrations of 12 μg/ml (see Table 2-17).[20] Twice that dose (20 mg/kg) produces 1-hour serum concentrations of 38 μg/ml in infants of similar birthweight and age. When cephalothin is administered intramuscularly to premature infants in a dose of 12.5 mg/kg, means serum levels of 22 µg/ml at 30 minutes, 2.5 µg/ml at 6 hours, and 0.5 µg/ml at 12 hours after the dose are observed.[41] When cephaloridine is administered to newborns in a dose of 12.5 mg/kg, a mean serum concentration of approximately 30 µg/ml is noted 1 hour after the dose is given.[42]

The pharmacokinetic properties of cefazolin in newborns have been studied.[43] A 20-mg/kg dose given intramuscularly to neonates results in mean serum concentrations of approximately 30–35 µg/ml 1 hour after the dose is given. The mean 12-hour serum values are approximately 2–3 µg/ml.

Cephalexin given orally to newborns gives a mean peak serum level of approximately 10 µg/ml (range, 5–14 µg/ml) 4 hours after a 14-mg/kg dose is given.[44] When the dose is increased to 50 mg/kg, an average serum concentration of approximately 30 µg/ml (range, 22–44 µg/ml) is detected at 2 hours after the dose is given. The concentration of cephalexin in urine ranges from 1300 to 4000 µg/ml, and 18–66 percent of the total dose is excreted within 24 hours.

Calculation of half-life values from pharmacokinetic data presented in the literature reveals that the serum half-life of cephalothin is approximately 1.5–2.0 hours during the first week of life.[20] The half-life of cefazolin is 4.5–5.0 hours in infants during the first week of life, and approximately 3 hours in infants 3–4 weeks old.[43]

Because of the limited experience with the first generation cephalosporins in newborns little information is available concerning toxicity. Published reports do not mention adverse reactions; however, the investigators were primarily concerned with the pharmacokinetic properties rather than the safety of these agents in this age group.

The first generation cephalosporins have limited usefulness for newborns (Tables 2-17 and 2-18). Because of their poor ability to penetrate the blood-brain barrier, these cephalosporins should *never* be used as initial therapy for suspected or proved neonatal bacterial diseases unless meningitis has been ruled out of consideration.

Second Generation Cephalosporins

This group of beta-lactam antibiotics consists principally of cefamandole nafate, cefoxitin, cefuroxime, and cefaclor. These drugs have increased activity against gram-negative bacilli by virtue of their relative resistance to beta-lactamases. Cefamandole has activity against gram-positive bacteria, particularly staphylococci, that is comparable to cephalothin, and it is active against many gram-negative enteric bacilli, including *Enterobacter cloacae* and *Serratia* species. *H. influenzae* are highly susceptible to cefamandole, but the MBC values to beta-lactamase positive strains may be 4–

Table 2-17
Dosage Recommendations for Cephalothin Sodium

Individual dose	20 mg/kg
Intervals	Every 12 h for infants 0–7 days and < 2000 g; every 8 h for infants ≥ 2000 g and 0–7 days or for those < 2000 g and > 7 days; every 6 hours for infants > 2000 g and > 7 days
Route	IV preferred; IM
Total daily dose	40 mg/kg for infants 0–7 days an < 2000 g; 60 mg/kg for infants ≥ 2000 g and 0–7 days or for those < 2000 g and > 7 days; 80 mg/kg for infants > 2000 g and > 7 days
Comments/cautions	The manufacturer recommends 80–160 mg/kg/day for infants and children but does not specify a dosage for neonates; IM injection painful; limited efficacy and safety data in neonates.
Trade name	Kelfin (Lilly)
Supplied as	Kelfin for IV use and Kelfin Neutral for IV or IM use, 1-g vials for reconstitution

8 μg/ml or greater. Cefoxitin, a cephamycin, is unique for its excellent *in vitro* activity against *Bacteroides fragilis* species (MIC 0.25 μg/ml or less) and indole-positive *Proteus* organisms. Cefoxitin is considerably less active than cefamandole against gram-positive bacteria and *Enterobacter* species. Cefuroxime (approval for use in infants and children pending as of June 1983) is effective *in vitro* against gram-positive bacteria, including *S. aureus* (MIC 1.5 μg/ml or less), *H. influenzae,* and many gram-negative enteric

Table 2-18
Dosage Recommendations for Cefazolin Sodium

Individual dose	20 mg/kg
Intervals	Every 12 h for all infants except those ≥ 2000 g and > 7 days (every 8 h)
Route	IV (preferred as 15–30-min infusion); IM
Total daily dose	40 mg/kg for all infants except for infants > 2000 g and > 7 days (60 mg/kg)
Comments/cautions	The manufacturers do not recommend use in infants under 1 month old; less painful than cephalothin on intramuscular injection
Trade name	Ancef (Smith Kline and French), Kefzol (Lilly)
Supplied as	250-mg vials for reconstitution

bacteria. When tested against 116 strains of coliform bacteria isolated from CSF of neonates with meningitis, 15 (13 percent) were resistant to cefuroxime (MIC_{90} greater than 20 µg/ml), 18 (16 percent) to cefamandole (MIC_{90} greater than 20 µg/ml), 32 (28 percent) to ampicillin (MIC_{90} greater than 20 µg/ml), and 2 (10 percent) to gentamicin (MIC_{90} greater than 2.5 µg/ml).[45] Cefaclor, a new orally administered cephalosporin derived from cephalexin, has substantially greater *in vitro* activity against pneumococci, *H. influenzae* (MIC_{90} 0.5–16.0 µg/ml) and certain of the *Enterobacter* species than does the parent compound. Cefaclor has considerably less activity (MIC_{90}, 8 µg/ml) against *S. aureus* than does cephalothin (MIC_{90} 0.125 µg/ml).

Cefamandole. This drug is rarely used in newborn infants. Hence there are few published studies on pharmacokinetics, safety, and efficacy in this age group. Agbayani and associates[46] determined serum concentrations in 23 newborns after 17-mg/kg or 33-mg/kg doses given intravenously or intramuscularly. After a 33-mg/kg intravenous dose, a mean peak serum concentration of 106 µg/ml occurred at 0.25 hour and the level at 8 hours was 0.5 µg/ml. The mean serum half-life was 56 minutes, and the distribution volume was 260 mg/kg. The bioavailability after intramuscular administration was similar to that after an intravenous infusion. The 17-mg/kg intravenous dose produced serum concentrations that were approximately one-half those of the 33 mg/kg dose.

CSF concentrations of cefamandole at 75–140 minutes after a 33-mg/kg intravenous dose ranged from 0.6 to 7.4 µg/ml in infants, children, and adults with bacterial meningitis.[47] The concentrations correlated directly with the CSF protein content.

Cefoxitin. There are no published data on the clinical pharmacology of cefoxitin in newborn infants. Feldman and coworkers[48] studied infants from 3 to 151 months (mean, 26 months) of age. After 37.5-mg/kg doses given intravenously, a mean peak serum concentration of 82 µg/ml occurred at 0.25 hours and declined rapidly to 1.4 µg/ml at 4 hours. The mean half-life was 42 minutes, the distribution volume was 5540 ml, and the plasma clearance was 242 ml/min/M^2. Similar values were seen after intramuscular administration. On the basis of experience with beta-lactam drugs in newborn infants, one would predict larger serum concentrations and more prolonged half-life times for cefoxitin in neonates than in older infants.

Cefuroxime. This drug has been evaluated in 104 neonates by Renlund and Pettey in Helsinki, Finland.[49] Serum concentrations at 30–60 minutes after intramuscular administration of 10-mg/kg doses ranged from

15 to 25 µg/ml and were inversely related to birthweight. For example, infants with birthweights of less than 1000 g had mean concentrations of 25.6 µg/ml, compared with 19.5 µg/ml in infants weighing more than 4000 g. The mean half-life in the first 2 days of life was 5.6 hours, compared with 4.2 hours in infants 4–6 days of age.

In 3 patients with meningitis Renlund and Pettey observed CSF concentrations of from 2.3 to 5.3 µg/ml, representing from 12 to 25 percent of the simultaneous serum level.[49] The concentrations in CSF were smaller (0.4–1.5 µg/ml) in those without meningeal inflammation.

Wilkinson and coworkers[50] studied 26 neonates who received cefuroxime in a total dosage of 100 mg/kg/day (information is not provided on the amount of drug in each dose). Peak concentrations were highly variable and impossible to interpret. In 1 patient with *E. coli* meningitis, a CSF concentration of 20 µg/ml was observed after the third dose of cefuroxime.

Cefaclor. This drug is seldom used in the newborn infant, and there are no published data on serum concentrations in this age group. We have determined the pharmacokinetics of cefaclor in infants and children who were from 4 to 63 months of age (mean, 21 months)[51] Mean peak serum concentrations of 10.8 and 13.1 µg/ml were seen at 0.5 hours after 10- and 15-mg/kg doses, respectively, in fasting subjects. The peak levels were somewhat smaller when drug was given with milk, but the bioavailability of cefaclor was similar in fasting and fed children. The half-life of cefaclor was 36–46 minutes, and the average total clearance time was from 450 to 550 ml/min/1.73M^2. Studies in infants with otitis media showed that approximately 75 percent of middle ear fluid specimens obtained in the first 2 hours after 10–15 mg/kg doses contained concentrations of 0.63 µg/ml or greater, a level that should inhibit all pneumococci, *H. influenzae,* and many coliform bacteria.[52]

Because of limited experience with these second generation cephalosporins in newborn infants, we do not recommend them for routine use. A dosage of approximately 30 mg/kg cefamandole given every 8 hours to low birthweight (under 2000 g) infants who are 0–7 days of age, and every 6 hours to all others, should result in therapeutically effective and safe serum levels (Table 2-19). Because of only modest penetration and unpredictable activity in CSF of infants with coliform meningitis, alternative agents should be selected (Chap. 5, Sepsis and Central Nervous System Infections).

There are no data on which to base dosage recommendations for cefoxitin in neonates, and the drug has not been approved for use in this age group. As of March, 1983, cefuroxime has not been approved for use in the United States, and the manufacturer is not seeking approval for use in infants less than 3 months of age.

Table 2-19
Dosage Recommendations for Cefamandole Nafate

Individual dose	Approximately 30 mg/kg
Intervals	Every 8 h in low birthweight (< 2000 g) infants 0–7 days of age and every 6 h to all others (provisional, insufficient data precludes definitive schedules)
Route	IV as 15–30-min infusions; IM
Total daily dose	90 mg/kg for infants < 2000 g and 0–7 days and 120 mg/kg for all others
Comments/cautions	Not recommended for routine use. Additional experience required to evaluate efficacy and safety.
Trade name	Mandol (Eli Lilly)
Supplied as	Mandol for injection, 500-mg vial for reconstitution

In our opinion cefaclor is preferred therapy for acute suppurative otitis media in the infant less than 6 weeks of age who can be managed with oral medication. Cefaclor provides satisfactory activity against the conventional middle ear pathogens (*Streptococcus pneumoniae* and *H. influenzae*) as well as against coliforms and *S. aureus*.The dosage is 15 mg/kg given 3 times daily (total daily dose, 45 mg/kg) either on an empty stomach or with milk (Table 2-20).

Third Generation Cephalosporins

There are a large number of new cephalosporin derivatives that offer remarkably increased *in vitro* activity against gram-negative enteric bacilli. Two of these agents have been approved for use in neonates: moxalactam

Table 2-20
Dosage Recommendations for Cefaclor

Individual dose	15 mg/kg
Intervals	Every 8 h
Route	Orally while fasting or with milk
Total daily dose	45 mg/kg
Comments/cautions	Recommended for use in otitis media; serum sickness–like reaction said to occur on readministration in approximately 3/1000 subjects
Trade name	Ceclor (Eli Lilly)
Supplied as	Ceclor, oral suspension, 125-mg/5 ml and 250 mg/ml in 75- and 150-ml sizes, for reconstitution

(a 1-oxa-β-lactam) and cefotaxime. It is likely that others among this class of drugs will also be approved in 1983 and 1984.

The *in vitro* activity of some of these drugs was determined against 116 gram-negative enteric bacilli, including 84 *E. coli* strains, that were recovered from cultures of CSF from neonates with meningitis.[45] The MIC_{90} values were 0.25 μg moxalactam/ml, 0.06 μg ceftriaxone/ml, and 0.12 μg cefotaxime/ml. These values were superior to those of the second generation cephalosporins, to ampicillin (MIC_{90} more than 20 μg/ml), and to the aminoglycosides (e.g., gentamicin, MIC_{90} 2.5 μg/ml; amikacin, 5 μg/ml).[45] With the exception of cefoperazone, ceftazidime, and cefsulodin,[53-54] these new cephalosporin derivatives are not active against *P. aeruginosa*.

There is unfortunately a trade-off for the enhanced activity against gram-negative bacteria; these agents have only modest activity against *S. aureus* (usual MIC values from 1 to more than 8 μg/ml) and one drug, moxalactam, is relatively ineffective against group B streptococci and *S. pneumoniae*.[55-56] All *Listeria* and enterococci are resistant to this new class of antibiotics.[55]

Moxalactam. The pharmacokinetics for this drug were determined by Schaad and coworkers[57] in 74 infants, 62 percent of whom were neonates. Peak serum concentrations at completion of 50-mg/kg, 10-minute infusions were approximately 125 μg/ml; the serum concentration time curves after intramuscular and intravenous administration were comparable. The half-life times were inversely related to postnatal age and were approximately 7 to 8 hours in low birthweight (under 2000 g) infants who were 0–7 days old, and 4 hours in those more than 7 days of age (Table 2-21). The plasma clearances increased with increasing birthweight and chronologic age.

Moxalactam penetrates well into CSF in the presence of inflamed meninges; CSF levels are approximately 10 percent of the corresponding serum concentration after the first dose and 30 percent after multiple doses (steady state.).[57] The mean concentrations in lumbar CSF or ventricular fluid are approximately 25 μg/ml; the values vary from 3 to 74 μg/ml depending on the time at which the specimens are obtained after 50-mg/kg doses (unpublished data from the third Neonatal Meningitis Cooperative Study).

The dosage of moxalactam for neonates is 50 mg/kg given intravenously every 12 hours for infants 0–7 days old and every 8 hours for those 7 days of age or older (Table 2-22). An initial dose of 100 mg/kg is given for therapy of meningitis. During therapy moxalactam may suppress the normal bacterial flora of the gastrointestinal tract, allowing growth of enterococci or *Pseudomonas* organisms. Prolongation of the prothrombin

Table 2-21

Pharmacokinetic Properties of Moxalactam (Dose, 50 mg/kg) in Newborns

Age/Birthweight Categories	Peak Serum Concentration* (μg/ml)	Serum Half-life (h)	Volume of Distribution (ml/kg)	Plasma Clearance (ml/min/1.73 M^2)
0–7 days				
< 2000 g	123	7.6	537	16
≥ 2000 g	128	5.4	515	28
7–28 days	122	4.4	517	31

* Mean values

38

Table 2-22
Dosage Recommendations for Moxalactam Disodium

Individual dose	50 mg/kg
Intervals	Every 12 h for infants 0–7 days and every 8 h for infants > 7 days
Route	IV infusion over 15–30-min; IM
Total daily dose	100 mg/kg for infants 0–7 and 150 mg/kg for infants > 7 days
Comments/cautions	An initial 100-mg/kg dose is given for therapy of meningitis. Moxalactam inhibits bacterial flora of gastrointestinal tract with overgrowth of enterococcus or *Pseudomonas*.
Trade name	Moxam (Eli Lilly)
Supplied as	Moxam for injection, 1-g, 250-, 500-, vials, requires reconstitution

time has been observed in 2 infants receiving moxalactam therapy; neither infant had bleeding problems, and a single dose of vitamin K corrected the prothrombin time.

Cefotaxime. This drug has been used by European physicians for therapy of neonatal sepsis and meningitis. Kafetzis and coworkers[58] found mean peak serum concentrations of from 50 to 80 μg/ml in neonates after 25-mg/kg doses. The elimination half-life was 5.7 hours in preterm infants less than 1 week old and 2 hours in term infants who were 1–4 weeks old. The volumes of distribution ranged from 530 to 690 ml/kg.

CSF concentrations of cefotaxime were measured in 5 infants with meningitis.[58] At 1–2 hours after 50-mg/kg doses, the concentrations ranged from 7.1 to 30.0 μg/ml (mean, 18.2 μg/ml), and the ratio of CSF to serum concentrations ranged from 0.27 to 0.63 (mean, 0.45).

Pharmacokinetic data obtained from infants in our nurseries (Table 2-23)[59] were similar to those of Kafetzis and associates.[58] After 50-mg/kg doses, mean peak concentrations were 116 μg/ml in low birthweight infants (under 2000 g) and 133 in average birthweight babies. The half-life values were 4.6 hours in the former and 3.4 hours in the latter infants. These values correlated inversely with the plasma clearance values.

The dosage of cefotaxime is similar to that of moxalactam: 50 mg/kg every 12 hours in infants 0–7 days old and every 8 hours thereafter for the remainder of the newborn period (Table 2-24). This agent appears to be well tolerated in newborn infants.

Table 2-23

Pharmacokinetic Properties of Cefotaxime (Dose, 50 mg/kg) in Newborns

Birthweight/Age Category	Peak Serum Concentration* ($\mu g/ml$)	Serum Half-life (h)	Volume of Distribution (ml/kg)	Plasma Clearance (ml/min/1.73 M^2)
0–7 days				
< 2000 g (mean, 1103 g)	116	4.6	400	23
≥ 2000 g (mean, 2561 g)	133	3.4	392	44

* Mean values

Table 2-24
Dosage Recommendations for Cefotaxime Sodium

Individual dose	50 mg/kg
Intervals	Every 12 h for infants 0–7 days and every 8 h for infants > 7 days
Route	IV infusion over 15–30-min; IM
Total daily dose	100 mg/kg for infants 0–7 days and 150 mg/kg for infants > 7 days
Comments/cautions	Well tolerated in neonates. Experience in United States is limited.
Trade name	Claforan (Hoechst-Roussel)
Supplied as	Claforan for injection, 1-g vial for reconstitution

Cefoperazone. Although this drug has not been approved by the FDA for use in infants, there are considerable data on its pharmacokinetics in this age group. In unpublished data from our laboratories, mean peak concentrations of approximately 110 μg/ml were observed after 50-mg/kg doses, and half-life times ranged from 8.1 hours in infants weighing less than 1500 g and 0–5 days of age to 4.9 hours in those weighing 2000 g or more and over 5 days of age.

Rosenfeld and colleagues[60] showed similar peak serum concentrations after a dose of 50 mg of cefoperazone/kg in infants who were 33 weeks gestational age or older. In infants less than 33 weeks gestational age, however, the mean peak levels were 159 μg/ml. The mean half-life in these latter infants was 8.9 hours. These authors interpreted their data as demonstrating the kidneys as the major route of excretion in infants less than 33 weeks gestational age and the liver as the principal route after 33 weeks.[60]

Cefoperazone was also studied by Bosso and coworkers[61] in 14 premature infants. After doses of 50 or 250 mg/kg, they calculated a mean half-life time of 5.5 hours, volume of distribution of 650 ml/kg, and a total body clearance of 91 ml/h/kg. In another study, mean CSF concentrations of cefoperazone in infants and children with meningitis were 4.4 μg/ml after 1 dose and 10.5 μg/ml after 3 doses given in the first 2 days of treatment.[62] At the end of therapy, the mean CSF level was 4.8 μg/ml after 3 additional doses (50 or 100 mg/kg) of cefoperazone were given. The calculated penetration into CSF was approximately 3–5 percent. Rosenfeld and associates[60] measured CSF concentrations of from 2.8 to 9.5 μg/ml in 4 neonates with meningitis and of less than 2 μg/ml in 2 infants without meningeal inflammation. There is not sufficient information to permit us to make specific dosage recommendations for neonates.

Table 2-25

Pharmacokinetic Properties of Ceftriaxone (Dose, 50 mg/kg) in Newborns

Birthweight/Age Categories	Peak Serum Concentration* (μg/ml)	Serum Half-life (h)	Volume of Distribution (ml/kg)	Plasma Clearance (ml/min/1.73 M^2)
< 1500 g				
1–4 days (3.2 days)*	145	7.7	608	17
6–8 days (6.7 days)	136	8.4	530	14
≥ 1500 g				
2–4 days (2.8 days)	158	7.4	520	17
5–45 days (22.5 days)	173	5.2	497	20

* Mean values

Ceftriaxone.   This drug is an investigational cephalosporin derivative that has been extensively studied in older infants and children. There are no published data on the pharmacokinetics in newborn infants. Preliminary information from our nurseries indicates that serum concentrations of from 100 to 130 μg/ml were seen at 0.5 hours after 50-mg/kg doses and that mean half-life values ranged from 5 to 8 hours (Table 2-25).[63] In some low birthweight (under 1300 g), premature (under 33 weeks) infants, however, half-life times as long as 60 hours occurred in the first several days of life. The volumes of distribution ranged from 500 to 600 ml/kg and plasma clearances from 14 to 20 ml/min/$1.73M^2$.

A single daily 50-mg/kg dose of ceftriaxone should be adequate for therapy of most neonatal infections. An exception might be meningitis, where an every-12 hour schedule would be preferred. Additional information is required to substantiate these suggested regimens.

Conclusions.   There are no conditions in the neonate for which a third generation cephalosporin represents the initial drug of choice. Although these agents have extraordinary activity against gram-negative enteric bacilli, they have not been shown to be superior to ampicillin used with an aminoglycoside for therapy of sepsis or meningitis caused by these organisms. Unpublished data from the third Neonatal Meningitis Cooperative Study show that ampicillin and amikacin are as effective as moxalactam in neonates with coliform meningitis. Either of the presently approved agents, moxlactam or cefotaxime, is appropriate for therapy of coliform sepsis or meningitis if the organism is resistant to the aminoglycosides or has not responded to conventional therapy.

Ureidopenicillins

Mezlocillin and azlocillin are alpha-amino-substituted ampicillins that have broad antimicrobial activity. Mezlocillin has been approved for use in newborn infants; there are no data for azlocillin in this age group. Mezlocillin is similar to carbenicillin and ticarcillin in its breadth of activity, but the former is more active *in vitro* against *B. fragilis*, some *Klebsiella-Enterobacter* species, enterococci, *Listeria*, and some *Serratia* strains.[64] *In vitro* susceptibility studies performed in our labortory with bacteria isolated from blood or CSF of neonates revealed similar MIC and MBC values of mezlocillin and ampicillin for *Listeria*, group B streptococci, and enterococci. Mezlocillin was more active than ampicillin against *P. aeruginosa*, *Citrobacter diversus*, *Serratia* species, and some *Klebsiella-Enterobacter* species.

Rubio and associates[65] studied the pharmacokinetics of mezlocillin in 60 newborn infants. The mean serum concentration at 0.5 hours after 75–100-mg/kg doses given intravenously or intramuscularly was approximately 140 μg/ml. The mean half-life time in infants less than 7 days of age, regardless of birthweight, was 4.3 hours, whereas that in infants older than 7 days was approximately 2.5 hours. Preliminary data from our institution in 18 newborns indicate that serum concentrations at 0.5 hours after 75-mg/kg doses were 175–225 μg/ml; these values are considerably larger than those reported by Rubio et al.[65]

There is scant information on concentrations of mezlocillin in CSF of neonates and young infants. In one study, CSF concentrations of from 20 to 80 μg/ml were found at varying intervals after 75-mg/kg doses; in 6 of the 9 specimens analyzed the levels were 20–30 μg/ml.[66] Weingartner reported CSF values of from 0 to 13.7 μg/ml (mean, 5.5 μg/ml) after doses of from 50 to 200 mg/kg of mezlocillin.[67]

Although mezlocillin has broad antimicrobial activity that is greater in scope but comparable in activity to that of ampicillin, experience with this agent is too meager to justify routine use in neonates. Unlike others of the new beta-lactam antibiotics, mezlocillin is unstable to the common beta-lactamases and thus would usually be ineffective against multiply-resistant coliform bacteria. In the few instances in which mezlocillin might be used in newborn infants, a dose of 75 mg/kg is provisionally recommended as an intravenous infusion every 12 hours in the first week of life and every 8 hours thereafter. Additional data are required to establish the proper dosage schedule in neonates.

Other New Beta-Lactam Antibiotics

A number of other beta-lactam drugs are presently under investigation. These include piperacillin, a piperazine derivative, and ceftazidime and cefsulodin, both of which are cephalosporin derivatives. These three agents have excellent *in vitro* activity against *P. aeruginosa,* but only piperacillin and ceftazidime have broad antimicrobial activity against gram-positive and gram-negative bacteria. There are insufficient pharmacokinetic, safety, and efficacy data in newborn infants to permit further comment regarding their use in newborns.

AMINOGLYCOSIDES

During the past 3 decades the aminoglycosides have been relied on for therapy of neonatal septicemia and meningitis because of their activity against gram-negative enteric bacilli. Approximately 10 percent of all newborn infants in a tertiary care center receive at least 1 course of a penicillin and aminoglycoside for suspected sepsis. Use of each successive aminoglycoside has been limited by a low therapeutic index and by the emergence of resistance. The margin between the therapeutic concentration of these agents in serum and the toxic concentration is narrow. Thus it is prudent to monitor serum levels of the aminoglycosides, particularly in low birth-weight premature infants who require repeated or prolonged antimicrobial therapy.

Streptomycin is no longer used because of the prevalence of resistant strains and the drug's toxicity. Similarly, kanamycin is used infrequently in nurseries because of its lack of activity against *P. aeruginosa* and development of resistant coliform strains in many nurseries during the 1970s.[68] Presently gentamicin or tobramycin is the aminoglycoside of choice in most North American nurseries. Because amikacin is resistant to degradation by most of the plasmid-mediated bacterial enzymes that inactivate kanamycin, gentamicin, and tobramycin, it has been held in reserve for treatment of hospital-acquired gram-negative infections that are suspected or proved to be multiply-resistant. Gentamicin resistance occurs frequently enough in some European and Latin American centers to warrant use of amikacin in these areas as a first-line drug for therapy of life-threatening infections such as meningitis.

The use of aminoglycosides in the late 1950s and 1960s was a chronicle of the inherent problems of adapting dosages derived from adults to newborn infants. Irreversible ototoxicity in neonates was caused by excessive dosages of streptomycin or kanamycin. By contrast the pharmacokinetics of gentamicin, tobramycin, and amikacin were carefully defined in the neonate prior to routine use of these drugs, which provided a scientific basis for the safe and effective dosage regimens. There have been no documented cases of ototoxicity in neonates directly attributed to gentamicin, tobramycin, or amikacin when these drugs were administered in the proper dosage.

Antimicrobial Activity

Aminoglycosidic antibiotics act on microbial ribosomes to irreversibly inhibit protein synthesis. There are 3 possible mechanisms by which drug resistance can develop either naturally or in the laboratory: (1) alteration of the ribosomal site; (2) changes in the cell surface properties; and (3) development of enzymes that inactivate the drug. Antibiotic resistance in clinical situations is most often due to extrachromosomally controlled (R factor) enzymes. Phosphorylation, adenylation, and acetylation are the three most common enzymatic mechanisms encountered. In order for the newer aminoglycosides to be clinically useful, they must not be suitable substrates for these commonly encountered microbial enzymes.

In general, gentamicin, tobramycin, netilmicin, sisomicin, and amikacin have good antimicrobial activity against approximately 90 percent or more of gram-negative enteric bacillary strains recovered from infants in North American nurseries, whereas kanamycin is active against a lower percentage of strains of enteric bacilli, and all *P. aeruginosa* are resistant.

On a weight-for-weight basis, tobramycin has the greatest anti-*Pseudo-monas* activity, and amikacin is the only drug of this class that reliably provides activity against nosocomially-acquired, multiply-resistant coliforms. *S. aureus* is the only gram-positive organism that has been considered susceptible to aminoglycosides by *in vitro* testing. This is no longer true in our center, where 10 percent of *S. aureus* and 20 percent of *S. epidermidis* are resistant to gentamicin. Staphylococcal infections, furthermore, usually do not respond satisfactorily to aminoglycoside therapy. Synergistic bactericidal activity between aminoglycosides and the penicillins has been demonstrated *in vitro* and in animals against *S. aureus*,[69] group B streptococcus,[70] *L. monocytogenes*,[71] and enterococci,[24] despite resistance of the microorganisms to the aminoglycoside alone.

General Pharmacokinetic Considerations

The intramuscular route has traditionally been preferred for the administration of aminoglycosidic antibiotics in order to avoid potentially toxic peak serum levels. Pharmacokinetic studies of kanamycin,[72] gentamicin,[72-73] and netilmicin,[74] have demonstrated that the serum concentration time curves (bioavailability) following an intramuscular injection are similar to those after a 20-minute intravenous infusion. Although serum concentrations at the end of infusion may at times be larger than the desired peak, this elevation is transient and is not therapeutically significant. The concentrations from 0.5 to 6 hours after the dose, the half-life values, and the area-under-the-curve values are equivalent.

These drugs cannot be administered orally for treatment of systemic infection because they are not absorbed from the intact gastrointestinal tract. Minimal systemic absorption has been demonstrated in adults by recovering 1–2 percent of a single orally administered dose of gentamicin from the urine.[75] Absorption through an inflamed gastrointestinal mucosa has been demonstrated by studies of infants with gastroenteritis who were treated orally with neomycin[76-77] and of infants with shigellosis[78] and necrotizing enterocolitis[79] who were treated orally with gentamicin. More than 10 percent of the administered dose of gentamicin was excreted in the urine during the acute phase of *Shigella* dysentery as compared to only 2 percent after the acute inflammation had subsided. Hansen and associates[79] measured peak serum gentamicin levels of more than 10 μg/ml in 4 of 9 infants with necrotizing enterocolitis who received a total dose of 15 mg/kg/day of gentamicin (2.5 mg/kg every 4 hours) through a nasogastric tube in addition to 7.5 mg/kg/day gentamicin by the intramuscular route. The mean peak level, 8.5 μg/ml, was significantly greater than the 6.6 μg/ml value measured in a control group of infants, but there was no significant difference in the mean trough values.

Recent studies have utilized two-compartment model pharmacokinetics to demonstrate a prolonged washout phase in neontes who received nctilmicin[74] or gentamicin.[80] Mean terminal half-lives of 62–110 hours and detectable serum and urine drug levels for as long as 11 and 14 days, respectively, after discontinuation of these drugs werc found. This probably represents release of drug that was bound to tissue, most likely renal, during the steady state. The practical significance of these findings is unknown. Persistence of drug in tissues may conceivably place the infant who requires a second course of therapy at increased risk of developing aminoglycoside-associated toxicity. It is also likely that the subinhibitory concentrations of aminoglycosides that persist in urine exert selective pressure for development of resistant enterobacteriaceae in intensive care units for high-risk infants.

Several studies, finally, have indicated that aminoglycoside pharmacokinetics in very low birthweight premature infants (under 1500 g, less than 34 weeks gestation) arc highly variable due to renal immaturity and unpredictable extracellular fluid volumes.[7, 81-85] Frequent measurements of serum concentrations is therefore indicated in these infants in order to individualize the dosage regimens. The pharmacokinetics of gentamicin, kanamycin, amikacin, and nctilimicin in low birthweight, premature infants are compared in Table 2-26.

Pharmacokinetic Properties

Neomycin

Although neomycin is no longer used parenterally in newborn infants, pharmacokinetic data determined after intramuscular administration are presented for historical and comparative purposes. A mean peak serum level of approximately 12 μg/ml was observed 2 hours after an intramuscular injection of 7 mg/kg. Serum concentrations of 2–5 μg/ml persisted for 12 hours.[17] The serum half-life is inversely related to postnatal age: 5½ hours in 4–10-day-old infants, and 3½ hours in 13–21-day-old infants.

Poor absorption after oral administration has made this antibiotic useful for the control of nursery outbreaks of diarrhea caused by enteropathogenic strains of E. coli. Although efficacy of this regimen has been questioned, a more rapid bacteriologic and clinical response was demonstrated in infants treated for 3–5 days than in those given placebo.[86] Occasionally neomycin may be absorbed from an inflamed gastrointestinal tract and cause ototoxicity or renal toxicity, particularly in patients with preexisting renal diseases.[77] Transient elevation of BUN occurred in 1 infant who received 10 times the recommended dosage for several days in our institution.

Table 2-26

Pharmacokinetics of Selected Aminoglycosides in Low Birthweight (under 1500 g) Premature (under 34 weeks) Infants Treated 5 Days or Longer

Drug	Mean Birth-weight (g)	Mean No. Previous Doses	Median Serum Concentration (μg/ml)					Serum Half-life (h)
			Predose	0.5 h	1 h	2 h	6 h	
Gentamicin	1087	3	2.2	4.6	4.9	4.5	3.0	6.8
		12	2.4	6.3	5.1	4.3	3.5	7.7
Kanamycin	1243	3	5.7	15.2	13.4	11.4	7.6	6.1
		14	4.6	15.6	14.4	11.6	7.2	5.1
Amikacin	923	3	16.4	20.0	20.4	20.4	14.1	7.5
		18	10.2	23.2	20.8	14.0	11.6	6.0
Netilmicin	1176	3	2.1	11.4	8.6	4.3	—	3.6
		14	5.0	9.6	8.5	5.3	—	5.1

Courtesy of Siegel JD: Unpublished data, University of Texas Health Science Center at Dallas.

Streptomycin

Despite the common use of streptomycin during the 1950s, there have been few studies of its pharmacokinetic properties in newborn and young infants. Serum concentration time curves are similar to those after kanamycin administration. Peak serum concentrations of 17–42 µg/ml (mean, 29 µg/ml) occur 2 hours after a 10-mg/kg dose is given to premature infants.[87] Following a 6.6-mg/kg streptomycin dose given to full-term infants, Hunt and Fell[88] documented serum concentrations of 18–25 µg/ml 6 hours after the dose.

The half-life of streptomycin in serum of premature infants is approximately 7 hours.[87] Preterm infants 1–3 days old excrete approximately 30 percent of the administered dose within 12 hours, compared with approximately 70 percent excretion by older children and adults.

Kanamycin

For approximately 20 years kanamycin has been effectively and safely employed in treatment of newborns. The history of kanamycin therapy in neonates is illustrative of the clinical and pharmacologic problems that may occur if an antibiotic is not carefully evaluated before and during its routine use in this age group. When kanamycin was first given to infants in the late 1950s, there were no pharmacologic data upon which to base dosage regimens. Thus excessively large dosages were used, resulting in irreversible ototoxicity in some cases. In the mid-1960s the pharmacokinetic properties of kanamycin were first published, resulting in a reduction of dosages.[89-90] A 7.5-mg/kg dose given every 12 hours to all neonates, regardless of birthweight and chronological age, was applied in virtually all nurseries in North America. After many years of routine use, emergence of kanamycin-resistant coliform organisms was observed in a number of neonatal units.[68] In some nurseries more than 70 percent of E. coli strains were resistant to kanamycin. This necessitated selection of a different aminoglycoside for therapy of infections in newborns. At the time that these changing susceptibilities to kanamycin were first documented, a suitable alternative, gentamicin, was commercially available, but insufficient data about its pharmacologic properties, effectiveness, and safety in newborn infants were available to recommend its routine use. These data were rapidly accumulated, and gentamicin became a mainstay of therapy in most nurseries. Subsequently a reappraisal of the clinical pharmacology of kanamycin showed that the dosage employed during the previous decade was insufficient for many neonates, particularly full-term infants older than 7 days.[91] From 1971 to 1973, when kanamycin in nurseries was infrequent, there was a return to the use of kanamycin susceptibility among coliform organisms. At the present time (1983), approximately 80 percent of coliform bacteria are susceptible to this agent.

In 1966 Simon and Axline[89] showed that 6.3–8.5 mg/kg doses given

Table 2-27

Pharmacokinetic Properties of Kanamycin (Dose, 10 mg/kg) in Newborns

Birthweight/Age Groups	Peak Serum Concentration* (µg/ml)	Serum Half-life (h)	Volume of Distribution (ml/kg)	Plasma Clearance (ml/min/1.73 M^2)
≤ 2000 g				
1–3 days	25.8	8.6	715	23
4–7 days	26.3	6.7	519	24
> 7 days	22.3	5.2	547	25
> 2000 g				
1–3 days	21.6	5.7	623	29
4–7 days	20.9	5.0	460	36
> 7 days	19.6	3.8	497	46

* Mean values

to premature infants produced mean serum concentrations of 17.5 μg/ml at 1 hour, and approximately 6 μg/ml at 12 hours after the dose. Serum kanamycin half-life values were inversely correlated to postnatal age. Values as high as 18 hours in preterm infants under 48 hours old, and approximately 6 hours in infants 5–22 days old were measured. Eichenwald[90] found similar kanamycin serum concentration time curves in a larger number of premature and full-term infants.

During the early 1970s we monitored the serum concentrations of kanamycin in infants within our nurseries.[91] Unexpectedly it was found that 7.5-mg/kg doses given to full-term infants produced peak serum concentrations below 20 μg/ml and frequently in a subtherapeutic range of 8–15 μg/ml. On the basis of these findings, pharmacokinetic studies of premature and full-term infants were undertaken.

After a 10-mg/kg kanamycin dose was given to low birthweight (2000 g or less) infants older than 7 days and to all infants more than 2000 g at birth, mean peak serum concentrations of from 19–22 μg/ml were noted (Table 2-27).[68, 91] The mean concentration of kanamycin in serum 12 hours after this dose fell to 3–6 μg/ml. By contrast, the 10-mg/kg dose to infants 2000 g or less at birth and 0–3 days old resulted in mean peak serum levels of 26 μg/ml (range, 23–30 μg/ml), and the 12-hour serum level was approximately 10 μg/ml.

The half-life of kanamycin in serum correlates inversely with birthweight and chronological age. Mean half-life values of approximately 8–9 hours are found in infants 2000 g or less at birth and 0–3 days old, compared to values of 3–4 hours in larger birthweight babies older than 7 days. These half-life values correlate inversely with the clearance of kanamycin from plasma (Table 2-27).

The volume of kanamycin distribution is greatest during the first 3 days of life; the largest values are observed in low birthweight babies. Although the plasma clearances increase during the postnatal period, these changes are not significant for low birthweight babies. The largest clearance values are seen in infants more than 2000 g at birth and older than 7 days.

Following a 7.5-mg/kg dose, peak concentrations of kanamycin in CSF 3–4 hours later are approximately 3–12 μg/ml (mean, 5.6 μg/ml).[91] The penetration of kanamycin into CSF correlates roughly with the degree of meningeal inflammation as determined by the CSF cell count and protein content. Penetration of drug into CSF, expressed as a percentage of the simultaneous serum concentration, ranges from 8 to 170 percent. The mean peak CSF concentration of 5.6 μg/ml is 43 percent of the mean peak serum concentration of 13 μg/ml after a 7.5-mg/kg dose. The 5.6-μg/ml mean CSF value is smaller than the MIC_{90} value for E. coli strains recovered from CSF cultures of neonates with meningitis. This observation may account for some of the clinical failures that have occurred with kanamycin therapy. Comparable data for the 10 mg/kg dose are not available.

Table 2-28
Dosage Recommendations for Kanamycin Sulfate

Individual dose	7.5 mg/kg for infants ≤ 2000 g and 0–7 days; 10 mg/kg for others
Intervals	Every 12 h for infants 0–7 days; every 8 h for infants > 7 days
Route	IV infusion over at least 20 min; IM
Total daily dose	15 mg/kg for infants < 2000 g and 0–7 days; 20 mg/kg for infants ≥ 2000 g and 0–7 days; 30 mg/kg for infants > 7 days
Comments/cautions	These dosages are greater than the 15 mg/kg/day recommended by the manufacturer, but they have found effective and safe; risk of nephrotoxicity and ototoxicity increased in patients with poor renal function and those treated longer than 10 days.
Trade name	Kantrex (Bristol)
Supplied as	Kantrex Pediatric Injection, 75 mg/2 ml vial

On the basis of the above pharmacokinetic data, we recommend a 7.5-mg/kg dose of kanamycin for infants who are 2000 g or less and 0–7 days old, and a 10-mg/kg dose for all other neonates (Table 2-28). These doses should be administered intravenously or intramuscularly every 12 hours to all infants who are 0–7 days and every 8 hours to infants of 15 mg/kg is recommended for infants who are 2000 g or less at birth and 0–7 days old; 20 mg/kg for infants weighing more than 2000 g at birth and 0–7 days old; and 30 mg/kg for infants older than 7 days.

It should be emphasized that although these revised dosages are greater than the 15-mg/kg/day dosage recommended by the manufacturer, they have been found safe and effective in our nurseries. Long-term follow-up studies utilizing these dosages are not available; however, the risk of ototoxicity is unlikely if the total dose does not exceed 500 mg/kg. It is wise to monitor serum concentrations of kanamycin in low birthweight, premature infants and in neonates with coliform meningitis who require kanamycin therapy for more than 10 days. Adjustments in dosage may be necessary to maintain peak serum values in the therapeutic range of 15–25 μg/ml.

Gentamicin

Gentamicin was the first aminoglycosidic drug to have been methodically studied in newborn infants before release for uncontrolled use in hospital nurseries. Both one- and two-compartment model pharmacokinetic data accumulated during the last decade have been analyzed with respect to birthweight, body surface area, gestational age, chronological age, and renal function.[72-73, 82, 92-95, 102, 112-117] Mean peak serum concentrations of 3.5–6.0 µg/ml occur within 1 hour after a 2.5-mg/kg dose. Mean serum values 12 hours after this dose range from 0.5 to 1.0 µg/ml. Although most studies have not demonstrated drug accumulation during a 5–7 day course of therapy, Coyer and associates[81] showed accumulation in small (mean birthweight, 1365 g) preterm (mean gestational age, 31 weeks) infants after a constant-rate, 1-hour intravenous infusion of 2.5 mg/kg. Because gentamicin levels are reduced by 21–62 percent following a two-volume exchange transfusion, whenever possible this procedure should be timed to precede the next scheduled dose of gentamicin.[98]

Urinary concentrations of gentamicin vary from 2 to 135 µg/ml. When expressed as a percentage of the administered dose, urinary excretion correlates directly with postnatal age and rates of creatinine clearance but is independent of birthweight and dosage.[93] Approximately 10 percent of the dose administered to infants 0–3 days old is excreted within 12 hours compared to 40 percent excreted during the same period by infants 5–40 days of age. After the final dose of gentamicin, urinary concentrations decrease in a biphasic pattern and remain detectable for 11 days.[99]

The serum half-life of gentamicin correlates inversely with the rate of creatinine clearance, birthweight, and postnatal age (Table 2-29).[92-93] During the first week of life, half-life values as long as 14 hours have been observed in infants with birthweights of 800–1500 g, compared with 4.5 hours in full-term infants. After the first 2 weeks of life, the half-life of gentamicin is approximately 3 hours, regardless of body weight. Because of unpredictable and prolonged half-life values, one group of investigators recommended dosing intervals of 18 hours for infants of less than 34 weeks gestation because trough serum gentamicin concentrations were greater than 2 µg/ml in 31 (91 percent) of 34 such infants, compared with 13 (32.5 percent) of 40 infants who were greater than 34 weeks gestational age.[82]

CSF concentrations of gentamicin in infants with meningitis range from 0.3 to 3.7 µg/ml (mean, 1.6 µg/ml) 1–6 hours after a 2.5 mg/kg dose.[100-101] Peak levels are observed 4–6 hours after the dose and are directly correlated with the degree of meningeal inflammation and size of dose.

Between 1970 and 1980 the Neonatal Meningitis Cooperative Study Group evaluated lumbar intrathecal and intraventricular gentamicin in comparative studies with systemic antibiotic therapy alone. Neither intrathecal nor intraventricular therapy proved superior to systemic therapy for neonates with meningitis caused by gram-negative enteric organisms.[18-19] However, these studies provided valuable data on lumbar CSF and ventricular fluid concentrations of gentamicin after local instillations (Table 2-

Table 2-29

Pharmacokinetic Properties of Gentamicin (Dose, 1.5 mg/kg) in Newborns

Age/Birthweight Groups	One-hour Serum Concentration (μg/ml)	Serum Half-life (h)	Volume of Distribution (ml/kg)	Plasma Clearance (ml/min/1.73 M^2)
≤ 1 week				
800–1500 g	1.7	13.9	782	12.2
1501–2000 g	2.2	10.5	693	16.5
2001–2500 g	2.5	5.4	610	30.9
2501–3500 g	2.7	4.5	519	34.0
> 1 week				
All infants	3.0	3.2	488	56.2

Note: Recommended dosage is 2.5 mg/kg/dose.

54

Table 2-30

CSF Concentrations (μg/ml) of Gentamicin in Infants with Meningitis Treated with Systemic Gentamicin with or Without Lumbar Intrathecal or Intraventricular Gentamicin Administration

Type of Fluid	Systemic Therapy	Lumbar Intrathecal Administration (1 mg)		Intraventricular Administration (2.5 mg)	
		2–4 h	18–24 h	1–6 h	16–24 h
Lumbar CSF	1.6 (0.3–3.7)	30* (18.4–> 40)	1.6 (0.5–3.4)	32 (8–85)	3.2 (1.8–4.2)
Ventricular fluid	1.1 (0.1–3.0)	—	—	48 (10–130)	8.1 (1–24)

Note: The dose of systemic gentamicin was 2.5 mg/kg given every 12 h or 8 hours, depending on postnatal age.
* Four samples only.

Table 2-31
Dosage Recommendations for Gentamicin Sulfate

Individual dose	2.5 mg/kg
Intervals	Every 12 h for infants ≤ 1 week; every 8 h for infants > 1 week
Route	IV as 20–30-min infusion; IM
Total daily dose	5 mg/kg for infants ≤ 1 week; 7.5 mg/kg for infants > 1 week
Comments/cautions	Manufacturer recommends 6 mg/kg/day for neonates; extensive experience indicates no ototoxicity or nephrotoxicity when our recommended dosages are given for 7–10 days; increased potential for toxicity with more prolonged administration; inactivates carbenicillin when the two drugs are combined in an IV infusion; reduce dose for impaired renal function
Trade name	Garamycin (Schering)
Supplied as	Garamycin Pediatric Injectable, 20 mg/2 ml multiple dose vials

30). The mean concentration in lumbar CSF obtained 2–4 hours after a 1-mg dose instilled into the lumbar intrathecal space was 30 μg/ml. By 18–24 hours the mean CSF concentration decreased to 1.6 μg/ml, a value similar to that seen after systemic therapy alone. Daily instillation of 2.5 mg gentamicin directly into the ventricles resulted in a mean ventricular fluid concentration of 48 μg/ml (range, 10–130 μg/ml) at 1–6 hours after the dose, compared with 1.1 μg/ml (range 0.1–3.0 μg/ml) after systemic therapy only. An average concentration of 8.1 μg/ml (range, 1–24 μg/ml) was measured 16–24 hours after the intraventricular dose. As a rule the larger ventricular fluid concentrations were observed in infants who had reduced outflow of fluid from the ventricles, resulting in accumulation of gentamicin after 2 or 3 doses. It is evident that attainment of CSF gentamicin levels that greatly exceed the MBCs of most coliform organisms was not an assurance of successful outcome. Lack of clinical efficacy in these infants must be attributed to other factors.

On the basis of these pharmacologic and safety studies, the recommended individual dose of gentamicin is 2.5 mg/kg given every 12 hours for infants who are less than 1 week old, and every 8 hours for infants older than 1 week (Table 2-31). A 20-minute intravenous infusion of gentamicin is preferred to repeated intramuscular injections.

Although the manufacturer recommends 6 mg/kg/day for neonates, extensive experience indicates that the agent is not ototoxic or nephrotoxic when administered in the larger doses for periods of 7–10 days. Increased potential for toxicity occurs with more prolonged administration. Serum concentrations should be monitored in low birthweight preterm infants to maintain peak values of from 4–8 μg/ml.

Tobramycin

Tobramycin resembles gentamicin in antimicrobial activity, pharmacology, clinical efficacy, and toxicity. It is somewhat more active *in vitro* against strains of *P. aeruginosa* than is gentamicin or amikacin and may have a lower ototoxic potential. Studies in adults suggest that tobramycin is less nephrotopic than gentamicin.[102] Comparable data are not available for newborn and young infants.

Mean peak serum concentrations of 4–6 μg/ml are observed at 0.5–1.0 hour after a 2-mg/kg tobramycin dose is administered intramuscularly.[103] The mean concentrations of tobramycin in serum 12 hours after the dose are 1.5–2 μg/ml in infants with birthweights of 2000 g or less and 0.5–1.0 μg/ml in larger birthweight babies (see Table 2-32).

The concentrations of tobramycin in urine vary from 25 μg/ml to 132 μg/ml after a 2-mg/kg dose. Excretion of tobramycin in urine expressed as a percentage of the dose correlates directly with postnatal age. Average excretion values are 15–25 percent of the administered dose during the first week of life and 25–40 percent in older neonates.

The half-life of tobramycin in serum correlates inversely with birthweight and postnatal age. In infants who are less than 1500 g at birth, the half-life values may be as long as 9–17 hours. By contrast, half-lives of 3.0–4.5 hours are noted in older neonates who are 2500 g or more at birth. Half-life values correlate inversely with clearance of tobramycin from plasma.[103]

The average distribution volumes of tobramycin in neonates range from 339–435 ml/kg. There is no apparent relation between the distribution volumes and postnatal age. Plasma clearance values increase during the postnatal period. Clearances of 9–11 ml/min/1.73 M^2 are demonstrated in infants who are less than 1500 g at birth, compared to 25–35 ml/min/1.73 M^2 in heavier birthweight babies.

The manufacturer's recommended dosage of tobramycin is 2 mg/kg every 12 hours for all neonates.[104] On the basis of the known pharmacokinetics of aminoglycosides in neonates, it is likely that tobramycin should be administered every 8 hours for infants with birthweights of more than 2000 g and older than 7 days (Table 2-33). There are, however, no pharmacologic data to substantiate this recommendation. We recommend that physicians determine peak and trough (predose) serum concentrations in low birthweight preterm infants and in those requiring prolonged therapy in order to select dosages that produce safe and therapeutic levels.

Table 2-32
Pharmacokinetic Properties of Tobramycin (Dose, 2 mg/kg) in Newborns

Age/Birthweight Categories	Peak Serum Concentration* (μg/ml)	Serum Half-life (h)	Volume of Distribution (ml/kg)	Plasma Clearance (ml/min/1.73 M^2)
≤ 1 week				
< 1500 g	4.9	8.5	431	11
1500–2500 g	5.6	8.6	378	11
> 2500g	4.9	5.1	390	25
> 1 week				
> 1500 g	5.0	9.8	385	9
1500–2500 g	5.4	6.0	339	14
> 2500g	4.5	4.0	435	36

* Mean values

Table 2-33
Dosage Recommendations for Tobramycin Sulfate

Individual dose	2 mg/kg
Intervals	Every 12 h for infants 0–7 days and every 8 h for infants > 7 days
Route	IV as 20–30 min infusion; IM
Total daily dose	4 mg/kg for infants 0–7 days and 6 mg/kg for those > 7 days
Comments/cautions	The 6 mg/kg/day schedule suggested for older infants has not been tested extensively, but pharmacokinetic data indicates that it should produce satisfactory serum concentrations without significant accumulation; there are no long-term safety data; there is potential ototoxicity and nephrotoxicity; limited efficacy data; reduce dose for impaired renal function.
Trade name	Nebcin (Lilly)
Supplied as	Nebcin Pediatric Injection 20 mg/2 ml rubber-stoppered ampules

Although tobramycin has not been used as extensively as gentamicin in neonates, data in adults indicates that this aminoglycoside should be as safe and effective as gentamicin when proper dosages are used. The greater *in vitro* activity of tobramycin against *P. aeruginosa* compared with that of gentamicin has not been shown to correlate with superior clinical efficacy. No studies have addressed this issue in neonates.

Amikacin

Clinical experience with amikacin in neonates is limited because this drug has been reserved for therapy of infections caused by multiply-resistant strains of enterobacteriaceae. From available data it appears that the pharmacokinetics, safety, and efficacy of amikacin are similar to those of kanamycin from which it is derived.

Mean peak serum concentrations of approximately 15–20 μg/ml occur at 0.5–1.0 hour after 7.5-mg/kg doses of amikacin (Table 2-34).[105-106] The average trough concentrations 12 hours after the dose is given are 3–6 μg/ml. Urinary amikacin concentrations range from 50–650 μg/ml, and the average urinary excretion of the drug after 12 hours is 30–50 percent of the dose.[105] In 1979 Cookson and associates[85] reported subtherapeutic peak serum levels after 7.5-mg/kg doses were administered to infants weighing less than 1500 g at birth. Doses of 10 mg/kg at 12-hour intervals were required to achieve a mean peak value of 21.5 μg/ml and an average trough concentration of 3.3 μg/ml.

Table 2-34

Pharmacokinetic Properties of Amikacin (Dose, 7.5 mg/kg) in Newborns

Birthweight/Age Groups	Peak Serum Concentration* (μg/ml)	Serum Half-life (h)	Volume of Distribution (ml/kg)	Plasma Clearance (ml/min/1.73 M^2)
≤ 2000 g				
1–4 days	17	7.1	563	21
4–7 days	17	6.1	568	23
> 7 days	19	5.5	502	25
> 2000 g				
1–4 days	18	6.5	509	27
4–7 days	20	5.1	567	30
> 7 days	17	4.9	594	36

* Mean values

Table 2-35
Dosage Recommendations for Amikacin Sulfate

Individual dose	7.5 mg/kg for infants < 2000 g and 0–7 days; 10 mg/kg for all others
Intervals	Every 12 h for infants 0–7 days and every 8 h for infants > 7 days
Route	IV infusion over 20–30-min; IM
Total daily dose	15 mg/kg for infants < 2000 g and 0–7 days; 20 mg/kg for infants ≥ 2000 g and 0–7 days; 30 mg/kg for infants > 7 days
Comments/cautions	Limited long-term toxicity data available. Serum concentrations should be monitored in low birthweight preterm infants.
Trade name	Amikin (Bristol)
Supplied as	Amikin, 100-mg/2-ml vials

Serum half-life values for amikacin in newborns are inversely correlated with gestational and chronological age. For example, values of 7–8 hours are seen in low birthweight infants 1–3 days old and of 4–5 hours in full-term infants who are 7 days or older.

The volumes of amikacin distribution in neonates do not change appreciably during the first 30 days of life. The values range from 500–600 ml/kg. The plasma clearance rates of amikacin lie within the narrow range of 20–36 ml/min/1.73M^2 during the neonatal period (Table 2-34).

There are few reports of CSF amikacin concentrations in neonates.[106–108] Penetration appears to be erratic. In the presence of uninflamed meninges in 1-day-old infants, CSF concentrations ranged from 0.2 to 2.7 μg/ml or less when measured at 1–4 hours after a single 10-mg/kg dose administered by slow intravenous infusion.[108] Simultaneous concentrations in serum ranged from 15 to 29 μg/ml. The largest concentration reported has been 9.2 μg/ml after a 7.5-mg/kg dose was administered intramuscularly to an infant with meningitis.[106] Amikacin concentrations in ventricular fluid 12 hours after 1- or 2-mg intraventricular doses and 2–8 hours after intramuscular doses varies from 4.5 to 11.6 μg/ml (mean, 7.3 μg/ml).

The dosage schedule for neonates has not been firmly established. The 10-mg/kg loading dose that was initially recommended by the manufacturer has been abandoned (Table 2-35). Because of the similarity of amikacin and kanamycin pharmacokinetics, we recommend the following schedule: 7.5-mg/kg for infants less than 2000 g and 0–7 days of age, and 10-mg/kg for all other infants. A 12-hour dosing interval should be used for all neonates in the first week of life and an 8-hour interval thereafter. Dosage schedules may require individualization for infants less than 1500 g at birth or less than 30 weeks gestational age regardless of postnatal age, because of the highly variable serum concentrations and half-life values seen in these infants. This dosage schedule has been used in some infants enrolled in the Third Neonatal Meningitis Cooperative Study. The peak serum concentrations have been in the safe and therapeutic range of 15–25 μg/ml.

Netilmicin

Netilmicin has been extensively studied in adults, but there have been few studies in neonates.[74, 109-110] The drug was recently approved for clinical use and will be marketed under the trade name of Netromycin (Schering Corporation). Mean peak serum concentrations range from 5.6 to 6.9 μg/ml in infants tested at 0.5 hour after intramuscular administration of 3 mg/kg (Table 2-36).[74] Average serum values of 1.0–1.5 μg/ml are observed 12 hours after the dose. The serum half-life of netilmicin is inversely related to birthweight, gestational age, and chronologic age and ranges from 4.7 hours in infants 2000 g or less at birth in the first week of life to 3.8 hours in infants more than 2000 g at birth and 7 days of age and older. The serum concentration curve following the last dose declines in a biphasic manner. The average terminal half-life of 62.4 hours is within the range determined for gentamicin in adults.[74] In spite of this long terminal half-life and tissue accumulation, dosing intervals of 2–3 times the elimination half-life appear to be appropriate for most neonates.

The steady state serum concentration time curves after 3-mg/kg doses of netilmicin or gentamicin are similar, with mean peak serum concentrations of 6.9 and 6.3 μg/ml and serum half-life values of 4.0 and 3.5 hours for gentamicin and netilmicin, respectively.[74] Greater variability in serum concentrations was observed with gentamicin than with netilmicin; this has been noted in adults as well.

The average concentrations of netilmicin in urine are 46 μg/ml and 29 μg/ml for the first and second 3-hour study periods, respectively, after a 3-mg/kg dose. These values increase to 69 μg/ml and 103 μg/ml after a 4-mg/kg dose.[74] Netilmicin remains detectable in the urine for 14 days after the last dose of antibiotic is given.

Drug accumulation has been documented in very low birthweight premature infants.[74] After 4-mg/kg doses of netilmicin given every 12 hours for an average of 6.4 days, the mean trough value in premature infants (mean weight, 1415 g, mean gestational age, 32 weeks) increased from 2.2 μg/ml on the second day of therapy to 5.6 μg/ml on the final day. These infants did not show the expected decrease in serum creatinine observed in full-term infants during the first 2 weeks of life, and they all required mechanical ventilation for their underlying conditions. Thus, hypoxemia

Table 2-36
Pharmacokinetic Properties of Netilmicin (Dose, 3 mg/kg) in Newborn Infants

Birthweight/Age Groups	Peak Serum Concentration* (μg/ml)	Serum Half-life (h)	Plasma Clearance (ml/min/1.73 M^2)
≤ 2000 g			
< 7 days	6.0	4.7	30.8
≥ 7 days	5.6	4.1	34.1
> 2000 g			
< 7 days	6.9	3.4	38.8

* Mean values

superimposed on immature renal function is a possible explanation of drug accumulation in this group of babies.

On the basis of these pharmacokinetic studies, a dosage schedule of 2.5–3.0 mg/kg administered every 12 hours to infants 0–7 days of age and every 8 hours to those older than 7 days should produce serum levels that are within the therapeutic range. Greater experience with this regimen will be necessary to confirm these recommendations.

Safety of the Aminoglycosides

The major adverse effects of aminoglycosidic antibiotics are nephrotoxicity, ototoxicity, and rarely, neuromuscular blockade. Adverse hepatic and hematologic effects are not associated with this group of drugs. Acute toxic reactions are rare in the neonate.

The immature kidney of the neonate appears to be protected from major toxic effects of aminoglycosides.[111] Transient cylindruria and proteinuria may occur after prolonged administration of any of these drugs, but significant elevations in BUN and creatinine values are rarely observed. The criteria of maintaining peak serum gentamicin concentrations less than 10 μg/ml and trough concentrations less than 2 μg/ml to prevent nephrotoxicity[112] have not been systematically assessed in infants.

Because renal excretion accounts for the elimination of approximately 80 percent of an aminoglycoside dose, the greatest risk of toxicity occurs when drug elimination is impaired by reduction in renal function. In infants and children with a constant serum creatinine value, the gentamicin serum half-life value may be estimated at 3.8 times the serum creatinine value.[113] There is, however, no correlation between the half-life of gentamicin in serum and the serum creatinine concentrations during periods of unstable creatinine values (progressively changing by 0.5 mg or more/dl/24 hr). We have not evaluated the relation between serum half-life and serum creatinine concentrations for the other aminoglycosides in infants and children. As a rule it is wise to measure serum concentrations to determine the proper intervals of administration.

Neomycin,[76-77,114] streptomycin,[115] kanamycin,[116] and gentamicin[100] have been implicated as a cause of sensorineural hearing loss in infants and children. Gentamicin has also been associated with vestibular impairment in adults. It is, however, difficult to incriminate the aminoglycoside as the single causative agent of hearing loss in most studies because of other high-risk factors present in these patients. For example, asphyxia, hyperbilirubinemia, or incubator noise exposure have been associated independently with ototoxicity.[117] Although animal studies have demonstrated a synergistic effect of noise combined with neomycin or kanamycin on development of ototoxicity, this has not been substantiated in the human neonate exposed to both incubator noise and kanamycin. A familial predisposition to cochlear damage has been observed following therapy with streptomycin[115,118] but not with the other aminoglycosides.

Johnsonbaugh et al.[119] performed follow-up studies on 98 infants who received short courses of streptomycin sulfate during the neonatal period. The mean total dose was 118 mg/kg given for an average of 3.2 days, or 37 mg/kg/day. Hearing loss ascribable to the drug was not observed in these subjects when they were evaluated at 7½–8 years of age.

Kanamycin rarely causes toxicity when given in a dosage of 15 mg/kg/day for 10 or 12 days.[120] Ototoxicity is primarily related to total dose; high-frequency sensorineural hearing loss in infants with normal renal function is more likely if the total dose exceeds 500 mg/kg.[116] In a prospective evaluation of long-term toxicity of kanamycin and gentamicin, 86 infants who received one of these two drugs during the neonatal period underwent yearly audiometric, vestibular, and psychometric evaluations for 4 years.[120] Neither gentamicin nor kanamycin could be incriminated as the sole agent responsible for sensorineural hearing impairment. Because the infants in this study received doses lower than those currently recommended (for gentamicin, 5–6 mg/kg/day versus the recommended dosage of 5.0–7.5 mg/kg/day; for kanamycin, 15 mg/kg/day versus the current recommended dosage of 15–30 mg/kg/day), continued evaluation is necessary for these as well as for the newer aminoglycosides. Elfving and associates[121] found vestibular dysfunction in 2 of 28 children evaluated 2–4 years after having received gentamicin in the neonatal period. Both infants had complicated neonatal hospital courses, making a definitive association impossible. Results of the first Neonatal Meningitis Cooperative Study[100] revealed only 1 (1.3 percent) of 79 infants who received a minimum of 5.0–7.5 mg/kg/day of gentamicin for 3 weeks or longer developed profound deafness that may have been drug related. It is impossible to establish a direct causal relationship in such patients.

Documentation of aminoglycoside ototoxicity in neonates has been limited by our ability to detect impairment in the very young infant. The development of brainstem response audiometry has, however, facilitated assessment of hearing during the neonate's hospital stay.[122] Interpretation of results of this examination depends on the definition of responses of normal controls carefully matched for gestational and chronological age and for other factors such as hyperbilirubinemia. A blinded prospective study of brainstem-evoked responses in neonates who were treated with amikacin or netilmicin has recently been completed in our institution. Analysis of the data combined with careful follow-up and correlation with traditional audiometry should provide further insight into drug-induced ototoxicity in neonates. Bernard and coworkers[123] used brainstem-evoked response audiometry in 15 neonates who were treated with 7.5 mg/kg/day of either gentamicin or tobramycin for 6–10 days and in 14 untreated controls. A significantly delayed response was found in the treated group. The clinical implications remain to be determined.

There are a few reports of aminoglycoside-associated neuromuscular blockade.[124-126] The very young postoperative surgical infant with a highly variable fluid volume and renal function is at highest risk. The aminoglycoside may act alone or synergistically with other neuromuscular blocking agents. Diagnosis is made by nerve conduction studies that reveal a progressive fatigue and post-tetanic facilitation characteristic of a nondepolarizing curarelike neuromuscular block. Reversal is achieved by neostigmine or calcium. Prophylactic treatment with calcium is not indicated because this cation may interfere with the antimicrobial activity of aminoglycosides against certain organisms. Because of their effect on the neuromuscular junction, the aminoglycosides should not be used in patients with suspected or proved infant botulism.[127]

Finally, a direct toxic effect of gentamicin on brain tissue following intrathecal administration has been reported in rabbits and a human adult.[128] It is possible but unproved that such toxicity accounts for the higher mortality rate in neonates with coliform meningitis treated with intraventricular gentamicin.[10]

MISCELLANEOUS ANTIBIOTICS

Chloramphenicol

Background

The history of the use of chloramphenicol in newborns illustrates the "therapeutic orphan" principle. When the drug was first used in young infants in the 1950s, the dosage was calculated from that used in normal adults rather than from carefully performed pharmacokinetic studies in babies; the results were disastrous.

In mid-1959 Sutherland[129] reported on three full-term infants who developed unexplained peripheral vascular collapse after they had received doses of chloramphenicol that were substantially greater than those usually given to newborns. Later in 1959 Burns, Hodgman, and Cass[130] described a significantly increased mortality rate in premature infants with respiratory distress syndrome who were treated prophylactically with chloramphenicol, compared to the mortality rate in untreated infants or to those receiving penicillin and streptomycin. The course of illness in those infants was characteristic and was soon to be recognized as the *gray syndrome*. Vomiting begins 2–9 days after start of therapy. This is followed by refusal to suck, respiratory distress, abdominal distension, and passage of loose green stools. The infants become gravely ill within 24 hours after onset of symptoms. If chloramphenicol is discontinued at this time, most babies survive with diminution in clinical findings over a 24–36 hour period. No permanent adverse effects are apparent in survivors. On the other hand, if chloramphenicol is continued, flaccidity, ashen color, and hypothermia ensue in the next 12 hours, followed by death. This syndrome of cardiovascular collapse associated with chloramphenicol has been documented in both premature and full-term infants during the first week of life and in a very small number of older infants. The oldest pediatric patient with the gray syndrome was 25 months old.[131] Despite repeated warnings against treating neonates with chloramphenicol without monitoring serum concentrations, the syndrome is still seen today.[132]

The pathogenesis of the gray syndrome was not understood until the pharmacokinetic properties of chloramphenicol in neonates were defined. The succinate ester is absorbed well after intramuscular administration and is hydrolyzed to the free, active chloramphenicol, which is then conjugated to acid glucuronate. The free drug is excreted by glomerular filtration, and the conjugate is eliminated by tubular mechanisms.

Three interrelated factors accounted for the large number of gray syndrome babies seen in the late 1950s: excessive doses, immaturity of the hepatic glucuronyl transferase system, and diminished glomerular and tubular function. As a result, elevated serum concentrations of both free and conjugated chloramphenicol occurred. Available evidence indicates that toxicity is due to the free drug rather than to its metabolic products.[133] Toxicity is observed most frequently in young premature infants in whom enzyme systems and physiologic processes are most immature.

Chloramphenicol has broad antimicrobial activity against both gram-positive and gram-negative bacteria and against all species of *Rickettsia* and *Chlamydia*. The following are representative chloramphenicol MIC values against commonly encountered pathogens: *S. aureus*, 4–12 μg/ml; *Streptococcus pyrogenes*, 2–4 μg/ml; *S. pneumoniae*, 1–4 μg/ml; *H. influenzae*, 0.2–0.5 μg/ml; *E. coli*, 0.8–8.0 μg/ml; *Klebsiella* species, 0.5–30.0

μg/ml; and *P. aeruginosa,* 50–125 μg/ml. The agent is principally bacteriostatic but is bactericidal against some coliforms and against *S. pneumoniae, Neisseria meningitidis,* and *H. influenzae. In vitro* studies indicate that chloramphenicol may interfere with the bactericidal activity of ampicillin against group B streptococci[134] and *L. monocytogenes.*[135] The clinical significance of this *in vitro* antagonism is uncertain. We recently observed delayed sterilization of CSF (positive CSF culture after 36 hours and negative culture after 72 hours of therapy) in a 3-year-old infant who was initially treated with ampicillin and chloramphenicol for what later proved to be *Listeria* meningitis. The CSF bactericidal titer against the pathogen was 1:2 while the patient was receiving ampicillin and chloramphenicol and 1:8 when ampicillin and gentamicin were given.

One mechanism of microbial resistance to chloramphenicol is by plasmid or R factor mediated acetyltransferase that catalyzes the acetylation of the drug. Although resistance is said to develop slowly, it has been noted during the first 10 days of therapy in chloramphenicol-treated patients with meningitis and ventriculitis in whom ventricular catheters are placed for drainage.[136]

Pharmacokinetics

Chloramphenicol succinate is hydrolyzed in the body to the free active drug, which in turn is conjugated in liver to the glucuronide salt. Approximately 10 percent of the compound is directly excreted by the kidneys as the succinate. The free drug is excreted by glomerular filtration, and the conjugate is eliminated by tubular secretion. Approximately 65 percent of the total chloramphenicol in the serum of neonates is free drug, compared to 90 percent in adults. This is because excretion of the glucuronide by tubular mechanisms is considerably reduced in the first weeks of life.

Recent studies have emphasized the large variability in serum concentrations and half-life values of chloramphenicol after recommended dosages are given to newborn infants.[137-138] This is particularly true of low birthweight, preterm infants, in whom concentrations ranged from 11 to 36 μg/ml after 14–25-mg/kg doses in the first week of life. Half-life times ranged from 10 hours to more than 48 hours; patients with long half-life times tended to accumulate drug in serum between doses. Friedman and coworkers[137] found half-life values of from 2.5 to 15 hours (mean, 8 hours) in 8 neonates, 5 of whom were premature. An inverse correlation exists between serum half-life and postnatal age and weight.

Studies in the early 1960s using less sensitive assay methods than are available today, showed surprisingly similar pharmacokinetics.[139-140] After 25-mg/kg does were given to premature infants, serum concentrations of from 14 to 27 μg/ml (mean, 20 μg/ml) at 3 hours, 7 to 21 μg/ml (mean, 14 μg/ml) at 9 hours, and 2 to 18 μg/ml (mean, 6 μg/ml) at 21 hours were

Table 2-37
Dosage Recommendations for Chloramphenicol

Individual dose	25 mg/kg
Intervals	Every 24 h for all infants 0–14 days and those ≤ 2000 g and 15–30 days; every 12 h for infants > 2000 g and 15–30 days, and those ≤ 2000 g and 15–30 days who have meniingitis
Route	IV (preferred) as 15–30-min infusion; PO
Total daily dose	25 mg/kg for infants ≤ 2000 g (regardless of age), and those > 2000 g and 0–14 days; 50 mg/kg for infants > 2000 g and 15–30 days
Comments/cautions	Our dosage recommendations are contrary to manufacturer's; measure blood concentrations if possible; clinical and laboratory monitoring for gray syndrome and blood dyscrasia; reserved for infections resistant or unresponsive to antibiotics with lesser toxicity
Trade name	Chloromycetin (Parke-Davis)
Supplied as	Chloromycetin sodium succinate, 1-g vial for reconstitution; oral suspension chloromycetin palmitate, 150 mg/5 ml

observed after the intramuscular dose. The half-life values were estimated to be approximately 24 hours in the first week of life and 14 hours thereafter.

The metabolism of chloramphenicol is altered by coadministration of other drugs that compete for hepatic enzyme binding sites. Thus, phenytoin will increase the serum chloramphenicol concentrations to potentially toxic levels, whereas coadministration of phenobarbitol reduces concentrations below the therapeutic range of 15–25 μg/ml.[141]

Chloramphenicol concentrations in CSF are approximately 65 percent of those in serum. This highly diffusible drug attains levels in CSF of from 5 to more than 20 μg/ml after 10–20-mg/kg doses. These concentrations are usually bacteriostatic against most gram-negative enteric bacilli.

Because of the variation in serum concentrations and half-life values in neonates, particularly low birthweight, preterm babies or in those receiving anticonvulsants, it is advisable to monitor serum concentrations in order to determine the proper dosage schedule. The dosage recommendations presented in Table 2-37 are designed as a guide only. Chloramphenicol should not be routinely used in the neonate without laboratory facilities adequate to provide serum concentration data promptly.

There are no primary indications for chloramphenicol therapy of the neonate. Treatment with chloramphenicol represents alternative therapy for coliform infections that have not adequately responded to the amino-glycosides. In this situation we prefer one of the third generation cephalo-sporins (discussed earlier in this chapter), which are more effective and safer. If chloramphenicol is used in a newborn, the infant should be followed closely for early signs of gray syndrome. In addition, a complete blood count should be performed twice weekly in order to detect blood dyscrasias. Recent evidence suggests that charcoal hemoperfusion is superior to exchange transfusion for removal of chloramphenicol from the blood and for reversing the shock and acidosis that accompany the gray syndrome.[142]

Polymyxins

The polymyxins are cyclic polypeptides that are used infrequently in pediatrics today. Polymyxin B and polymyxin E (colistin) have identical pharmacologic and antimicrobial properties. These drugs are uniquely bactericidal because of their detergent-like action on bacterial cell membranes, causing disruption in osmotic properties that leads eventually to cell lysis and death. The polymyxins are active *in vitro* against many *E. coli, Pseudomonas, Klebsiella, Enterobacter, Salmonella,* and *Shigella* strains isolated from newborns and young infants. These drugs are ineffective *in vitro* against *Proteus* species and gram-positive bacteria. Emergence of microbial resistance to the polymyxins occurs only rarely and is not a clinical problem.

Unpublished data by Eichenwald demonstrate that a 2-mg/kg polymyxin B intramuscular dose in full-term infants results in peak serum concentrations of approximately 6 µg/ml 2 hours after the dose is given. The concentration after 6 hours is 2 µg/ml, and after 12 hours the concentrations are 0.25–0.5 µg/ml.

After a single 2-mg/kg intramuscular dose of colistimethate, average concentrations of colistin in serum are 5.3 µg/ml at 0.5 hours, 3.9 µg/ml at 2 hours, 2.4 µg/ml at 4 hours, 1.2 µg/ml at 6 hours, and 1 µg/ml at 12 hours.[143] Multiple 2-mg/kg doses do not result in significant accumulation of drug in serum. Axline, Yaffe, and Simon[17] administered 5 mg/kg of colistimethate to premature infants. Peak serum values were 16.4 µg/ml in infants 4 days old and 14.8 µg/ml in infants 12–51 days old. Antimicrobial activity was measurable 12 hours after the dose was given, and serum half-life values of 2–3 hours did not change significantly with increasing postnatal age.

Neither polymyxin B nor colistin penetrates well into tissue or CSF even in the presence of inflammation. Flux et al.[144] administered a 5-mg/kg colistimethate dose to an infant and detected serum concentrations of 5 µg/ml after 6 hours, and of 1 µg/ml after 24 hours. CSF colistin concentrations in that patient were measurable at 12 hours and reached a peak of 1 μg/ml after 24 hours. When used for treatment of meningitis caused by *P. aeruginosa,* it is necessary to instill polymyxin B intraventricularly or in the lumbar intrathecal space in addition to intramuscular administration.

The polymyxins are potentially nephrotoxic; manifestations are diminished urinary output and rising BUN. These drugs should be cautiously used in patients with impaired renal function in order to prevent accumulation of drug in serum with resultant neurotoxic effects. Numbness of the extremities, transient circumoral paresthesias, dizziness, ataxia, and muscular weakness may occur in older patients. These manifestations have not been seen in neonates.

With the advent of ampicillin, the third generation cephalosporins, and the aminoglycoside drugs, the polymyxins have limited usefulness in neonates. Whereas they were once considered first-line agents for therapy of *Pseudomonas* infections, carbenicillin or ticarcillin alone or in combination with gentamicin, amikacin, or tobramycin are now the preferred agents. The only possible indication for systemic use of these drugs is for gram-negative bacteria that are resistant to the aminoglycosides and the new beta-lactam derivatives such as moxalactam, cefotaxime, mezlocillin, and others that will soon be approved for use in newborns. The dosage of polymyxin B is from 2.0 to 4.5 mg/kg/day. Colistin (as colistimethate) is given in a dosage of 5–8 mg/kg/day in 2 or 3 divided doses. Colistin sulfate, the formulation for oral administration, is an acceptable alternative to neomycin therapy of gastroenteritis caused by enteropathogenic strains of *E. coli.* Colistin sulfate is given orally in a dosage of 10–15 mg/kg/day divided into 3 or 4 doses. Colistin sulfate administered orally is effective treatment for gastroenteritis caused by enteropathogenic *E. coli.* It has also been used for prophylaxis in infants considered at high risk for necrotizing enterocolitis.[145] The efficacy and safety of this use is unproved.

Tetracyclines

The tetracyclines are a large family of closely related compounds. Because of their broad antimicrobial spectrum, these drugs were commonly used for chemoprophylaxis of infections in premature infants and in neonates with high-risk factors that allegedly predispose to infection. When it became apparent that these agents caused significant bone and dental abnormalities and were not effective in preventing infection, their popularity decreased. There is no indication for the systemic or oral use of the tetracyclines in newborns. Tetracycline ophthalmic preparations are used in some nurseries as prophylaxis against gonococcal conjunctivitis and for treatment of inclusion conjunctivitis due to *Chlamydia* organisms.

The tetracyclines have broad antimicrobial activity against many bacteria, actinomycetes, rickettsiae, mycoplasmas, and *Chlamydia* organisms. These agents are primarily bacteriostatic at the serum concentrations achieved with standard dosages. At considerably higher concentrations, they are frequently bactericidal. The tetracyclines are potent inhibitors of protein synthesis by reversible binding to ribosomes and messenger RNA. Emergence of bacteria resistant to the tetracyclines has become common. Organisms demonstrating substantial resistance to the tetracyclines are coliform bacteria, group A beta-hemolytic streptococci, pneumococci, B. fragilis, and coagulase positive staphylococci.

Sereni et al.[146] studied the comparative blood levels, kinetics of distribution in body fluid, and the urinary excretion of tetracycline-1-methylene-lysine in newborns, older infants, and children. The pharmacologic properties of this drug are similar to those of the other tetracyclines. Concentrations of 3–5 μg/ml are detected in serum of 1-day-old neonates after 7-mg/kg doses. With the same dosage, serum concentrations range from 2.0 to 3.5 μg/ml in infants, 2–11 months old. The half-life in serum is prolonged in the first days of life (15–18 hours), compared with values (6–8 hours) in patients 1 month to 11 years of age. The volume of distribution of tetracycline-1-methylene-lysine is smaller in newborns than in older infants and children. The average plasma clearance of tetracycline-1-methylene-lysine is 6.7 mg/min/1.73 M^2, compared to 31 ml/min/1.73 M^2 in older infants and 61.4 mg/min/1.73 M^2 in children 3–9 years of age.

Gidion and Marget[147] studied tetracycline and oxytetracycline in newborns. Mean serum concentrations of approximately 4 μg/ml at 1 hour, and 0.5–1.0 μg/ml at 12 hours were observed after a 10-mg/kg intramuscular dose was given. Intravenous administration resulted in higher serum concentrations at 0.5 hours after a 10 mg/kg dose, but the concentrations at 12 hours were similar to those after an intramuscular dose.

Gibbons and Riechelderfer[148] gave demethyl chlortetracycline hydrochloride (now called demeclocycline) orally to premature and full-term infants. This agent was selected for study because of its higher and better-sustained serum concentrations in adults compared with the other tetracyclines. With 1.5-mg/kg demeclocycline doses given orally every 6 hours, serum concentrations were 0.4–3.3 μg/ml (mean, 2.3 μg/ml) on the 4th day and 0.6–2.2 μg/ml (mean, 1.8 μg/ml) on the 10th day of treatment.

The toxicities of the various members of the tetracycline family are essentially identical. These drugs chelate with calcium and related cations, bind firmly to bone, and concentrate in areas of newly formed calcium complexes. Fluorescent residues of tetracycline localize and persist in bone for long periods after the drug has been cleared from the body.[149] As a result, the tetracyclines interfere with bone and tooth metabolism in fetal life and early childhood. Permanent discoloration and defective enamelization of the deciduous teeth may occur following administration during the latter half of pregnancy and in the first 6 months of life. If given at any time from age 6 months to approximately 6 years, the tetracyclines may cause discoloration of the permanent teeth. Discoloration and enamel hypoplasia appear to be related more to the total dose of drug than to the duration of therapy. Wallman and Hilton[150] examined 50 infants who were treated with tetracycline during the neonatal period: 46 had some degree of pigmentation with or without deformity of the teeth, 23 (46 percent) demonstrated deep pigmentation and deformity, 6 had moderate pigmentation and no deformity, and 7 showed slight pigmentation and no deformity. An additional 10 infants were reported to have pigmented teeth, but the investigators did not examine these cases. The average duration of therapy had been 6.5 days for patients with severe deformity, 6.1 days for those with moderate deformity, and 4.1 days for those with mild deformity. The average total doses were 189 mg/kg, 156 mg/kg, and 108 mg/kg for the severely, moderately, and mildly affected infants, respectively.

Tetracycline and demeclocycline are most toxic to rabbit teeth, followed by the other analogs such as oxytetracycline and chlortetracycline.[151]

In 1963 Cohlan, Bevelander, and Tiamsic[149] reported that tetracycline produces 40-percent depression of normal skeletal growth as measured by inhibition of fibula length in premature infants. This inhibition is reversible after short-term tetracycline administration. Further studies by these authors, of rats, demonstrated that when a 40-mg/kg/day tetracycline dose was given during the 10th–15th day of gestation there was a 28-percent reduction in fetal size at term. The permanent effects on skeletal growth after long-term administration of the tetracyclines during pregnancy in humans are unknown. Prolonged administration of the tetracyclines may result in inhibition of the microbial flora of the respiratory and gastrointestinal tracts, allowing for superinfection with resistant strains that are potentially more virulent. In addition, increased intracranial pressure (pseudotumor cerebri) in young infants has been described.[152] The tetracyclines may cause severe and often fatal hepatic toxicity after intravenous administration of excessive dosages to pregnant women, patients with renal failure, and occasionally patients with relatively minor infections who are otherwise healthy. Outdated tetracycline can produce Fanconi's syndrome from renal damage.

The tetracyclines are not recommended for systemic use in newborn and young infants. The infectious conditions for which tetracycline is indicated rarely occur in the neonate. The only use for tetracycline in newborns is topical application for gonococcal prophylaxis or for treatment of inclusion blenorrhea caused by *Chlamydia trachomatis* (see Chap 9).

Sulfonamides

In the late 1940s and 1950s the sulfonamides were commonly used for prophylaxis and treatment of neonatal bacterial disease. The availability of superior antimicrobial agents, emergence of resistant bacteria, and recognition that sulfonamides might be associated with development of kernicterus in neonates have greatly reduced the use of these agents in newborn and young infants.

The sulfonamides are bacteriostatic agents with a wide range of antimicrobial activity against gram-positive and gram-negative bacteria. Because these agents are structural analogs of para-aminobenzoic acid (PABA) they act competitively to inhibit normal utilization of PABA by bacteria. Synthesis of folic acid is inhibited at the dihydrofolinic acid step.

Microbial resistance to the sulfonamides occurs frequently. This is particularly true for gonococci, staphylococci, Shigella species, some streptococci, and group C meningococci. Resistance is more likely to develop if treatment is prolonged. In such circumstances it is likely that mutations occurring in random fashion give rise to resistant variants that are favored by selection in the presence of drug. Transfer of multiple drug resistance among strains of coliform bacilli was responsible for the emergence of sulfonamide-resistant Shigella strains in Japan during the early 1950s.

The sulfonamides are metabolized primarily by hepatic acetylation. The proportion of free to total serum sulfonamide is higher in neonates than in older children or adults, indicating that the degree of acetylation is limited during the neonatal period. This is probably explained by hepatic enzyme immaturity similar to that observed with glucuronidation of chloramphenicol in newborns. Fichter and Curtis studied the pharmacology of sulfadiazine in premature and full-term infants[153] An initial dose of 100 mg/kg, followed in 48 hours by 50-mg/kg doses every 24 hours for 3 days, produced mean peak serum levels of 15–17 mg/dl and trough concentrations of 9–11 mg/dl. The peak serum concentrations of sulfadiazine varied considerably and ranged from 4 to 20 mg/dl during the 5-day period of administration. The same dosage schedule administered to premature infants resulted in mean peak serum concentrations of 14–15 mg/dl and trough values of 6–9 mg/dl. As with the full-term infants, the individual serum concentrations varied considerably. The peak sulfonamide concentrations in blood ranged from 16 to 19 mg/dl of free drug and 25–29 mg/dl of total drug. The free sulfonamide concentrations were in general within the desired therapeutic range of 5–15 mg/dl. Serum concentrations of 11–18 mg/dl were found after an initial 100-mg/kg sulfadiazine dose given subcutaneously and followed in 48 hours by a 50-mg/kg dose of triple sulfonamide suspension given orally every 12 hours for 6 doses.

Serum concentrations of 6–12 mg/dl were observed after 75-mg/kg doses of sulfisoxazole were given every 12 hours.[154] A 100-mg/kg sulfisoxazole dose administered subcutaneously to infants less than 1000 g at birth resulted in serum concentrations of 10–20 mg/dl at 12–24 hours after the dose was given.

The sulfonamides are excreted primarily by renal mechanisms. Glomerular filtration is the major means of excretion for both the free and acetylated forms. Varying degrees of tubular reabsorption occur for most sulfonamides. The persistence of therapeutic concentrations of sulfonamide in serum of newborns is explained in part by the diminished renal function that is characteristic of this age group.

Plasma albumin binding of sulfonamides varies considerably. Bound drug, like the acetate conjugate, is antimicrobially inactive. The clinical importance of sulfonamide-albumin binding relates to competition with bilirubin for binding sites and distribution of sulfonamide in extravascular spaces such as CSF.[154] Sulfadiazine enters CSF more readily than does sulfisoxazole.

Subcutaneous administration of sulfadiazine or sulfisoxazole is well tolerated by neonates. Hematuria and crystalluria are uncommon in newborns. Use of the sulfonamides in neonates was greatly diminished after the demonstration by Silverman et al.[154] of a significantly increased incidence of kernicterus in premature infants prophylactically treated with penicillin and sulfisoxazole. It was not for many years after this observation that the mechanism for kernicterus was explained. Because sulfonamides compete with bilirubin for albumin binding sites, the displaced free bilirubin diffuses into extravascular sites such as the central nervous system ganglia, causing kernicterus.

Sulfonamides may also cause hemolysis in neonates who have erythrocyte glucose-6-phosphate dehydrogenase deficiency.

We do not recommend sulfonamide therapy for newborns except as topical application to the eyes for inclusion conjunctivitis caused by C. trachomatis. Acute urinary tract infections of newborns should be treated parenterally with ampicillin and an aminglycosidic drug.

Trimethoprim—Sulfamethoxazole

This combination of drugs provides sequential and synergistic inhibition of microbial folic acid synthesis. Trimethoprim—sulfamethoxazole (TMP-SMX) has been approved for use in the United States for therapy of chronic urinary tract infections, otitis media, shigellosis, Pneumocystis carinii infections, and acute exacerbations of chronic bronchitis in patients over 2 months of age. The drug comes under the "orphan clause" because of insufficient pharmacokinetic, safety, and efficacy data to permit approval of its use in neonates.

Springer and associates[155] reported on the pharmacokinetics of TMP-SMX in newborn infants (Table 2-38). After a dose of 5.25 mg/kg TMP with 26.25 mg/kg SMX, peak SMX concentrations of from 72 to 135 µg/ml were observed after the first dose and of 120 to 200 µg/ml after multiple doses on day 3. The corresponding TMP concentrations ranged from 3.0 to 4.5 µg/ml and 3.0 to 6.4 µg/ml, respectively. The serum half-life values

Table 2-38

Pharmacokinetic Properties of Trimethoprim (TMP)–Sulfmethoxazole (SMX)

Time of Study	Peak Serum Concentration* (μg/ml)		Serum Half-life (h)		Volume of Distribution (ml/kg)		Plasma Clearance (ml/min)	
	TMP	SMX	TMP	SMX	TMP	SMX	TMP	MSX
After first dose	3.4	107	19	16.5	2700	480	3.3	0.65
After 3 days	5	148	24.6	23.3	—	—	—	—

Note: Dosage was 5.25 mg TMP/kg with 26.25 mg SMX/kg.

* Mean values

were significantly longer after repeated doses than after the first dose (Table 2-38). TMP diffuses widely throughout the body fluids, as reflected by the volume of distribution value of 2700 ml/kg for TMP compared to (480 ml/kg) for SMX.

Because of its broad antimicrobial activity, demonstration of *in vitro* synergism between gentamicin and TMP against coliform bacilli,[156] and excellent diffusibility of TMP into most body fluids and tissues including CSF and brain, TMP-SMX has been used alone or in combination with an aminoglycoside for therapy of neonatal meningitis caused by gram-negative enteric bacilli.[157-158] These are not controlled studies, and most of the infants had previously received other antibiotic regimens before TMP-SMX was used. Failures of TMP-SMX therapy have been observed.[158]

The limited experience with this agent precludes its use in neonates except for extraordinary circumstances such as shigellosis, pneumocystis infection, or coliform meningitis that has failed to respond to other regimens. Springer and associates[155] suggested that an initial dose of approximately 2 mg/kg TMP with 10 mg/kg SMX followed by 0.6 mg/kg TMP with 3 mg/kg SMX be given every 12 hours. An infant with elevated bilirubin levels, even if they are below 10 mg/dl, may be at risk of developing kernicterus due to displacement of indirect bilirubin from albumin binding sites. Although SMX does not appear to displace bilirubin from albumin in *in vitro* systems,[155] the risk for this agent alone or in combination with TMP to do so in infants is unknown. Other side effects of this drug combination include anemia, hepatitis, and rash (including Stevens–Johnson syndrome). TMP is present in large concentrations in breast milk, amniotic fluid, and fetal serum after adminstration to the mother.[159]

Macrolide Antibiotics

The macrolide group of antimicrobial agents includes erythromycin, clindamycin, novobiocin, and oleandomycin. With the exception of the lincomycins, these drugs were used in the 1950s to treat neonatal staphylococcal infections when penicillin-resistant staphylococcal strains were prevalent and the penicillinase-resistant penicillins were not yet available. Novobiocin and oleandomycin are limited-purpose agents that have no current role in the antimicrobial therapy of neonatal bacterial infections. Clindamycin is noteworthy for its activity against *B. fragilis*, but there has been very little clinical experience with this drug in the neonate. Erythromycin has recently assumed an important role in the young infant for therapy of infections caused by *C. trachomatis* and *Bordetalla pertussis*. Erythromycin and clindamycin will be reviewed in this section, and novobiacin will also be discussed to give historical perspective.

Erythromycin

Erythromycin is primarily a bacteriostatic agent that acts by interfering with protein synthesis in a manner similar to that of chloramphenicol. Resistant strains develop *in vivo* but only after prolonged therapy. Resistance to the macrolide antibiotics is not associated with drug destruction by inactivating enzyme. Erythromycin is active against most gram-positive bacteria, including many penicillin-resistant strains of staphylococci. In addition, most strains of *H. influenzae, Neisseria* species, *B. pertussis,* and *C. trachomatis* are susceptible to this agent. Erythromycin is rarely administered parenterally due to the associated tissue toxicity.

Burns and Hodgman [160] administered erythromycin estolate (the lauryl sulfate salt of the propionyl ester of erythromycin) to premature infants. Serum erythromycin concentrations of 1–2 µg/ml were observed 3–4 hours after a 10-mg/kg-dose was given orally, and concentrations of 0.5 µg/ml or greater were measured for a minimum of 6 hours. Serum levels of erythromycin were independent of birthweight, postnatal age, and gastric acidity. Accumulation of drug in serum did not result from repeated doses every 6 hours for 8 days.

These data have been confirmed in a comparative pharmacokinetic study of erythromycin ethyl succinate and erythromycin estolate in 28 infants who were less than 4 months of age; 12 infants were between 12 and 30 days of age.[161] After 10-mg/kg doses, peak serum concentrations in infants receiving the estolate were larger (mean, 1.6 ± 0.6 µg/ml) than those given the ethyl succinate (mean, 1.1 ± 0.5 µg/ml). The peak concentrations increased slightly after multiple doses (steady state), and the time to the peak level for the estolate and the elimination half-life were significantly longer at steady state (Table 2-39). The larger area-under-the-curve values for the estolate indicate a superior bioavailability of this compound compared to erythromycin ethyl succinate.

Erythromycin is excreted in the urine and bile, but only a fraction of the total dose can be accounted for by these two excretory routes. Although erythromycin is uniformly distributed throughout most of the body, concentrations in CSF are small, even in the presence of inflammation. Drug concentrations in tears 1 hour after the dose were greater than the mean serum concentrations obtained concomitantly and ranged from 2.0 to 5.4 µg/ml (mean, 2.8) after the ethyl succinate and from 0.6 to 5.0 µg/ml (mean, 2.4) after the estolate.[161]

On the basis of these pharmacokinetic studies, we recommend that erythromycin estolate be given orally in a 10-mg/kg dose every 12 hours (20 mg/kg/day) or 8 hour (30 mg/kg/day). The ethyl succinate suspension should be given orally every 6 hours (40 mg/kg/day). These agents are recommended for therapy of chlamydial infections or of pertussis.

Table 2-39

Pharmacokinetic Properties of Erythromycin (EE) and Erythromycin Ethyl Succinate (ES) (Dose, 10 mg/kg) in Newborn and Young Infants

Time/Drug	Peak Serum Concentration* (μg/ml)	Absorption half-life (h)	Elimination half-life (h)	AUC† (μg × h/ml)
Initial dose				
EE	1.6	1.0	4.1	17.2
ES	1.1	0.6	2.3	6.3
Steady state				
EE	1.8	0.7	6.6	16.2
ES	1.3	0.3	2.4	5.4

* Mean value
† Area under the curve

Erythromycin estolate is well tolerated by newborns. Burns and Hodgman[160] were unable to demonstrate chemical alteration of hepatic function or abnormal bilirubin levels in newborns who were treated for 8 days or longer with erythromycin estolate. Both erythromycin esters administered orally in suspension form were well tolerated by infants with chlamydial conjunctivitis who were treated for 21 days.[162] Cholestatic jaundice resulting from hypersensitivity to this preparation occurs primarily in teenagers and adults and has not been reported in infants less than 6 weeks of age.[163]

Clindamycin

Until recently there were few data on the pharmacokinetics of clindamycin in young infants. Bell and associates[164] presented data showing maximum serum concentrations of approximately 13 μg/ml after 5–7-mg/kg-doses were administered intravenously. The trough concentrations ranged from 3 to 5 μg/ml. The mean serum half-life was 11 hours in premature infants and 4.7 hours in full-term babies. The clearance of clindamycin was 0.14 ml/min/kg in neonates compared with 0.22 ml/min/kg in older infants. These authors recommended a dosage of 15 mg/kg/day in 3 divided doses for all low birthweight, preterm infants and for full-term infants less than 1 week of age. Older full term infants would receive 20 mg/kg/day in 4 divided doses.

Although clindamycin has been associated with development of pseudo-membranous colitis or antibiotic-associated colitis, this is a rare disorder in infants, and when it does occur other antibiotics, notably ampicillin or amoxicillin, are more frequently implicated.[165] Because up to 20 percent of healthy neonates are colonized with C. difficile, the putative pathogen in antiobiotic-associated colitis,[166] it seems prudent to restrict the use of clindamycin and the orally administered ampicillins during this period. We do not recommend clindamycin for use in neonates. There is far greater experience with the beta-lactam antibiotics, and these drugs are preferred for therapy of staphylococcal diseases. We favor chloramphenicol or metronidazole for the B. fragilis infections that occur rarely in young infants. Furthermore, clindamycin does not penetrate well in CSF or brain and is relatively ineffective for management of B. fragilis ventriculitis.[167]

Novobiocin

Novobiocin has been used alone and in combination with other antimicrobial agents for prophylaxis and treatment of neonatal staphylococcal diseases. The drug is very active against S. aureus, most strains of which, in the absence of previous contact with the drug, are among the most susceptible bacteria.[168] Novobiocin is also effective against other gram-positive bacteria. Although inactive against most coliform bacilli, novobiocin is active in vitro against P. vulgaris.

Novobiocin is primarily a bacteriostatic drug that inhibits protein and nucleic acid synthesis. Significant albumin binding (90 percent) accounts for diminished *in vitro* antimicrobial activity in the presence of serum. Novobiocin may displace other substances, such as bilirubin, from protein binding sites. The clinical significance of this displacement is unknown.

Novobiocin is well absorbed from the gastrointestinal tract and attains high and sustained levels in the blood. Serum concentrations vary widely from patient to patient. For example, doses of approximately 6 mg/kg administered orally to neonates produce serum levels of 18–95 μg/ml at 2 hours and of 19–90 μg/ml at 6 hours after the dose.[169] Novobiocin is excreted mainly in bile, and the continual process of biliary excretion and gastrointestinal reabsorption results in sustained blood levels.

The major toxicity caused by novobiocin is hyperbilirubinemia in newborn infants. Sutherland and Keller[170] reported a 3-fold increase in neonatal hyperbilirubinemia after administration of novobiocin. This did not result from the yellow pigment inherent in the drug but was due to potent inhibition of glucuronyl transferase, the enzyme that catalyzes the conjugation of bilirubin.

Rifampin

Rifampin, a semisynthetic derivative of rifamycin, has gained popularity recently for therapy of tuberculosis and for prophylaxis against disease caused by *H. influenza* or *N. meningitidis*. It has broad antimicrobial activity against gram-positive and gram-negative bacteria. Tubercle bacilli are inhibited by 0.02–0.50 μg/ml of rifampin. These concentrations are readily achieved in serum and are usually attainable in CSF. Rifampin is 80 percent protein-bound in serum.

There is little information regarding the pharmacokinetics of rifampin in neonates and young infants. Acocella et al.[171] administered 10-mg/kg doses to 33 male full-term infants who were less than 3 days old. After a single oral dose, the serum concentrations increased progressively to a mean peak value of 5.8 μg/ml at 8 hours. By contrast, a mean peak concentration of 12.5 μg/ml was detected 2 hours after multiple 10-mg/kg daily doses. The serum concentrations at 8 and 12 hours after multiple doses were similar to the 8-hour values in infants who received a single dose. When a single 10-mg/kg dose of rifampin (suspension prepared in 85 percent sucrose solution or as powder in applesauce) was given to infants and children from 6 to 58 months old, mean peak serum concentrations were 10.7–11.5 μg/ml.[172] These values are approximately twice those in neonates after a single 10-mg/kg dose. The mean urinary concentrations of rifampin are approximately 50 μg/ml after 0–6 hours, and 85 μg/ml 6–12 hours after the dose is given. Approximately 35 percent of the administered dose of rifampin is recovered in urine during the first 12 hours after the oral dose is given.

The concentrations of rifampin[173] in CSF of patients with tuberculous meningitis are highly variable.[173] After 300-mg doses, the values range from 0.04–1.40 µg/ml. The average concentrations are 0.3–0.6 µg/ml. There are no data on CSF levels in neonates.

It is difficult to formulate dosage recommendations for rifampin in neonates. A 10-mg/kg oral daily dose appears to be adequate for therapy of tuberculosis in newborns. It is possible that accumulation of drug in serum will occur after multiple doses, particularly in preterm infants. Serum values should be monitored in these infants and in neonates with tuberculous meningitis, where the rifampin dosage may need to be increased to attain antituberculous activity in CSF. There is no information on the safety of this drug in neonates.

Metronidazole

Metronidazole, a nitroimidazole antibiotic, has excellent *in vitro* activity against anaerobic gram-positive and gram-negative bacteria and against certain protozoa. It is ineffective against aerobic bacteria. The drug has been selectively used in neonates for therapy of B. *fragilis* central nervous system infection[167] and occasionally of other conditions potentially involving anaerobes such as necrotizing enterocolitis.

Until 1981 there were no data on the pharmacokinetics of metronidazole in newborn infants. Because this compound is hydroxylated, conjugated, and excreted by the kidneys, processes that may be immature and functioning suboptimally in neonates, it was important to evaluate this drug in order to formulate dosage schedules.

Investigators from Westmead, Australia[174] studied 11 infants who were 1 to 3 days of age and had been given 7.5–15-mg/kg doses of metronidazole intravenously (Table 2-40). Peak serum concentrations were largest (mean, 30 µg/ml) in low birthweight, preterm infants, compared with those (mean, 20 µg/ml) in full-term babies. The elimination half-life values were prolonged in the preterm infants: 59 hours in 2 infants and 109 hours in a 3rd. By comparison, the mean half-life in full-term infants was 25 hours. The clearance of metronidazole is directly correlated with birthweight and gestational age.

The hydroxymetabolite of metronidazole was not measurable in plasma of infants who were less than 35 weeks gestational age. Thus, hepatic hydroxylation does not occur or functions poorly in these preterm infants, which explains in part the larger serum concentrations of metronidazole and the longer half-life values in these infants.

In 3 patients metronidazole was present in CSF in concentrations of 18, 14, and 11.5 µg/ml.[168] These values were comparable to or exceeded the concomitant serum concentrations. Feldman[167] noted ventricular fluid concentrations of 18 and 15 µg/ml approximately 2 hours after 15-mg/kg doses were given orally.

Table 2-40
Pharmacokinetic Properties of Metronidazole (Dose, 7.5-15 mg/kg) in Newborn Infants

Mean Birthweight* (g)/ Gestational Age (Weeks)	Peak Serum Concentration* (µg/ml)	Serum Half -life (h)	Volume of Distribution (ml/kg)	Clearance (ml/min)
1020/28–30	30	75	650	0.12
1860/32–35	18	35	710	0.44
3150/36—40	20	25	690	0.99

* Mean values

On the basis of these pharmacokinetic data, the following dosage schedule for metronidazole is suggested: an initial dose of 15 mg/kg given intravenously or orally, followed—48 hours later in preterm infants (those of less than 35 weeks gestational age) and 24 hours later in full-term infants—with 7.5-mg/kg doses given every 12 hours for the first week of life. There are no data for older neonates, but we suggest 15-mg/kg doses given every 12 hours (30 mg/kg/day), especially for therapy of central nervous system infections.

PLACENTAL TRANSPORT OF ANTIBIOTICS

More than 90 percent of pregnant women receive at least 1 drug during pregnancy, and approximately 4 percent of pregnant women are given 10 or more drugs by their physicians. Antimicrobial agents are commonly prescribed to pregnant women to treat a variety of conditions ranging from mild upper respiratory tract infections to bacterial disease of the genitourinary tract. The drugs are often prescribed in attempts either to prevent or treat amnionitis and intrauterine bacterial infections. In antibiotic selection the physician should take into consideration the transplacental passage of the drug from the mother to the fetus and the concentrations of drug in cord serum and amniotic fluid.

Drugs are either passively transported across the placenta by simple diffusion or actively transported by temporary combination with membrane constituents. Some of the factors influencing transplacental passage of drugs are lipid solubility, degree of ionization, molecular weight (substances with molecular weights greater than 600 to 1000 are impeded), placental blood flow, stage of pregnancy, and placental metabolism.[175]

Drug distribution within the fetus is dependent on several factors. The permeability of specialized membranes such as the blood–brain barrier appears to be increased in early pregnancy. Antibiotic concentrations in tissue are influenced by such factors as water and lipid solubility and specific binding to cellular and subcellular constituents. Changes in fetal circulation also influence distribution of drug. Fetal distribution of antimicrobial agents has been studied by autoradiography and bioassay techniques measuring either total or antimicrobially active drug. Tetracycline crosses the placenta readily and distributes in many fetal organs. Persistent fluorescence due to tetracycline has been observed in fetal bone.[176] Detectable clindamycin and erythromycin activity in fetal tissue has been demonstrated following maternal administration.[177] The concentrations were greater after multiple doses than after a single dose. The aminoglycosides are concentrated in the fetal kidney.[178,179]

Table 2-41

Transplacental Passage of Antimicrobial Agents

Relative Degree of Passage	Antimicrobial Agents	Infant/Maternal Peak Serum Concentration Ratios	Adverse Effects on Infants
HIGH			
	Ampicillin	0.3–0.9	None
	Carbenicillin	0.9	Unknown
	Chloramphenicol	0.3–0.5	Potential for circulatory collapse[129]
	Methicillin	0.5–0.8	None
	Nitrofurantoin	0.4–0.9	Hemolysis in G-6-P-D deficiency[191]
	Penicillin G	0.1–0.5	None
	Sulfonamides	0.5–1.0	Hemolysis in G-6-P-D deficiency,[190] potential kernicterus[154]
	Trimethoprim*– sulfamethoxazole	0.3–1.0	Teratogenic in animals*
	Tetracyclines	0.3–0.5	Depressed bone growth,[149] abnormal teeth[193]

84

MODERATE		
Gentamicin	0.4	Potential ototoxicity
Kanamycin	0.4	Ototoxicity[116]
Streptomycin	0.5	Ototoxicity[186]
Cefamandole	0.4	None
Cephalothin	0.05–0.4	None
Clindamycin	0–0.4	None
Colistimethate	0.3	None
LOW		
Dicloxacillin	0.07–0.1	None
Erythromycin	0–0.2	None
Nafcillin	0.2	None
Oxacillin	0.3	None
Amikacin	0.2	Potential ototoxicity
Tobramycin	0.2	Potential ototoxicity
Cephazolin	0.03–0.3	None

* Refers to trimethoprim levels only

Ratios of infant peak serum concentrations to maternal peak serum concentrations of commonly used antimicrobial agents are shown in Table 2-41. Maternal serum concentrations are generally smaller than those reported in nonpregnant adults, due to a larger plasma volume and to the increased renal plasma clearance observed during pregnancy.[180] The infant serum concentrations vary considerably because of differences in maternal dosage and route of drug administration, the time of gestation, the interval from administration of the dose to collection of the sample, and techniques of measuring antimicrobial activity.

Peak infant serum concentrations of sulfonamides,[181,182] trimethoprim,[159] nitrofurantoin,[183] and methicillin[184-185] approach those in maternal serum. The infant/maternal serum level ratio for methicillin (0.50:0.75)[185] is considerably larger than that for dicloxacillin (0.07:0.10);[185,186] this may be due to differences in serum protein binding (37 percent and 98 percent, respectively). The following drugs are not transported readily across the placenta, as reflected by low infant/maternal serum concentration ratios: erythromycin,[177,187] clindamycin,[177]cephalothin,[188] and colistimethate,[189] and nafcillin and dicloxacillin.[185,186]

Drugs may adversely affect the fetus or neonate in the following ways:[190, 191] (1) fetal death and abortion (aminopterin), (2) teratogenicity (thalidomide), (3) neonatal death (heroin), (4) neonatal disease such as kernicterus (sulfonamides), and (5) late infant effects such as discoloration of teeth (tetracyclines), and ototoxicity (kanamycin). Anecdotal clinical experience is not sufficient to assess properly the safety of antibiotics during pregnancy. Carefully planned prospective studies to evaluate potential fetal and neonatal toxicity are needed.

A number of antimicrobial agents have the potential for adversely affecting the fetus or newborn when administered to the pregnant mother. To date, only a few drugs have caused definite abnormalities. Streptomycin, when used for treatment of active tuberculosis during pregnancy, has been associated with deafness of the offspring. Conway and Birt[192] reported minor abnormalities of eighth nerve function in 8 of 17 children whose mothers received streptomycin during pregnancy. Caloric tests were abnormal in 6 children, and audiograms were abnormal in 4 individuals. Although it is possible that other factors could have contributed to these abnormalities, the evidence strongly suggests a casual relationship. Abnormalities of eight-nerve function have not as yet been demonstrated in infants and children of mothers who received either kanamycin or gentamicin during pregnancy; however, recent studies have demonstrated gentamicin and amikacin activity in the fetal brain after these drugs were given to the mother during the first trimester.[193] The aminoglycosides should be used cautiously in pregnant women until there is definite evidence that hearing or vestibular function is not disturbed.

Sulfisoxazole therapy has been associated with kernicterus in some neonates.[154] When this sulfonamide is given to mothers shortly before delivery, unconjugated bilirubin levels in the infant's serum are lower than those of babies born to untreated mothers.[194] Sulfonamides compete with bilirubin, which diffuses readily into the extravascular space. Because of the possibility that this free bilirubin will deposit in central nervous system ganglia, causing kernicterus, a sulfonamide alone or in combination with trimethoprin should not be administered to pregnant women in late pregnancy nor should these drugs be routinely given to newborns. Neonatal hemolytic anemia and jaundice have been reported in two black male infants with erythrocyte G-6-P-D deficiency whose mothers received sulfamethoxpyridazine.[195] This long-acting sulfonamide has also been associated with neonatal hyperbilirubinemia after maternal administration.[196] Because nitrofurantoin has been associated with hemolytic anemia in patients with erythrocyte G-6-P-D deficiency,[197] a G-6-P-D–deficient infant exposed in utero is at considerable risk of hemolysis.

The tetracyclines readily cross the placental barrier and concentrate in many tissues of the developing fetus.[198-199] Of particular interest is the deposition of tetracycline in fetal bones[200] and deciduous teeth.[201] Tetracycline administered during the last trimester of pregnancy deposits as a fluorophore throughout the human fetal skeleton. Cohlan, Bevelander, and Tiamsic[149] demonstrated a 40-percent depression of normal skeletal growth (measured by inhibition of fibula growth) when tetracycline was administered to premature infants. This growth inhibition was readily reversible on discontinuation of short-term therapy. Calcification of deciduous teeth begins during the fourth month of gestation, and crown formation of the anterior teeth is almost complete at term. Tetracycline given during this period of gestation can produce yellow discoloration, enamel hypoplasia, and abnormal formation of the deciduous teeth.[200,201] Tetracycline, oxytetracyline, and demethyl chlortetracycline have been documented as causing these effects.[200]

Chloramphenicol has been associated with circulatory collapse ("gray syndrome") and death in premature infants who received this drug during the first weeks of life.[129] This drug should not be administered during the last days of pregnancy because of the absence of glycuronyl transferase activity in the fetal liver and the potential danger of serum drug accumulation and shock in the newborn infant.

Selection of antimicrobial therapy in pregnancy must be based on a judgment as to which bacterial pathogens are likely to be causing the maternal disease and must also involve consideration of transport of the drug across the placenta and the risk of toxicity to the developing fetus. Although it is commonly stated that treatment of maternal infection will either prevent or treat fetal infection, there is little evidence to support this contention. Undoubtedly certain bacterial infections of the fetus will be treated effectively, particularly when the pathogen such as group A or B streptococcus or pneumococcus is highly suspectible to antimicrobial therapy. The presence of antimicrobial activity in the blood of the newborn may mask existing infection, however, resulting in delayed diagnosis and institution of appropriate therapeutic measures. It is for these reasons and the possibility of fetal toxicity that the physician must carefully consider the use of antibiotics during pregnancy.

EXCRETION OF ANTIBIOTICS IN HUMAN MILK

The nursing infant may be the unintended recipient of antibiotics excreted in milk of treated mothers. It is generally conceded that the concentration of antibiotics in milk is very low, making it seem unlikely that either therapeutic or harmful effects to the infant are possible. Determination of the concentration of the antibiotic in the milk, however, is not the only factor to be considered; the volume of milk ingested and the degree of absorption of the drug from the infant's gastrointestinal tract must also be taken into account. The safety of antibiotics in milk has been primarily determined by anecdotal clinical experience, rather than by carefully controlled long-term studies. For example, tetracyclines in milk may possible damage teeth if a sufficient amount is ingested. Although effects of ingested antibiotics on the gastrointestinal microbial flora of the newborn infant are unknown, Hawking and Lawrence[202] described diarrhea and "evil-smelling stools" in breast-fed infants of mothers receiving sulfapyridine.

Drugs are secreted into milk by active or passive mechanisms. Factors influencing the transfer of antibiotics from plasma to milk include concentration of the drug in maternal serum, solubility in fat and water, ionization of the drug (pK_a), its potential for binding protein in serum and milk, and molecular size of the drug.[203,204] As a rule the concentration of the drug in maternal serum influences the passage into milk of those drugs excreted primarily by passive diffusion. Drugs with a high lipid solubility concentrate in milk; this varies with the fat content of the milk. Ionization of organic acids and bases depends on the pH content of the milk and the drug dissociation constant (pK_a). Human milk has a pH of 7.37; drugs that are weak bases (pK_a greater than pH) will therefore ionize and concentrate in human milk. The opposite situation applies to weak acids.[204] Drugs that are highly serum protein-bound tend to remain in the intravascular space.

The concentrations of commonly administered antimicrobial agents in maternal serum and breast milk are listed in Table 2-42. The data for each drug are based on small numbers of patients. It is likely that the concentrations of antibiotic in milk vary considerably from patient to patient

Table 2-42
Excretion of Antimicrobial Agents in Human Milk

Antimicrobial Agent	Dose and Route	Concentrations in Maternal Specimens		Milk Serum Ratio
		Serum	Breast Milk	
Carbenicillin	1 g (IV)	NT*	0.27 µg/ml	—
Cephazolin	2 g (IV)	54 µg/ml	1.5 µg/ml	0.03
Chloramphenicol	250 mg (oral)	26–49 µg/ml	16–25 µg/ml	0.5
Dihydrostreptomycin	1 g (IM)	14–18 µg/ml	0.3–1.3 µg/ml	0.02–0.1
Erythromycin	400 mg (oral)	0.4–3.2 µg/ml	0.4–1.6 µg/ml	0.5
Kanamycin	1 g (IM)	55.2 µg/ml	18.4 µg/ml	0.3
Isoniazid	5–10 mg/kg (oral)	6–2 µg/ml	6–12 µg/ml	1.0
Metronidazole	—	NT	NT	1.0
Nalidixic acid	1 g (oral)	NT	4 µg/ml	—
Nitrofurantoin	100 mg (oral)	NT	0	—
Novobiocin	250 mg (oral)	12–52 µg/ml	3–5 µg/ml	0.1–0.25
Oxacillin	1 g (oral)	< 0.3–5.6 µg/ml	0.2 µg/ml	0.03–0.7
Quinine	300–600 mg (oral)	NT	0–1 µg/ml	—
Aqueous penicillin G	100,000 u (IM)	0.29–1.1 µg/ml	0.01–0.04 µg/ml	0.02–0.2
Phenoxymethyl penicillin	120–240 mg (oral)	NT	0.03–0.2 µg/ml	—
Tetracycline	500 mg (oral)	0.9–3.2 µg/ml	0.5–2.6 µg/ml	0.6–0.8
Sulfonamides				
Sulfanilamide	500 mg (oral)	80–50 µg/ml	90 µg/ml	1.0
Sulfapyridine	750 mg (oral)	30–130 µg/ml	30–130 µg/ml	1.0
Sulfisoxazole	1 g (oral)	NT	NT	0.06†
Trimethoprim–sulfamethoxazole	—	NT	NT	> 1.0

* NT - Not tested
† 0.22 for metabolite, N^4 - acetyl sulfisoxazole

89

because of individual differences in attainable maternal serum levels, pH values in milk, and the fat content and volume of breast milk produced. The concentrations of sulfanilamide, sulfapyridine, and isoniazid in breast milk are similar to those in maternal serum (milk/serum ratio, 1) while concentrations of chloramphenicol, erythromycin, and tetracycline are approximately 50 percent of those in maternal serum (milk/serum ratio, 0.5).[203] Available data suggest that the concentrations of penicillin[205] and of the aminoglycosides[206] in human milk are low. Poor gastrointestinal tract absorption of aminoglycosides further decreases the risk of toxicity to the infant. By contrast, recovery of 96 percent of the total amount of sulfisoxazole in maternal milk from the nursing infant's urine during a 24-hour period is indicative of the efficient absorption of this drug from the infant's gastrointestinal tract.[207] Only about 1 percent of the maternal dose of sulfisoxazole is actually secreted in milk, however.

There are no data pertaining to antibiotic levels in colostrum. Because blood flow and permeability are increased during the colostral phase,[204] it is possible that these drugs are present in concentrations equal to or greater than those found in milk.

There are very few reported instances of adverse effects to infants who are breast fed by mothers receiving antimicrobial agents. Hemolytic anemia in 2 infants receiving breast milk from mothers being given antimicrobial therapy has been reported. The first neonate has documented G-6-P-D deficiency, and sulfamethoxypryidazine, which had been given to the mother for 6–13 days postpartum, was present in the milk.[208] The second case of hemolytic anemia was ascribed to ingestion of nalidixic acid in breast milk of a mother with pyelonephritis.[209] There are undoubtedly other examples of infant toxicity from antibiotics in milk that have not been recognized or reported.

The decision to allow or stop breast feeding must be based on the above considerations. Although the physician should be cautious in recommending breast feeding if the mother is treated with a drug that attains concentrations in milk similar to those in her serum, in practice this does not appear to be a problem, with the possible exception of the tetracyclines and most sulfonamides. Sulfisoxazole has traditionally been contraindicated for the nursing woman. Kauffman and associates,[207] however, recently reported a milk/serum ratio of 0.06. This was explained by the high degree of water solubility and resistance to diffusion across biologic membranes of sulfisoxazole as compared to the other sulfonamides. Although such concentrations of sulfisoxazole would not endanger a normal infant, the risk to the G-6-P-D–deficient, infected, stressed, or premature infant has not been evaluated. By contrast, the concentrations of the penicillins and cephalosporins in breast milk are too small to be dangerous to the newborn. The severity of the woman's infection rather than the drug that she is receiving is most often the more important contraindication to breast feeding.

REFERENCES

1. Radetsky MS, Istre GP, Johanson TL, et al: Multiply resistant pneumococcus causing meningitis: Its epidemiology within a day-care center. Lancet 2:771–773, 1981

2. Anderson KC, Mauer MJ, Dajani AS: Pneumococci relatively resistant to pencillin: A prevalence survey in children. J Pediatr 97:939–941, 1980

3. Tarpay MM, Welch DF, Marks MI: Antimicrobial susceptibility testing of *Streptococcus pneumoniae* by micro-broth dilution. Antimicrob Agents Chemother 18:570–581, 1980

4. Siegel JD, Shannon KM, DePasse BM: Recurrent infection associated with penicillin-tolerant group B streptococci: A report of two cases. J Pediatr 99:920–924, 1981

5. McCracken GH, Ginsburg C, Chrane DF, et al: Clinical pharmacology of pencillin in newborn infants. J Pediatr 82:692–698, 1973

6. Grossman M, Ticknor W: High doses of penicillin G in the neonate. Antimicrob Agents Chemother 59–63, 1966

7. Barnett HL, McNamara H, Shultz S, et al: Renal clearances of sodium penicillin G and inulin in infants and children. Pediatrics 3:418–422, 1949

8. Nelson JD, Hieber JP: A pharmacologic evaluation of penicillin in children with purulent meningitis. New Engl J Med 297:410–413, 1977

9. Troug WE, Davis RF, Ray CG: Recurrence of group B streptococcal infections. J Pediatr 89:185–196, 1976

10. Kaplan JM, McCracken GH: Clinical pharmacology of benzathine penicillin G in neonates with regard to its recommended use in congenital syphilis. J Pediatr 82: 1069–1072, 1973

11. Klein JO, Schaberg MJ, Buntin M, et al: Levels of penicillin in serum of newborn infants after single intramuscular doses of benzathine penicillin G. J Pediatr 82:1065–1068, 1973

12. McCracken GH, Kaplan JM: Penicillin treatment for congenital syphilis: A critical reappraisal. JAMA 288:855–858, 1974

13. Huang NN, High RH: Comparison of serum levels following the administration of oral and parenteral preparations of penicillin to infants and children of various age groups. J Pediatr 42:657–668, 1953

14. McCracken GH, Ginsburg CM, Clahsen JC, et al: Pharmacologic evaluation of orally administered antibiotics in infants and children. Pediatrics 62:738–743, 1978

15. McCracken GH, Mize SG, Threlkeld N: Intraventricular gentamicin therapy in gram negative bacillary meningitis of infancy. Lancet 1:787–791, 1980

16. Boe RW, Williams CPS, Bennett JV, et al: Serum levels of methicillin and ampicillin in newborn and premature infants in relation to postnatal age. Pediatrics 39:194–201, 1967

17. Axline SG, Yaffe SJ, Simon HJ: Clinical pharmacology of antimicrobials in premature infants: II. Ampicillin, methicillin, oxacillin, neomycin, and colistin. Pediatrics 39:97–107, 1967

18. Kaplan JM, McCracken GH, Horton LS, et al: Pharmacologic studies in neonates given large dosages of ampicillin. J Pediatr 84:517–577, 1974

19. Wilson HD, Haltalin KC: Ampicillin in *Haemophilus influenzae* meningitis. Am J Dis Child 29:208–215, 1975

20. Grossman M, Ticknor W: Serum levels of ampicillin, cephalothin, cloxacillin and nafcillin in the newborn infant. Antimicrob Agents Chemother 214–219, 1965

21. Silverio J, Poole JW: Serum concentrations of ampicillin in newborn infants after oral administration. Pediatrics 51:578–580, 1973

22. Ginsburg CM, McCracken GH, Thomas ML, et al: Comparative pharmacokinetics or amoxicillin and ampicillin in infants and children. Pediatrics 64:627–631, 1979

23. Nelson JD, McCracken GH: Clinical pharmacology of carbenicillin and gentamicin in the neonate and comparative efficacy with ampicillin and gentamicin. Pediatrics 52:801–812, 1973

24. McCracken GH, Nelson JD, Thomas ML: Discrepancy between carbenicillin and ampicillin activities against enterococci and *Listeria*. Antimicrob Agents Chemother 3:343–349, 1973

25. Morehead CD, Shelton S, Kusmiesz H, et al: Pharmacokinetics of carbenicillin in neonates of normal and low birthweight. Antimicrob Agents Chemother 2:267-271, 1972

26. Yoshioka H, Takimoto M, Shinizu T, et al: Pharmacokinetics of intramuscular carbenicillin in the newborn. Infection 7:27–29, 1979

27. Ervin FR, Bullock WE, Nuttall CE: On activation of gentamicin by penicillins in patients with renal failure. Antimicrob Agents Chemother 9:1004–1011, 1976

28. Pickering LK, Gearhart P: Effect of time and concentration upon interaction between gentamicin, tobramycin, netilmicin, or amikacin and carbenicillin or ticarcillin. Antimicrob Agents Chemother 15:592–596, 1979

29. Nelson JD, Kusmeisz H, Shelton S, et al: Clinical pharmacology and efficacy of ticarcillin in infants and children. Pediatrics 61:858–863, 1978

30. Sabath LD, Wheeler N. Laverdiere, et al: A new type of penicillin resistance of *Staphylococcus aureus*. Lancet 1:443–447, 1977

31. Sarff LD, McCracken GH, Thomas ML, et al: Clinical pharmacology of methicillin in neonates. J Pediatr 90:1005–1008, 1977

32. Sarff LD, McCracken GH: Methicillin-associated nephropathy or cystitis. J Pediatr 90:1031–1032, 1977

33. Kitzing W, Nelson JD, Mohs E: Comparative toxicities of methicillin and nafcillin. Am J Dis Child 135:52–55, 1981

34. Yow MD, Taber LH, Barrett F, et al: A ten-year assessment of methicillin-associated side effects. Pediatrics 58:329–334, 1976

35. Burns, LE, Hodgman JE, Wahrle PF: Treatment of premature infants with oxacillin. Antimicrob, Reports Chemother 192–194, 1964

36. O'Conner WJ, Warren GH, Mandala PS, et al: Serum concentrations of

nafcillin in newborn infants and children. Antimicrob Agents Chemother 188–191, 1964

37. Sarff LD: Nafcillin pharmacokinetics in neonates: Dosage recommendations. Presented to the Nineteenth Interscience Conference on Antimicrobial Agents and Chemotherapy, Boston, Oct 1979

38. Banner W, Gooch WM, Burckart G, et al: Pharmacokinetics of nafcillin in infants with low birthweights. Antimicrob Agents Chemother 17:691–694, 1980

39. Schaad UB, McCracken GH, Nelson JD: Clinical pharmacolgy and efficacy of vancomycin in pediatric patients. J Pediatrics 96:119–126, 1980

40. Schaad UB, Nelson JD, McCracken GH: Pharmacology and efficacy of vancomycin for staphylococcal infections in children. Rev Infect Dis 3 (suppl):S282–S287, 1982

41. Sheng KT, Huang NN, Promadhattavedi V: Serum concentrations of cephalothin in infants and children and placental transmission of the antibiotic. Antimicrob Agents Chemother 200–206, 1964

42. Walker SH, Maisog VT: Cephaloridine dosage in infants and children. Md State Med J 18:65–69, 1969

43. Nakazawa S, Ika S, Sato H, et al: Studies on cefazolin in the pediatric field. Chemotherapy 18:659-678, 1970

44. Marget W: Special aspects of cephalosporin therapy in infants and children. Postgrad Med J 47:54–58, 1971

45. Shelton S, Nelson JD, McCracken GH: In vitro susceptibility of gram-negative bacilli from pediatric patients to moxalactam, cefotaxime, RO 13–9904, and other cephalosporins. Antimicrob Agents Chemother 18:476–479, 1980

46. Agbayani MM, Khan AJ, Kemawikasit P, et al: Pharmacokinetics and safety of cefamandole in newborn infants. Antimicrob Agents Chemother 15:674–676, 1979

47. Steinberg EA, Overturf GD, Baraff LJ, et al: Penetration of cefamandole into spinal fluid. Antimicrob Agents Chemother 11:933–935, 1977

48. Feldman WE, Moffit S, Sprow N: Clinical and pharmacokinetic evaluation of parenteral cefoxitin in infants and children. Antimicrob Agents Chemother 17:669–674, 1980

49. Renlund M, Pettey O: Pharmacokinetics and clinical efficacy of cefuroxime in the newborn period. Proc R Soc Med 70 (suppl no 9):179–182, 1977

50. Wilkinson PJ, Belohradsky BH, Marget L: A clinical study of cefuroxime in neonates. Proc R Soc Med 70 (suppl no 9):183–185, 1977

51. McCracken GH, Ginsburg CM, Clahsen JC: Pharmacokinetics of cefaclor in infants and children. J Antimicrob Chemother 4:515–521, 1978

52. Ginsburg CM, McCracken GH, Nelson JD: Pharmacology of oral antibiotics used for treatment of otitis media and tonsillopharyngitis in infants and children. Ann Otol Rhin Laryngol 5:37–43, 1981

53. Scribner RK, Marks MI, Weber AH, et al: Activities of various β-lactams and aminoglycosides, alone and in combination, against isolates of *Pseudomonas aeruginosa* from patients with cystic fibrosis. Antimicrob Agents Chemother 21:939–934, 1982

54. Barry AL, Jones RN, Thronsberry C: Cefsulodin: Antibacterial activity and tentative interpretive zone standards for the disc susceptibility test. Antimicrob Angents Chemother 20:525–529, 1981

55. Schaad UB, McCracken GH, Loock CA, et al: Pharmacokinetics and bacteriologic efficacy of moxalactam, cefotaxime, cefoperazone and rocephin in experimental bacterial meningitis. J Infect Dis 143:156–163, 1981

56. McCracken GH, Nelson JD, Grimm L: Pharmacokinetics and bacteriologic efficacy of cefoperazone, cefuroxime, ceftriaxone, and moxalactam in experimental *Steptococcus pneumoniae* and *Haemophilus influenzae* meningitis. Antimicrob Agents Chemother 21:262–267, 1982

57. Schaad UB, McCracken GH, Threlkeld N, et al: Clinical evaluation of a new broad-spectrum oxa-beta-lactam antibiotic, moxalactam, in neonates and infants. J Pediatr 98:129–136, 1981

58. Kafetzis DA, Brater DC, Kapiki AN, et al: Treatment of severe neonatal infections with cefotaxime: Efficacy and pharmacokinetics. J Pediatr 100:438–489, 1982

59. McCracken GH, Threlkeld NE, Thomas ML: Pharmacokinetics of cefotaxime in newborn infants. Antimicrob Agents Chemother 21:683–684, 1982

60. Rosenfeld W, Batheja R, Jhaveri R, et al: Pharmacokinetics of cefoperazone in neonates. Presented at the Twenty-first Interscience Conference on Antimicrobial Agents and Chemotherapy. Chicago, Nov 1981

61. Bosso JA, Chan GM, Matsen JM: Pharmacokinetics of cefoperazone in premature neonates. Presented at the Twenty-second Interscience Conference on Antimicrobial Agents and Chemotherapy. Miami, Oct 1982

62. Chartrand S, Johnson J, Marks MI, et al: Cefoperazone pharmacokinetics in bacterial meningitis. Presented at the Twenty-second Interscience Conference on Antimicrobial Agents and Chemotherapy. Miami, Oct 1982

63. McCracken GH, Siegel JD, Threlkeld N: Clinical pharmacology of ceftriaxone in newborn infants. Presented at the Twenty-second Interscience Conference on Antimicrobial Agents and Chemotherapy. Miami, Oct 1982

64. Wise R, Andrews JM: Activity of mezlocillin against gram-negative and gram-positive organisms: Comparison with other penicillins. J Antimicrob Chemother 9 (suppl A):1–9, 1982

65. Rubio T, Wirth F, Karotkin E: Pharmacokinetic studies of mezlocillin in newborn infants. J Antimicrob Chemother 9 (suppl A):241–244, 1982

66. Chiu T, Garrison RD, Fakhreddine F, et al: Mezlocillin in neonatal infections: Evaluation of efficacy and toxicity. J Antimicrob Chemother 9 (suppl A):251–255, 1982

67. Weingartner L: Clinical aspects of mezlocillin: Therapy in childhood. J Antimicrob Chemother 9 (suppl A):257–262, 1982

68. Howard JB and McCracken GH: Reappraisal of kanamycin usage in neonates. J Pediatr 86:949–956, 1975

69. Watanakunakorn C, Glotzbecker C: Enhancement of the effects of anti-staphylococcal antibiotics by aminoglycosides, Antimicrob Agents Chemother:802–806, 1974

70. Scheld WM, Allegro GM: Ampicllin-gentamicin syngerism in experimental

group B streptococcal meningitis. Presented to the Twentieth Interscience Conference on Antibiotic Agents and Chemotherapy. New Orleans, Sept 22–24, 1980

71. Scheld WM, Fletcher DD, Fink FN, et al: Response to therapy in an experimental rabbit model of meningitis due to *Listeria monocytogenes*. J Infect Dis 140:291–294, 1979

72. McCracken GH, Threlkeld N, Thomas ML: Intravenous administration of kanamycin and gentamicin in newborn infants. Pediatrics 60:463–466, 1977

73. Paisley JW, Smith AL, Smith DH: Gentamicin in newborn infants: Comparison of intramuscular and intravenous administraton. Am J Dis Child 126:473–477, 1973

74. Siegel JD, McCracken GH, Thomas ML, et al: Pharmacokinetic properties of netilmicin in newborn infants. Antimicrob Agents Chemother 15:246–253, 1979

75. Black J, Calesnick B, Williams D, et al: Pharmacology of gentamicin, a new broad-spectrum antibiotic. Antimicrob Agents Chemother 138–147, 1963

76. Beutow KC, Cheung C, Finberg R: Prolonged use of neomycin in premature infants. Am J Dis Child 104:76–81, 1962.

77. King JF: Severe deafness in an infant following oral administration of neomycin. J Med Assoc Ga 51:530–531, 1962

78. Nunnery AW, Riley HD: Gentamicin: Pharmacologic observations in newborns and infants. J Infect Dis 119:402–405, 1969

79. Hansen TN, Ritter DA, Speci ME, et al: A randomized controlled study of oral gentamicin in the treatment of neonatal necrotizing enterocolitis. J Pediatr 97:836–839, 1980

80. Haughey DB, Hilligass DM, Grassi A, et al: Two-compartment gentamicin pharmacokinetics in premature neonates. J Pediatr 96:325–330, 1980

81. Coyer WF, Wesbey GE, Cech KL, et al: Intravenous gentamicin pharmacokinetics in the small preterm infant. Pediatr Res 12:403, 1978

82. Szefler SJ, Wynn RJ, Clarke DF, et al: Relationship of gentamicin serum concentrations to gestational age in preterm and term neonates. J Pediatr 97:312–315, 1980

83. Arbeter AM, Saccar CL, Eisner S, et al: Tobramycin dosage regimens in very small premature infants. Presented to the Twentieth Interscience Conference on Antimicrobial Agents and Chemotherapy. New Orleans, Sept 22–24, 1980

84. Williams GL, Stroebel AB, Richardson H, et al: Pharmacokinetics of tobramycin in low birthweight newborn infants. Presented to the Nineteenth Interscience Conference on Antimicrobial Agents and Chemotherapy. Boston, Oct 1–5, 1979

85. Cookson BD, Tupp JH, Teung T: Pharmacokinetic aspects of amikacin in low and very low birthweight infants. Presented to the Nineteenth Interscience Conference on Antimicrobial Agents and Chemotherapy. Boston, Oct 1–5, 1979

86. Nelson JD: Duration of neomycin therapy for enteropathogenic *Escherichia coli* diarrheal disease: A comparison study of 113 cases. Pediatrics 48:248–258, 1971

87. Axline SG, Simon HJ: Clinical pharmacology of antimicrobials in premature infants. I. Kanamycin, streptomycin and neomycin. Antimicrob Agents Chemother 135–141, 1964

88. Hunt AD, Fell B: Streptomycin intramuscular dosage per unit body weight correlated with serum levels in infants and children. Pediatrics 4:163–169, 1949

89. Simon HJ, Axline SG: Clinical pharmacology of kanamycin in premature infants. Ann NY Acad Sci 132:1020–1027, 1966

90. Eichenwald HF: Some observations on dosage and toxicity of kanamycin in premature and fullterm infants. Ann NY Acad Sci 132:984–991, 1966

91. McCracken GH, Threlkeld N: Kanamycin dosage in newborn infants. J Pediatrics 89:313–314, 1976

92. McCracken GH, Chrane DF, Thomas ML: Pharmacologic evaluation of gentamicin in newborn infants. J Infect Dis 124 (suppl):S214–S223, 1971

93. McCracken GH, West NR, Horton LJ: Urinary excretion of gentamicin in the neonatal period. J Infect Dis 123:257–262, 1971

94. Klein JO, Herschel M, Theraken RM et al: Gentamicin in serious neonatal infections: Absorption, excretion and clinical results in 25 cases. J Infect Dis 124 (suppl):S224–S231, 1971

95. Milner RDG, Ross J, Froud DLR, et al: Clinical pharmacology of gentamicin in the newborn infant. Arch Dis Child 47:927–932, 1972

96. Zoumboulakis D, Anagnostakis D, Arseni A, et al: Gentamicin in the treatment of purulent meningitis in neonates and infants. Acta Paediatr Scand 62:55–58, 1973

97. Chang MJ, Escobedo M, Anderson DC, et al: Kanamycin and gentamiacin treatment of neonatal sepsis and meningitis. Pediatrics 56:695–699, 1975

98. Kliegman RM, Bertino JS, Fanaroff AA, et al: Pharmacokinetics of gentamicin during exchange transfusions in neonates. J Pediatr 96:927–930, 1980

99. Siegel JD, McCracken GH: Unpublished observations

100. McCracken GH Jr, Mize SG: A controlled study of intrathecal antibiotic therapy in gram negative enteric meningitis of infancy. Report of the Neonatal Meningitis Cooperative Study Group. J Pediatr 89:66–72, 1976

101. McCracken GH Jr, Mize SG, Threlkeld N: Intraventricular gentamicin therapy in gram negative bacillary meningitis of infancy. Lancet 1:787–791, 1980

102. Smith CR, Lipsky JJ, Laskin OL, et al: Double blind comparison of the nephrotoxicity and auditory toxicity of gentamicin and tobramycin. New Engl J Med 302:1106–1109, 1980

103. Kaplan JM, McCracken GH, Thomas ML, et al: Clinical pharmacology of tobramycin in newborns. Am J Dis Child 125:656–660, 1973

104. McCracken GH, Nelson JD: Commentary, an appraisal of tobramycin usage in pediatrics. J Pediatr 88:315–317, 1976

105. Howard JB, McCracken GH: Pharmacologic evaluation of amikacin in neonates. Antimicrob Agents Chemother 8:86–90, 1975

106. Howard JB, McCracken GH, Trujillo H, et al: Amikacin in newborn infants: Comparative pharmacology with kanamycin and clinical efficacy in 45 neo-

nates with bacterial disease. Antimicrob Agents Chemother 10:205–210, 1976

107. Trujillo H, Manotas R, Londono R, et al: Clinical and laboratory studies with amikacin in newborns, infants and children. J Infect Dis 134 (suppl):S406–S411, 1976

108. Yow MD: An overview of pediatric experience with amikacin. Am J Med 62:954–958, 1977

109. Rubio T, Wirth F, Wellman L, et al: Pharmacokinetics of netilmicin in newborn infants. Abstract, Eighteenth Interscience Conference on Antimicrobial Agents and Chemotherapy. Atlanta, Oct 1979

110. Schauf V, Chindasilpa V, Hamilton L, et al: Netilmicin pharmacology in pediatric patients. Pediatr Res 12:408, 1978

111. Cowan RM, Jukkola AF, Arant BS: Pathophysiologic evidence of gentamicin nephrotoxicity in neonatal puppies. Pediatr Res 14:1204–1211, 1980

112. Dahlgren JG, Anderson ET, Hewitt WL: Gentamicin blood levels: A guide to nephrotoxicity. Antimicrob Agents Chemother 8:58–62, 1975

113. Sirinavin S, McCracken GH, Nelson JD: Determining gentamicin dosage in infants and children with renal failure. J Pediatr 96:331–334, 1980

114. Buekelaer MM, Travis LB, Dodge WF, et al: Deafness and acute tubular necrosis following parenteral administration of neomycin. Am J Dis Child 121:250–252, 1971

115. Robinson GC, Cambon KG: Hearing loss in infants of tuberculous mothers treated with streptomycin during pregnancy. N Engl J Med 271:949–951, 1964

116. Yow MD, Tengg NE, Bangs J, et al: The ototoxic effects of kanamycin sulfate in infants and children. J Pediatr 60:230–242, 1962

117. Winkel S, Bonding P, Larsen PK, et al: Possible effects of kanamycin and incubation in newborn children with low birthweight. Acta Paediatr Scand 67:709–715, 1978

118. Johnsonbaugh RE, Drexler HG, Light IJ, et al: Familial occurrence of drug-induced hearing loss. Am J Dis Child 127:245–247, 1974

119. Johnsonbaugh RE, Drexler HG, Sutherland JM, et al: Audiometric study of streptomycin-treated infants. Am J Dis Child 122:43–45, 1966

120. Finitzo-Hieber T, McCracken GH, Roeser RJ, et al: Ototoxicity in neonates treated with gentamicin in kanamycin: Results of a four-year controlled follow-up study. Pediatrics 63:443–450, 1979

121. Elfving J, Pettay O, Raivio M: A follow-up study on the cochlear, vestibular and renal function in children treated with gentamicin in the newborn period. Chemotherapy 18:141–153, 1973

122. Starr A, Amlie RN, Martin WH, et al: Development of auditory function in newborn infants revealed by auditory brainstem potentials. Pediatrics 60:831–839, 1977

123. Bernard PA, Pechere JC, Hebert R, et al: Detection of aminoglycoside antibiotics in newborns using brainstem response audiometry. Presented to the Nineteenth Interscience Conference on Antimicrobial Agents and Chemotherapy. Boston, Oct 1–5, 1979

124. Ream CR: Respiratory and cardiac arrest after intravenous administration of kanamycin with reversal of toxic effects by neostigmine. Ann Intern Med 59:384–387, 1963

125. Pittinger CB, Eryasa Y, Adamson R: Antibiotic-induced paralysis. Anesth Analg 49:487–501, 1970

126. Warner WA, Sanders E: Neuromuscular blockade associated with gentamicin therapy. JAMA 215:1153–1154, 1971

127. Santos JI, Swenson P, Glasgow LA: Potentiation of *Clostridium botulinum* toxin by aminoglycoside antibiotics: Clinical and laboratory observations. Pediatrics 68:50–54, 1981

128. Watanabe I, Hodges GR, Dworzack DL, et al: Neurotoxicity of intrathecal gentamicin. Ann Neurol 4:564–572, 1978

129. Sutherland JM: Fatal cardiovascular collapse in infants receiving large amounts of chloramphenicol. Am J Dis Child 97:761–767, 1959

130. Burns LE, Hodgman JE, Cass AB: Fatal circulatory collapse in premature infants receiving chloramphenicol. N Engl J Med 261:1318–1321, 1959

131. Morton K: Chloramphenicol overdosage in a 6-week-old infant. Am J Dis Child 102:430, 1961

132. Krasinski K, Perkin R, Tubledge J: Gray baby syndrome revisited. Clin Pediatr (Phila) 9:571–572, 1982

133. Weiss CF, Glazko AJ, Weston JK: Chloramphenicol in the newborn infant. N Engl J Med 262:787–794, 1960

134. Weeks JL, Mason EO, Baker CJ: Antagonism of ampicillin and chloramphenicol for meningeal isolates of group B streptococci. Antimicrob Agents Chemother 20:281–285, 1981

135. Winslow DL, Dieckman E, Damme J, et al: Delayed bactericidal activity of beta-lactam antibotics against *Listeria monocytogenes.* Presented to the Twenty-second Interscience Conference on Antimicrobial Agents and Chemotherapy, Miami, Oct 1982

136. McGee ZA, Kaiser AB, Rubeno C, Farrar WE: Emergence of chloramphenicol resistance during chloramphenicol treatment of gram negative bacillary meningitis. Presented to the Seventeenth Interscience Conference on Antimicrobial Agents and Chemotherapy, New York, Oct 12–14, 1977

137. Friedman CA, Lovejoy FC, Smith AL: Chloramphenicol disposition in infants and children. J Pediatr 95:1071–1077, 1979

138. Glazer JP, Danish MA, Plotkin SA, et al: Disposition of chloramphenicol in low birthweight infants. Pediatrics 66:573–578, 1980

139. Hodgman JE, Burns LE: Safe and effective chloramphenicol dosages for premature infants. Amer J Dis Child 101:140–148, 1961

140. Ziegra SR, Storm RR: Dosage of chloramphenicol in premature infants. J Pediatr 58:852–857, 1961

141. Krasinski K. Dusmiesz H, Nelson JD: Pharmacologic interactions among chloramphenicol, phenytoin and phenobarbital. Pediatr Infect Dis 1:232–235, 1982

142. Mauer SM, Chavers BM, Kjellstrand CM: Treatment of an infant with severe chloramphenicol intoxication using charcoal column hemoperfusion. J Pediatr 96:136–139, 1980

143. Katsampes CP: Personal communication, 1971
144. Flux M, Riley HD, Bracken EC, et al: Clinical and laboratory evaluation of colistin in infants and children. Antimicrob Agents Chemother 455–465, 1962
145. Grylack LJ, Scanlon JW, Neugebauer DL: Oral gentamicin and colistin in the prevention of neonatal necrotizing enterocolitis. Pediatr Res 14:599, 1980
146. Sereni F, Perletti L, Manfredi N, et al: Tissue distribution and urinary excretion of a tetracycline derivative in newborn and older infants. J Pediatr 67:299–304, 1965
147. Gidion R, Marget W: Sur Frage der Dosierung injizierbarer Tetracycline im Sauglingsalter. Meunchen Med Wschr 103:967–971, 1961
148. Gibbons RJ, Reichelderfer TE: Transplacental transmission of demethylchlortetracycline and toxicity studies in premature and fullterm newly born infants. Pediatrics 7:618–622, 1960
149. Cohlan SQ, Bevelander G, Tiamsic T: Growth inhibition of prematures receiving tetracycline. Am J Dis Child 105:453–461, 1963
150. Wallman IS, Hilton HB: Teeth pigmented by tetracycline. Lancet 1:827–829, 1962
151. Ibsen KH, Urist MR, Sognnaes RF, et al: Differences among tetracyclines with respect to the staining of teeth. J Pediatr 67:459–462, 1965
152. Fields JP: Bulging fontanel: A complication of tetracycline therapy in infants. J Pediatr 58:74–76, 1961
153. Fichter EG, Curtis JA: Sulfonamide administration in newborn and premature infants. Pediatrics 18:50–57, 1956
154. Silverman WA, Anderson DH, Blanc WA, et al: A difference in mortality rate and incidence of kernicterus among premature infants allotted to two prophylactic antibacterial regimens. Pediatrics 18:614–624, 1956
155. Springer C, Eyal F, Michel J: Pharmacology of trimethoprim–sulfamethoxazole in newborn infants. J Pediatr 100:647–650, 1982
156. Paisley JW, Washington JA: Synergistic activity of gentamicin with trimethoprim or sulfamethoxazole–trimethoprim against Escherichia coli and Klebsiella pneumonia. Antimicrob Agents Chemother 14:656–658, 1978
157. Sabel KG, Brandberg A: Treatment of meningitis and septicemia in infancy with a sulfamethoxazole/trimethoprim combination. Acta Paediatr Scand 64:25–32, 1975
158. Ardata KO, Thirumoorthi MB, Dajani AS: Intravenous trimethoprim–sulfamethoxazole in the treatment of serious infections in children. J Pediatr 95:801–806, 1979
159. Gleckman R, Alvarez P, Joubert DW: Drug therapy reviews: Trimethoprim–sulfamethoxazole. Am J Hosp Pharm 36:893–906, 1979
160. Burns L, Hodgman J: Studies of prematures given erythromycin estolate. Am J Dis Child 106:80–88, 1963
161. Patamasucon P, Káojarern S, Kusmiesz H, et al: Pharmacokinetics of erythromycin ethylsuccinate and estolate in infants under 4 months of age. Antimicrob Agents Chemother 19:736–739, 1981
162. Patamasucon P, Rettig PJ, Faust KL, et al: Oral vs. topical erythromycin

therapies for chlamydial conjunctivitis. Am J Dis Child 136:817–821, 1982

163. Krowchuk D, Seashore JG: Complete biliary obstruction due to erythromycin estolate administration in an infant. Pediatrics 64:956–958, 1979

164. Bell M, Shakelford P, Smith R, et al: Pharmacokinetics of clindamycin phosphate in infants. Presented at the Twenty-second Interscience Conference on Antimicrobial Agents and Chemotherapy, Miami, Oct 1982

165. Vescidi RP, Bartlett JG: Antibiotic-associated pseudomembranous colitis in children. Pediatrics 67:381–386, 1981

166. Donta ST, Myers MG: Clostridium difficile toxin in asymptomatic neonates. J Pediatr 100:431–434, 1982

167. Feldman WE: Bacteroides fragilis ventriculitis and meningitis. Am J Dis Child 130:880–883, 1976

168. Garrod LP, Lambert HP, O'Grady F: Antibiotic and Chemotherapy (ed 3). Edinburgh and London, Churchill Livingstone, 1981

169. Teixeira GC, Scott RB: Further clinical and laboratory studies with novobiocin. Antibiotic Med and Clin Ther 5:577–585, 1958

170. Sutherland JM, Keller WH: Novobiocin and neonatal hyperbilirubinemia. Am J Dis Child 101:447–453, 1961

171. Acocella G, Buniva G, Flauto U, et al: Absorption and elimination of the antibiotic rifampin in newborns and children, in Proceedings of the Sixth International Congress of Chemotherapy. Baltimore, University Park Press, 1970

172. McCracken GH, Ginsburg CM, Zwieghaft TC, et al: Pharmacokinetics of rifampin in infants and children: Relevance to prophylaxis against Haemophilus influenzae type b disease. Pediatrics 66:17–21, 1980

173. D'Oliveira JJG: Cerebrospinal fluid concentrations of rifampin in meningeal tuberculosis. Am Rev Respir Dis 106:432–436, 1972

174. Jager-Roman E, Doyle PE, Baird-Lambert J, et al: Pharmacokinetics and tissue distribution of metronidazole in the newborn infant. J Pediatr 100:651–654, 1982

175. Juchau MR, Dyer DC: Pharmacology of the placenta. Pediatr Clin North Am 19:65–79, 1972

176. Totterman LE, Saxen L: Incorporation of tetracycline into human fetal bones after maternal drug administration. Acta Obstet Gynecol Scand 48:542–549, 1969

177. Philipson A, Sabeth LD, Charles O: Transplacental passage of erythromycin and clinidamycin. N Engl J Med 288: 1219–1221, 1973

178. Bernard B, Abate M, Threlen PF, et al: Maternal–fetal pharmacological activity of amikacin. J Infect Dis 135:925–932, 1977

179. Bernard B, Garcia-Cazares SF, Ballard CA, et al: Tobramycin: Maternal–fetal pharmacology. Antimicrob Agents Chemother 11:688–694, 1977

180. Phillipson A: Pharmacokinetics of ampicillin during pregnancy. J Infect Dis 136:370–372, 1977

181. Speert H: Placental transmission of sulfathiazole and sulfadiazine and its significance for fetal chemotherapy. J Obstet Gynecol 45:200–207, 1943

182. Spaar RA, Pritchard JA: Maternal and newborn distribution and excretion of sulfamethoxypryidazine (Kynex). Obstet Gynecol 12:131–134, 1958

183. Perry JE, LeBlanc AL: Transfer of nitrofurantoin across the human placenta. Tex Rep Biol Med 25:265–267, 1967

184. MacAulay MA, Molloy WB, Charles D: Placental transfer of methicillin. Am J Obstet Gynecol 115:58–65, 1953

185. Depp R, Kind AC, Kirby WMM, et al: Transplacental passage of methicillin and dicloxacillin into the fetus and amniotic fluid. Am J Obstet Gynecol 107:1054–1057, 1970

186. MacAulay MA, Berg SR, Charles D: Placental transfer of dicloxacillin at term. Am J Obstet Gynecol 102:1162–1168, 1968

187. Kiefer L, Rubin A, McCoy JB, et al: The placental transfer of erythromycin. Am J Obstet Gynecol 69:174–177, 1955

188. Morrow S, Palmisano P, Cassady G: The placental transfer of cephalothin. J Pediatr 73:262–264, 1968

189. MacAulay MA, Charles D: Placental transmission of colistimethate. Clin Pharmacol Ther 8:578–586, 1967

190. Apgar V: Drugs in pregnancy. JAMA 190:840–841, 1964

191. Sutherland JM, Light IT: The effect of drugs upon the developing fetus. Pediatr Clin North Am 12:781–806, 1965

192. Conway N, Birt DN: Streptomycin in pregnancy: Effect on the fetal ear. Br Med J 2:260–263, 1965

193. Bernard B, Abate M, Ballard CA, et al: Maternal–fetal pharmacology of BB-K8. Fourteenth Interscience Conference on Antimicrobial Agents and Chemotherapy. San Francisco, 1974

194. Kantor IIL, Sutherland DA, Leonard JT, et al: Effect of bilirubin metabolism in the newborn of sulfisoxazole administered to the mother. Obstet Gynecol 17:494–500, 1961

195. Brown AK, Cefik N: Hemolysis and jaundice in the newborn following maternal treatment with sulfamethoxypyridazine (Kynex). Pediatrics 36:742–744, 1965

196. Duna PM: The possible relationship between the maternal administration of sulfamethoxypyridazine and hyperbilirubinemia in the newborn. J Obstet Gynaecol Br Commonw 71:128–131, 1964

197. McCracken GH Jr, Eichenwald HF, Nelson JD: Antimicrobial therapy in theory and practice. I. Clinical pharmacology. J Pediatr 75:742–757, 1969

198. LeBlanc AL, Perry JE: Transfer of tetracycline across the human placenta. Tex Rep Biol Med 25:541–545, 1967

199. Charles D: Placental transmission of antibiotics. J Obstet Gynaecol Br Commonw 61:750–757, 1954

200. Kline AH, Blattner RJ, Lunin M: Transplacental effect of tetracyclines on teeth. JAMA 188:178–180, 1964

201. Kutscher AH, Zegarelle EV, Tovell HMM, et al: Discoloration of deciduous teeth induced by administration of tetracycline antepartum. Am J Obstet Gynecol 96:291–292, 1966

202. Hawking F, Lawrence JS: The Sulfonamides. New York, Grune & Stratton, 1951, p 95–96

203. Knowles JA: Excretion of drugs in milk: A review. J Pediatr 66:1068–1081, 1965

204. Catz CS, Giacoia GP: Drugs and breast milk. Pediatr Clin North Am 19:151–166, 1972

205. Greene HJ, Burkhart B, Hobby GL: Excretion of penicillin in human milk following parturition. Am J Obstet Gynec 51:732–736, 1946

206. O'Brien JE: Excretion of drugs in human milk. Am J Hosp Pharm 31:844–862, 1974

207. Kauffman RE, O'Brien C, Gilford P: Sulfisoxazole secretion into human milk. J Pediatr 97:839–841, 1980

208. Harley JD, Robin H: "Late" neonatal jaundice following maternal treatment with sulfamethoxypyridazine. Pediatrics 37:855–856, 1966

209. Belton EM, Jones RV: Hemolytic anemia due to nalidixic acid. Lancet 2:691, 1965

PART II

Laboratory Aspects

3

Diagnostic Methods

BACTERIAL CULTURES

The diagnosis of bacterial disease is established by isolation of the pathogen from the affected site. All infants with suspected septicemia should have blood, urine, and cerebrospinal fluid (CSF) cultures prior to initiation of antimicrobial therapy. Blood for culture should be obtained from a peripheral vein rather than from the umbilical vessels, since the distal several millimeters of the umbilicus are rapidly colonized with bacteria after birth. Blood should not be taken from indwelling umbilical catheters, particularly if these have been in place for several days or longer.

The skin overlying the vessel to be punctured should be carefully cleansed with an antiseptic such as povidone-iodine. The material should be allowed to dry for at least 20 seconds before needle puncture. Improper skin preparation frequently results in blood cultures contaminated by *Staphylococcus epidermidis*, *Bacillus* species, diphtheroids, and other commensals of the skin.

We do not recommend routine cultures of skin, umbilicus, nasopharynx, ear canal, or rectum of neonates who are suspected of having systemic bacterial disease. Group B streptococci, *Escherichia coli*, and other potential pathogens can be cultured from these sites in 5–30 percent of healthy babies, and yet fewer than 1 percent of these colonized infants have invasive disease. Isolation of these organisms from superficial surfaces has no predictable relationship to results of blood or CSF cultures and therefore is of limited value.

Examination of gastric aspirates for leukocytes and bacteria has been advocated as a means of identifying infants who are at risk of developing systemic bacterial disease. The leukocytes in the infant's stomach are of

105

maternal origin, and the bacteria observed on stained smears and cultures are most likely carried from the nasopharynx to the stomach during intubation. Thus the results of gastric aspirate examinations and cultures should be interpreted with the same caution as findings from cultures of skin and mucosal surfaces.

Urine for culture is often obtained in a sterile plastic bag attached on the cleansed perineum of the baby. Contamination of the specimen by rectal bacteria is likely if urine is not collected within a 20–30-minute period. Infants with positive urine cultures obtained by this technique should have a percutaneous bladder aspiration of urine for repeat culture in order to establish firmly the presence of urinary tract infection.

Anaerobic bacteria have been incriminated in 3–26 percent of all cases of neonatal bacteremia.[1-3] The incidence of neonatal anaerobic bacteremia in one institution was 1.8 cases for each 1000 live births.[1] *Bacteroides* species and peptostreptococci are the most frequently isolated organisms either singly or in combination with aerobic bacteria. The significance of anaerobes in blood cultures from neonates in unknown. In the majority of cases these organisms are considered to be either contaminants or to be responsible for a transient bacteremia. Anaerobes, however, have been clearly implicated as pathogens of neonatal septicemia,[4-6] meningitis,[7-8] peritonitis,[2] and soft-tissue infections.[9] Accordingly, blood for culture should be inoculated into aerobic (vented) and anaerobic (nonvented) culture bottles, and CSF should be inoculated into thioglycolate broth. If pus or peritoneal fluid is suspected to contain anaerobes, the specimens should be taken immediately to the laboratory and the bacteriologist informed of the possibility of anaerobic infection.

Once a specific etiologic diagnosis has been established and therapy started, it is important to obtain follow-up cultures in order to document bacteriologic cure. In infants with septicemia, blood cultures are repeated 24–48 hours after therapy has been started. Possible causes of persistent bacteremia include resistance of the pathogen to the prescribed drugs, incorrect administration of the antibiotics, or occult sites of infection that require surgical drainage.

All infants with purulent meningitis should have a repeat examination and culture of spinal fluid within 24–36 hours after initiation of therapy and approximately every 24 hours thereafter until cultures are sterile. Documentation of bacteriologic cure in neonatal meningitis has important therapeutic and prognostic implications.[10] Most neonates with meningitis caused by gram-positive bacteria have sterile spinal fluid cultures within 24–36 hours after start of therapy. By contrast, many infants with gram-negative enteric meningitis have positive cultures for 3–4 days and a few infants for 7–10 days. Outcome from disease is correlated directly with persistence of bacteria in CSF.[10]

The single most effective method of establishing therapeutic success in patients with urinary tract infection is to repeat a urine culture after 48–72 hours of therapy. This culture should contain either no bacteria or a significantly reduced number of bacteria to those recovered at diagnosis. Continued bacteriuria may signify inappropriate therapy, unrecognized obstruction, or abscess formation.

VIRAL CULTURES

Viral cultures are useful for several diseases of neonates, but in several conditions discussed in the following section immunologic methods are more practical. Urine cultures for cytomegalovirus are generally positive within 24–48 hours when infants are symptomatic and have large quantities of virus in urine. In asymptomatic infants cytomegalovirus may not be detectable for many days or weeks.

Herpes simplex virus is easily and rapidly cultivated from vesicles. When an infant with herpes encephalitis has no skin lesions, however, brain biopsy is necessary for culture confirmation of the diagnosis, since cultures of CSF may be negative.

Cultures of respiratory secretions can be useful for diagnosis of respiratory syncytial virus and other respiratory viruses, but rapid diagnostic methods of antigen detection are more practical in most situations. CSF and stool specimens should be cultured in cases of suspected enterovirus infection.

For most other viral infections, immunologic methods are preferred to culture. Rotavirus has not been successfully cultivated *in vitro*.

IMMUNOLOGIC METHODS

Seriologic tests for syphilis are extremely valuable (see Chap. 6), but for other congenital infections such as rubella, toxoplasmosis, cytomegalovirus, and herpes simplex infections, the utility of antibody studies is severely limited. Antibodies are common in the general population so that babies acquire antibodies passively. Reliable IgM-specific antibody tests are not readily available for most diseases, but they can be obtained from specialized laboratories. It is likely that IgM antibody tests for several antigens will be adapted soon to kits suitable for ordinary laboratories.

Comparing antibody titers in infant and maternal sera does not reliably distinguish passively aquired antibodies from those produced by the fetus unless the titer in the infant's blood is several dilutions greater than that in maternal serum, and this is rarely the case in congenital infections. Serial

Table 3-1
Rapid Methods for Diseases Occurring in Neonates

Tests	Bacteria	Viruses	Miscellaneous Pathogens
Reverse immunoelectrophoresis	*Haemophilus influenzae b* *Streptococcus pneumoniae* *Neisseria meningitidis* Group B streptococcus	Varicella-zoster	*Candida* species
Fluorescent antibody	*Bordetella pertussis*	Varicella-zoster Cytomegalovirus Respiratory viruses	*Rickettsia rickettsii*
Latex agglutination	*H. influenzae b* Group B streptococcus III	—	*Cryptococcus neoformans*
Bacterial coagglutination	*H. influenzae b* *S. pneumoniae* *N. meningitidis* Group B streptococcus	—	—
Enzyme-linked immunosorbent assay or radioimmunoassay	*H. influenzae b*	Herpes simplex Rotavirus Hepatitis B Respiratory syncytial Varicella-zoster Epstein–Barr	*Candida* species

Adapted from Friedman AD, Ray CB: Rapid laboratory diagnosis of infections. Pediatr Infect Dis 1:366–373, 1982

determinations of titers in an infant's blood over several months occasionally discriminates between passively acquired and actively produced antibodies but gives no useful information in the newborn period, and the possibility of postnatal infection confounds interpretation.

Antibody titers in serum specimens from acutely ill and convalescent patients are useful for retrospective diagnosis of several respiratory virus infections.

Several rapid diagnostic methods based on immunologic methods are outlined in Table 3-1.[11-17] The enzyme-linked immunosobent assay method (ELISA) for rotavirus antigen in feces[17] and the latex agglutination test for group B streptococcal antigen in body fluids[12-13] are commercially available, easily performed in ordinary laboratories, specific, and more sensitive than counterimmunoelectrophoresis (CIE). Webb and Baker[12] detected group B streptococcal antigen by latex agglutination in 27 percent of serum, 80 percent of CSF, and 93 percent of concentrated urine specimens from infants with proved group B streptococcal infections.

The *Limulus* lysate test for endotoxin in CSF has been used successfully in cases of gram-negative meningitis.[18]

REFERENCES

1. Chow AW, Leake RD, Yamanchi T, et al: The significance of anaerobes in neonatal bacteremia: Analysis of 23 cases and review of the literature. Pediatrics 54:736–745, 1974

2. Thirumoorthi MC, Keen BM, Dajani AS: Anaerobic infections in children: A prospective survey. J Clin Microbial 3:318–323, 1976

3. Dunkle LM, Brotherton TJ, Feigin RD: Anaerobic infections in children: A prospective study. Pediatrics 57;311–320, 1976

4. Freedman S, Hollander M: *Clostridium perfringens* septicemia as a postoperative complication of the newborn infant. J Pediatr 71:576–578, 1967

5. Harrod JR, Stevens DA: Anaerobic infections in the newborn infant. J Pediatr 85:399–402, 1974

6. Pearson HE, Anderson GV: Perinatal deaths associated with *Bacteroides* infections. Obstet Gynecol 30:486–491, 1967

7. O'Grady LR, Edward RD: Anaerobic meningitis and bacteremia caused by *Fusobacterium* species. Am J Dis Child 130:871–883, 1976

8. Feldman WE: *Bacteroides fragilis* ventriculitis and meningitis. Am J Dis Child 130:880–883, 1976

9. Lee Y, Berg RB: Cephalhematoma infected with *Bacteroides*. Am J Dis Child 121:77–78, 1971

10. McCracken GH: The rate of bacteriologic response to antimicrobial therapy in neonatal meningitis. Am J Dis Child 123:547–553, 1972

11. Friedman AD, Ray CG: Rapid laboratory diagnosis of infections. Pediatr Infect Dis 1:366–373, 1982

12. Webb BJ, Baker CJ: Commercial latex agglutination test for rapid diagnosis of group B streptococcal infection in infants. J Clin Microbiol 12:442–444, 1980

13. Bromberger PI, Chandler B, Gezon H, et al: Rapid detection of neonatal group B streptococcal infections by latex agglutination. J Pediatr 96:104–106, 1980

14. Edwards MS, Kasper DL, Baker CJ: Rapid diagnosis of type III group B streptococcal meningitis by latex particle agglutination. J Pediatr 95:202–205, 1979

15. Edwards MS, Baker CJ: Prospective diagnosis of early onset group B streptococcal infection by countercurrent immunoelectrophoresis. J Pediatr 94:286–288, 1979

16. Yolken RH: Enzyme immunoassays for the detection of infectious antigens in body fluids: Current limitations and future prospects. Rev Infect Dis 4:35–68, 1982

17. Chiba S, Sakuma Y, Kogasaka R, et al: Fecal shedding of virus in relation to the days of illness of infantile gastroenteritis due to calicivirus. J Infect Dis 142:247–249, 1980

18. Dyson D, Cassady G: Use of *Limulus* lysate for detecting gram-negative neonatal meningitis. Pediatrics 58:105–109, 1976

4

Clinical Applications of Laboratory Tests

ANTIMICROBIAL ASSAYS

Development of methods for antimicrobial assays by microtechniques has facilitated formulation of accurate and safe antibiotic dosage schedules in newborns. Measurement of antibiotics in body fluids by chemical, microbioassay, or enzymatic techniques can now be done in many hospital laboratories. Measurement of serum antibiotic concentrations is especially helpful for managing infants with renal failure and patients who have received an overdosage of a drug.

Antimicrobial Therapy in Renal Failure

Of the antibiotics frequently prescribed to neonates, the aminoglycosides are affected most by alterations of renal function. It has been appreciated for many years that glomerular and tubular functions during the early weeks of life are greatly reduced compared to these processes in older infants and children.[1-2] For example, creatinine clearance values in babies are approximately one-third of those in older individuals.[3] Because half-life values of the aminoglycosides in serum are inversely correlated with the rates of creatinine clearance, the half-lives of these drugs in neonates are prolonged.[4] Further reduction in renal function results in accumulation of drug in serum unless the dosage schedule is altered.

Nomograms relating serum creatinine or creatinine clearances to antibiotic doses and intervals of administration are available for older children and adults[5-7] but have not been formulated for newborn and young infants.

111

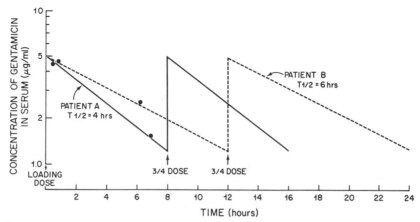

Figure 4-1. *Serum gentamicin concentration-time curves for two hypothetical patients with differing renal clearances of gentamicin. See text for formulation of dosage schedules in patients with renal failure.*

In order to calculate a dosage schedule for a neonate with renal failure, the physician must obtain for antibiotic assay at least 2 serum samples after the antibiotic has been given. The amount of drug and its frequency of administration are based on the desired peak and trough serum concentrations. Using gentamicin as an example, peak concentrations of 4–8 µg/ml and trough levels of 1–2 µg/ml are desirable for safe and effective therapy. The serum half-life curve calculated by the method of least mean squares from the peak and trough serum concentrations is plotted on a semilogarithmic graph (see Fig. 4-1). The slope is extended to the vertical axis, where the intercept represents the theoretical peak serum concentration (5 µg/ml) after an initial loading dose of 2.5 mg/kg gentamicin. This corresponds to an actual peak serum value of 4.0–4.5 µg/ml observed 0.5–1.0 hour after the dose is given. To maintain the serum level above 1 µg/ml in patient A, a second gentamicin dose should be given at eight hours after 2 half-lives have elapsed. Because the serum concentration at eight hours is approximately 25 percent of the theoretical peak value, the amount of gentamicin required to achieve the same peak level is three-quarters of the original dose.

In actual practice, repeating the full loading dose every 2 half-lives (i.e., every eight hours) in patient A results in only slightly increased peak serum concentrations for 2 successive doses, after which the steady state concentration is attained.[8]

If the half-life is prolonged to 6 hours, as in patient B, a second dose would be given 12 hours after the loading dose in order to maintain peak and trough serum concentrations in the desired range. In patients with renal failure, the half-life values may be longer than the example cited above. The pharmacologic principles outlined still apply to the formulation of the specific dosage and frequency of administration schedules for those patients.

An alternate approach would be to use Dettli's[9] nomograph for estimating the patient's individual elimination rate constant of a particular antibiotic. From the value the serum half-life, maintenance dose, and dose interval is calculated. We have found this nomograph useful in infants and children with compromised renal function, but we have only limited experience with using the graph in neonates with renal failure.

It can be helpful to estimate the concentrations of antibiotic in serum by performing a simple inhibitory test.[10] Twofold serial dilutions of the patient's serum are made in broth, and approximately 10^5 bacteria (the organism isolated from the patient or a stock laboratory strain) are inoculated into each tube or well (micromethod). After overnight incubation the serum inhibitory titer is read as the highest dilution showing no visible growth. If a bactericidal end-point is desired, the tubes or wells showing no visible growth are subcultured onto appropriate bacteriologic agar and incubated overnight. The highest dilution demonstrating no growth on agar is the bactericidal titer. For the penicillins and aminoglycosides, the inhibitory and bactericidal titers are usually within 1 dilution of each other. As a general rule, the antibiotic is in the effective and nontoxic range when titers against susceptible pathogens of 1:2–1:8 for the aminoglycosides and 1:8–1:64 for the penicillins or cephalosporins are attained.

Managing Antibiotic Overdoses

Occasionally an infant will be inadvertently given an overdose of an antibiotic. If the drug is a penicillin or a cephalosporin, there is very little chance of developing an adverse reaction. The main precautions would be to withhold one or two subsequent doses of that drug and observe the infant for possible neurologic or renal abnormalities. In contrast, an overdose of an aminoglycoside may potentially have serious consequences. These include possible acute nephrotoxicity and cochlear or vestibular damage. When an overdose is given, the error may not be realized for several hours. When the error is discovered, the physician must determine the amount of drug that was administered and the approximate serum concentration at that time. Is the serum concentration of antibiotic in the toxic range? How long will it take to fall to safe levels? Should dialysis or exchange transfusion be performed? These questions and others must be considered by the physician.

Figure 4-2 illustrates an actual case where an 1800-g, 3-day-old infant was given 10 times the recommended 2.5 mg/kg dose of gentamicin. We

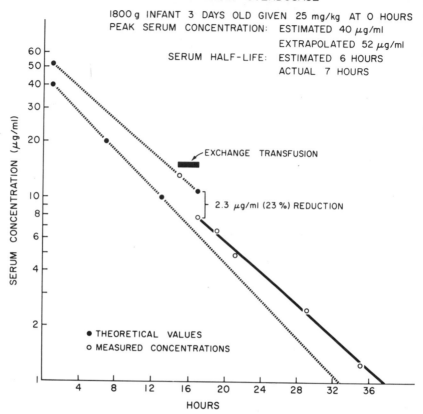

Figure 4-2. *Estimations and measured concentrations of gentamicin in serum following an accidental overdosage. See text for details.*

were consulted on the case, and our formulations were as follows. First, the approximate zero-time peak serum concentration of gentamicin was calculated by multiplying the anticipated peak concentration after a 2.5-mg/kg dose by the dosage error (4.0 μg/ml × 10 = 40 μg/ml). Next the half-life of gentamicin in the serum of this infant (less than 2000 g and younger than 7 days) was estimated to be 6 hours on the basis of the known pharmacokinetic properties of this drug in neonates (see Chap. 2). A serum concentration–time curve was constructed utilizing a 6-hour concentration of 20 μg/ml (1 half-life elapsed) and a 12-hour concentration of 10 μg/ml (2 half-lives elapsed). On the basis of this curve we determined that the concentration of gentamicin in serum would be within the safe range by 12–14 hours after the overdose, which was the time that had elapsed before the dosage error was discovered. We advised against exchange transfusion, since the infant's hourly urine output was normal. The primary physicians elected to perform an exchange transfusion at 14 hours. Serum specimens obtained before and after the procedure were assayed for gentamicin content. The actual concentrations of gentamicin in serum are shown in Figure 4-2. The serum half-life was calculated and used to extrapolate the serum concentration time curve back to the abscissa, the intersection of which represents the actual zero-time peak serum concentration in the patient (52 µg/ml). The estimated serum values were close to the true concentrations, which demonstrates the applicability of these simple formulations to managing infants with antibiotic overdoses.

By our calculations the serum concentration was reduced by the exchange transfusion by 2.3 µg/ml gentamicin, which is probably not enough to justify the 2-hour procedure in this infant. If the estimated concentration of drug at the time an exchange transfusion is contemplated is considerably greater than the upper limits of the safe range, then the procedure may be indicated. Peritoneal dialysis is not effective in removing gentamicin but may be effective for removal of kanamycin.[7] Hemodialysis cannot be performed in neonates in most centers.

The physician should withhold aminoglycoside therapy for as long a period as the drug is present in potentially toxic concentrations in serum of the patient. The clinical status and results of cultures should be reviewed. If there is no definite indication for antimicrobial therapy, these drugs should be stopped. There are no data on the long-term outcome of infants who have received aminoglycoside overdoses with which to assess the risk of drug toxicity.

SERUM INHIBITORY AND BACTERICIDAL TITERS

Aside from improvement of clinical signs, there are two objective ways in which to assess whether an infant with an infectious disease is receiving the proper antibiotic and in sufficient amounts to eradicate the infection. These methods are documentation of bacteriologic cure by repeated culture of the site of infection, and demonstration of serum bacteriostatic or bactericidal activity against the pathogen. The method for determining serum inhibitory and bactericidal activity was outlined earlier in this chapter and is presented in greater detail in several published reports.[10-13]

We have found the assay of antibacterial activity particularly useful in the management of infants with infections for which prolonged antimicrobial therapy is necessary. Other conditions where this test may be applied are septicemia and meningitis. In the latter, measurements of inhibitory and bactericidal activity in cerebrospinal or ventricular fluid are useful in guiding antibiotic dosage and administration route. The value of this test has been evaluated in adult patients with malignancy and infection.[13] When the peak titer of bacteriostatic activity in serum of these patients was 1:8 or greater, infection was cured in 80 percent or more of cases.

REFERENCES

1. Dean RFA, McCance RA: Inulin, diodone, creatinine and urea clearances in newborn infants. J Physiol 106:431–439, 1947
2. Leake RD, Trygstad CW, Oh W: Inulin clearance in the newborn infant: Relationship to gestational and postnatal age. Pediatr Res 10:759–762, 1976
3. Winberg J: The 24-hour true endogenous creatinine clearance in infants and children without renal disease. Acta Pediatr Scand 48:443–452, 1959
4. McCracken GH, West NR, Horton LJ: Urinary excretion of gentamicin in the neonatal period. J Infect Dis 123:257–262, 1971
5. Linquist JA, Siddiqui JL, Smith IM: Cephalex in patients with renal disease. N Engl J Med 283:720–723, 1970
6. Cutler RE, Gyselynck A, Fleet P, et al.: Correlation of serum creatinine concentration and gentamicin half-life. JAMA 219:1037–1041, 1972
7. Bennet WM, Singer I, Coggins CJ: A guide to drug therapy in renal failure. JAMA 230:1544–1553, 1974
8. O'Grady F: Antibiotics in renal failure. Br Bull Med 142–147, 1971
9. Dettli L: Individualization of drug dosage in patients with renal disease. Med Clin North Am 58:977–985, 1974
10. Jawetz E: Assay of antibacterial activity in serum. Am J Dis Child 103:81–84, 1962
11. Provonchee RB, Zinner SH: Rapid method for determining serum bactericidal activity. Appl Microbiol 27:185–186, 1974
12. Taub WH: Assay of the antibiotic activity of serum. Appl Microbiol 18:51–56, 1969
13. Klastersky J, Daneua D, Savings G, et al.: Antibacterial activity in serum and urine as a therapeutic guide in bacterial infections. J Infect Dis 129:187–197, 1974

PART III

Clinical Aspects

5

Sepsis and Central Nervous System Infections

Systemic bacterial diseases occur in from 1–10 infants in each 1000 live births. Approximately one-third of cases of bacteremia are associated with meningitis. The rates of neonatal bacterial disease vary from nursery to nursery and depend on the rate of prematurity, predisposing maternal conditions, and the extent of life-support procedures and monitoring devices required postnatally. These apparatuses have served as fomites of relatively nonpathogenic microorganisms that can cause nosocomial bacterial diseases. The frequency of these opportunistic infections varies and is usually sporadic.

EPIDEMIOLOGY

The gastrointestinal tract is the principal reservoir of *Escherichia coli*, group B streptococci,[1] and *Listeria monocytogenes*.[2] The group B streptococcus is found in the rectum or vagina of from 5–30 percent of asymptomatic pregnant women[3] and is vertically transmitted to 50–75 percent of infants born vaginally.[4] A similar mode of transmission has been demonstrated for *E. coli* K1 strains[5] and *L. monocytogenes*.[2] The risk of invasive group B streptococcal disease appears to be related to the number of sites from which the organism can be isolated and the quantity of bacteria recovered from each site.[6]

Many host defense systems have been shown to be abnormal in the neonatal period,[7] but the most important predisposing factor for group B streptococcal disease appears to be lack of circulating specific anticapsular antibody derived transplacentally from the mother.[8] As yet there are no comparable data for the pathogenesis of *E. coli* K1 infection or of other bacterial diseases of the newborn.

ETIOLOGY

Although the incidence of neonatal bacterial diseases has not substantially changed since the 1950s, for unknown reasons the responsible pathogens have varied considerably. Since 1965 group B streptococci and *E. coli* have accounted for approximately 60 percent of all cases of sepsis and meningitis. Other organisms that can cause these conditions include *Listeria, Klebsiella–Enterobacter* species, *Proteus* species, group D streptococci (enterococci and *Streptococcus bovis*), and non–group D alpha-hemolytic streptococci.[7] Less frequently encountered agents are *Haemophilus influenzae* (usually unencapsulated strains),[9] *Streptococcus pneumoniae*,[10] *Neisseria meningitidis*,[11] and *Pseudomonas aeruginosa*. *Citrobacter diversus*[12-13] can cause neonatal meningitis and is associated with brain abscess in up to 70 percent of meningitis cases. *Enterobacter sakazakii* was first encountered in our third Neonatal Meningitis Cooperative Study (1980–1982) and was associated with severe neurologic sequellae in the 2 patients studied.

Although anaerobes have been recovered from blood cultures of as many as 26 percent of neonates,[14] anaerobic bacteremia is usually self-limited and is rarely life-threatening. Exceptions are clostridial sepsis and meningitis caused by *Bacteroides fragilis*.[15] Additionally, nosocomial infections caused by multiply-resistant *Staphylococcus aureus* and gram-negative enteric bacilli occur sporadically and are frequently transmitted by use of respiratory therapy equipment and vascular lines that provide direct access to the pulmonary and systemic circulations

DIAGNOSIS

The early symptoms of bacterial disease in the neonate are usually nonspecific and include temperature instability, tachypnea, tachycardia, lethargy, vomiting, diarrhea, and unwillingness to nipple feed. Jaundice, petechiae, meningeal signs, bulging fontanel, and seizures are late signs and frequently denote a poor prognosis. Infection is difficult to recognize in infants receiving intensive care because of the severe underlying illness requiring intensive therapy and the frequent use of prophylactic antibiotics in these infants.

Many indirect indicators of bacterial infection of the neonate have been evaluated.[7] In our experience the peripheral white cell count is the most reliable of these screening tests. Elevation of the absolute neutrophil count and an increased ratio of immature to mature neutrophils are associated with bacterial disease.[16] A sepsis screen has been advocated by Philip and Hewitt,[17] but of the 5 tests suggested the peripheral white cell count is the most helpful. Stained smears and cultures of a gastric aspirate are frequently overinterpreted and reflect maternal origin of the cells and bacteria and fetal stress of noninfectious origin.[18]

Interpretation of cerebrospinal fluid (CSF) cell counts in newborns may be difficult. During the first several days of life, as many as 32 white blood cells in each cubic millimeter of CSF (mean, 9 cells/mm^3) may be found in both healthy and high-risk uninfected babies.[19] Approximately 60 percent of these cells are polymorphonuclear leukocytes. During the first week the CSF cell count slowly diminishes in full-term infants and increases in premature infants. Cell counts in the range of 0–10 cells/mm^3 are observed at age 1 month. The CSF protein concentration may be as great at 170 mg/dl, and the percentage ratio of CSF glucose to blood glucose ranges from 44 percent to more than 100 percent in both preterm and full-term infants, with an average of approximately 65 percent. A total evaluation of the CSF fluid examination is necessary in order to make an early diagnosis of neonatal meningitis. Although one or two elements of the CSF examination in infants with meiningitis may overlap with values in normal infants, fewer than 1 percent of babies with proved meningitis have a totally normal CSF study on the initial lumbar tap.[19]

It is important to examine carefully stained smears of CSF from every infant with suspected meningitis. Grossly clear fluid may contain few white blood cells and many bacteria. Bacteria are seen in the stained smears of CSF from approximately 80 percent of neonates with proved meningitis. Blood and urine cultures should be obtained from every infant with suspected meningitis.

Detection of the capsular polysaccharide antigens of group B streptococci, E. coli K1, and less frequently of S. pneumoniae, N. meningitidis, and type b H. influenzae in body fluids facilitates prompt diagnosis, particularly in pretreated newborn infants.[20-21] The techniques (reverse immunoelectrophoresis, latex agglutination, or enzyme-linked immunosorbent assay) to detect these antigens are available in many hospital laboratories. The concentration of antigen in CSF is a useful guide in predicting long-term outcome from meningitis.[20]

THERAPY

Before bacteriologic confirmation of the diagnosis of sepsis or meningitis and prior to the availability of microbial susceptibility studies, antimicrobial therapy should be initiated using a combination of a beta-lactam and an aminoglycoside. The choice of antibiotics must be based on the historical experience of the nursery and on the antimicrobial susceptibilities of bacteria that have been recently recovered from cultures of sick and healthy neonates. Emergence of resistant coliform organisms and staphylococci and recognition of drug tolerance among group B streptococcal and staphylococcal strains have made it necessary to develop alternative antibiotic strategies. For example, treatment with ampicillin and an aminoglycoside has been recommended for therapy of group B streptococcal or *Listeria* infections because *in vitro* synergism between these drugs, enhanced killing of bacteria, and longer survival of animals treated with combination drug therapy than with single-drug therapy have been demonstrated.[22-23] There have been no controlled clinical trials, however, to evaluate the applicability of these *in vitro* and animal studies.

Attention to general supportive therapy is of utmost importance in managing infants with sepsis or meningitis. Many of these patients, particularly those with early-onset group B streptococcal sepsis and those with meningitis, require management in an intensive care facility. Apnea, hypotension, acidosis, electrolyte imbalance, or seizures are difficult to control in newborn infants and often require the skills of trained physicians and nurses in intensive care units.

Sepsis

As initial antimicrobial therapy we prefer ampicillin combined with either gentamicin or tobramycin. Amikacin is reserved for situations in which aminoglycoside-resistant gram-negative enteric bacilli become prevalent in a nursery. Usually gentamicin and tobramycin-resistant strains are susceptible to amikacin; this must, however, be confirmed in the laboratory. Ampicillin is active *in vitro* against group B and group D streptococci and against *Listeria* as well as against approximately 60 percent of *E. coli* strains. When epidemiologic experience in the nursery or clinical findings suggest *Pseudomonas* infection, ticarcillin in combination with gentamicin or tobramycin is indicated. Because a small percentage of group B streptococcal strains are tolerant to penicillin or ampicillin[24] (inhibited but not killed by easily achievable concentrations of drug in blood or CSF), we routinely determine the minimum inhibitory concentration (MIC) and minimal bactericidal concentration (MBC) values for isolates before altering the initial antimicrobial regimen. Tolerant strains of streptococci are best treated with ampicillin and an aminoglycoside.

Many physicians favor the use of whole blood or fresh frozen plasma transfusions as adjuncts to management of septic infants. Whole blood exchange transfusions for critically ill neonates with sepsis has been advocated by some.[25] A recent report demonstrated the efficacy of irradiated granulocyte transfusions in septic infants with neutropenia and depletion of the neutrophil storage pool.[26] Results of this provocative study are promising but require verification before granulocyte transfusion can be recommended for routine use in such infants.

A repeat blood culture is suggested 24–48 hours after initiation of antimicrobial therapy. If the culture is not sterile, the antimicrobial susceptibilities of the pathogen should be checked, as should also the actual dosage of the drugs being administered. Persistence of septicemia should prompt a search for an unidentified focus of infection such as a perinephric abscess, an infected vascular line, or an intraabdominal process. Duration of therapy in the patient without complications is usually 7–10 days.

Meningitis

The principal goal of antibiotic therapy of neonatal meningitis is prompt eradication of the pathogen from CSF because persistence of bacteria is correlated with an increased incidence of complications during therapy and of long-term neurologic sequellae.[27] As a rule it takes longer to sterilize CSF in infants with meningitis caused by gram-negative enteric bacilli than in patients who have meningitis caused by gram-positive bacteria. The difference is related in part to the fact that the dosages of aminoglycosides used against coliform organisms produce considerably smaller CSF bactericidal titers, since there are only small concentrations of aminoglycosides in CSF relative to the MBC of the offending pathogen. The amount of drug administered cannot be substantially increased because of the narrow range between the therapeutic and toxic serum concentrations of the aminoglycosides. By contrast, there is a wide margin of safety with the beta-lactam drugs, thereby permitting large increases in doses in order to achieve adequate concentrations of drug and bactericidal activity in CSF against group B streptococci and other susceptible bacteria. Attempts to increase the concentrations of gentamicin in CSF of neonates with coliform meningitis by direct lumbar instillation[28] or by intraventricular administration[12] of gentamicin have proved no more effective clinically than systemic therapy alone.

The new beta-lactam derivates with enhanced *in vitro* activity against gram-negative enteric bacilli have been shown in experimental coliform meningitis to have superior CSF bactericidal activity and a greater bacteriologic efficacy than the aminoglycosides.[29] An uncontrolled trial of cefotaxime in neonates and young infants suggested that this agent is effective for therapy of group B streptococcal or coliform meningitis.[30] Because there is no information from randomized controlled studies in neonates, additional experience with cefotaxime is required. By contrast, the third Neonatal Meningitis Cooperative Study Group is conducting a prospective, randomized, controlled study of the effectiveness of ampicillin and amikacin compared with that of moxalactam in neonates with coliform meningitis. After 2 years (fall, 1982) 50 patients have been enrolled, and the results indicate that moxalactam is as effective as the conventional ampicillin–aminoglycoside regimen for management of this condition. Moxalactam should not be used for single-drug initial therapy in neonates, however, because of its inadequate *in vitro* activity against group B streptococci, enterococci, and *Listeria*.[29] A combination of ampicillin and moxalactam would be satisfactory, but because of insufficient experience with this regimen it cannot be considered first-line initial therapy at this time (see Chap. 2 for discussion of the other new beta-lactam derivatives).

All neonates should have a repeat CSF examination and culture at 24–36 hours after initiation of antibiotic therapy. If no organisms are seen on stained smears of CSF and the cultures are ultimately sterile, single-drug therapy can be used if laboratory studies indicate susceptibility (and nontolerance) of the pathogen. Ampicillin is suitable for group B streptococci, *Listeria,* and enterococci, while moxalactam or cefotaxime is an alternative to ampicillin aminoglycoside therapy for gram-negative enteric bacillary meningitis (with the exception of *Pseudomonas, Acinetobacter,* and some *Serratia* strains). If the stained smears of CSF obtained at 24–36 hours demonstrate bacteria, modification of the antimicrobial regimen may be necessary. Depending on the results of susceptibility studies, moxalactam or cefotaxime for coliforms, ticarcillin and an aminoglycoside for *Pseudomonas* or indole-positive *Proteus* species, and metronidazole for *B. fragilis* are suitable alternatives.

Although the CSF concentrations of chloramphenicol are nearly equivalent to those in serum, we do not recommend the use of this drug in neonates with meningitis unless serum concentrations can be monitored to maintain levels in the safe and effective range (15–25 μg/ml). Concomitant administration of phenobarbital lowers the serum concentrations, while therapy with phenytoin results in considerably larger values.[31] Additionally, there is evidence that chloramphenicol antagonizes the *in vitro* action of ampicillin against group B streptococci,[32] and data from animal studies suggest that this agent antagonizes the aminoglycosides against *Proteus* species.[33] Finally, chloramphenicol is bacteriostatic against most coliform bacilli, which may be disadvantageous in a neonate with abnormal immunologic mechanisms.

The duration of antimicrobial therapy for neonatal sepsis is usually 7–10 days, while that of meningitis is approximately 14 days for group B streptococcal and *Listeria* disease and 21 days for coliform or staphylococcal meningitis. Outcome is highly variable, but mortality from neonatal sepsis and meningitis ranges from 15–20 percent in centers with intensive care facilities to 30–50 percent in those without provision for specialized care.

Brain Abscess

Primary brain abscess in the neonate and young infant is rare. In 1970, Hoffman, Hendrick, and Hiscox[34] added 6 cases of solitary brain abscess in infants less than 3 months old to 17 cases that had been previously reported. Intracranial abscesses in young infants are frequently unsuspected because of their nonspecific clinical presentations. The infant is usually evaluated for septicemia or meningitis, and lumbar CSF may be purulent because of rupture of the abscess into the ventricle. Hence the infant may be treated for meningitis without recognition of the primary brain abscess. Initial clinical improvement after systemic antibiotic therapy is usually followed by deterioration due to the expanding mass and increased intracranial pressure.

Computed tomography (CT) with contrast is invaluable in diagnosing brain abscess in young infants. Early findings are usually of edema and cerebritis, whereas later a focal defect with circumferential enhancement is characteristic of abscess formation.

Although once considered rare in newborn infants, abscesses developing as a complication of meningitis have been encountered more frequently in recent years. Of 50 infants in the third Neonatal Meningitis Cooperative Study, 5 had brain abscesses. This increased incidence of secondary abscesses may be more apparent than real with the advent of CT scans in many hospital facilities. Of the 5 infants with secondary abscess, 3 had C. diversus meningitis, a condition that is known to be associated with abscesses in approximately 70 percent of cases.[12-13]

Therapy of brain abscess in neonates depends in part on the susceptibility of the causative agent. Possible pathogens include C. diversus, group B streptococcus, E. coli, and other coliform organisms. In cases of primary brain abscess, broad-spectrum coverage is started using the conventional beta-lactam–aminoglycoside combination. Response to this regimen is judged clinically and by repeated CT scans. Failure to respond adequately is indication for surgery to obtain material for an etiologic diagnosis and to provide drainage or excision if possible. Evolution of the abscess with encapsulation and diminution in size as judged by serial CT scans usually indicates that medical management alone is satisfactory. Duration of antimicrobial therapy is highly variable. Complete excision is followed by approximately 5–7 days of therapy, whereas 3 weeks or longer may be required when response to therapy is slow and surgery is not undertaken.

For dosages see Chapter 2 or Abbreviated Guide to Dosage on Inside Covers

REFERENCES

1. Badri MS, Zaweneh S, Cruz AC, et al: Rectal colonization with group B streptococcus: Relation to vaginal colonization of pregnant women. J Infect Dis 135:308–312, 1977
2. Bojsen-Møller J: Human listeriosis: Diagnostic, epidemiological and clinical studies. Acta Pathol Microbiol Scand [B] 229(suppl):1972
3. Anthony BF, Okada DM, Hobel C, et al: Epidemiology of group B streptococcus: Longitudinal observations during pregnancy. J Infect Dis 137:524–530, 1978
4. Siegel JD, McCracken GH, Threlkeld N, et al: Single-dose penicillin prophylaxis against neonatal group B streptococcal infections: A controlled trial in 18,738 newborn infants. N Engl J Med 303:769–775, 1980
5. Sarff LD, McCracken GH, Schiffer MS, et al: Epidemiology of *Escherichia coli* K1 in healthy and diseased newborns. Lancet 1:1099–1104, 1975
6. Pass MA, Gray BM, Khare S, et al: Prospective studies of group B streptococcal infections in infants. J Pediatr 95:437–443, 1979
7. Siegel JD, McCracken GH: Sepsis neonatorum. New Engl J Med 304:642–647, 1981
8. Baker CJ, Kasper DL: Correlation of maternal antibody deficiency with susceptibility to neonatal group B streptococcal infection. New Engl J Med 294:753–756, 1976
9. Lilien LD, Yeh TF, Novak GM: Early-onset *Haemophilus* sepsis in newborn infants: Clinical, roentgenographic and pathologic features. Pediatrics 62:299–303, 1978
10. Bortolussi R, Thompson TR, Ferrieri P: Early-onset pneumococcal sepsis in newborn infants. Pediatrics 60:352–355, 1977
11. Jones RN, Slepack J, Eades A: Fatal neonatal meningococcal meningitis. JAMA 236:2652–2653, 1976
12. McCracken GH, Mize SG, Threlkeld N: Intraventricular gentamicin therapy in gram negative bacillary meningitis of infancy. Report of the Second Neonatal Meningitis Cooperative Study Group. Lancet 1:787–791, 1980
13. Graham DR, Band JD: *Citrobacter diversus* brain abscess and meningitis in neonates. JAMA 245:1923–1925, 1981
14. Chow AW, Leake RD, Yamauchi T, et al: The significance of anerobes in neonatal bacteremia: Analysis of 23 cases and review of the literature. Pediatrics 54:736–745, 1974
15. Berman BW, King FH, Rubenstein DS, et al: *Bacteriodes fragilis* meningitis in a neonate successfully treated with metronidazole. J Pediatr 93:793–795, 1978
16. Manroe BL, Weinberg AG, Rosenfeld CR, et al: The neonatal blood count in health and disease. I. Reference values for neutrophilic cells. J Pediatr 95:89–98, 1979
17. Philip AGS, Hewitt JR: Early diagnosis of neonatal sepsis. Pediatrics 65:1036–1041, 1980
18. Mims LC, Medawar MS, Perkins JR, et al: Predicting neonatal infections by evaluation of the gastric aspirate: A study in 207 patients. Am J Obstet Gynecol 114:232–238, 1972

19. Sarff LD, Platt LH, McCracken GH: Cerebrospinal fluid evaluation in neonates: Comparison of high-risk infants with and without meningitis. J Pediatr 88:473–477, 1976

20. McCracken GH, Sarff LD, Glode MP, et al: Relation between *Escherichiae coli* K1 capsular polysaccharide antigen and clinical outcome in neonatal meningitis. Lancet 2:246–250, 1974

21. Siegel JD, McCracken GH: Detection of group B streptococcal antigens in body fluids of neonates. J Pediatr 93:491–492, 1978

22. Scheld WM, Alliegro GM, Field MR, et al: Synergy between ampicillin and gentamicin in experimental meningitis due to group B streptococci. J Infect Dis 146:100, 1982

23. Scheld WM, Fletcher DD, Fink FN, et al: Response to therapy in an experimental rabbit model of meningitis due to *Listeria monocytogenes*. J Infect Dis 140:287–294, 1979

24. Kim KS, Anthony BF: Penicillin tolerance in group B streptococci isolated from infected neonates. J Infect Dis 144:411–419, 1981

25. Vain NE, Mazlumian JR, Swarner OW, et al: Role of exchange transfusion in the treatment of severe septicemia. Pediatrics 66:693–697, 1980

26. Christensen RD, Rothstein G, Anstell HB, et al: Granulocyte transfusions in neonates with bacterial infection, neutropenia and depletion of mature marrow neutrophils. Pediatrics 70:1–6, 1982

27. McCracken GH: The rate of bacteriologic response to antimicrobial therapy in neonatal meningitis. Am J Dis Child 123:547 551, 1972

28. McCracken GH, Mize SG: A controlled study of intrathecal antibiotic therapy in gram negative enteric meningitis of infancy. J Pediatr 89:66–72, 1976

29. Schaad UB, McCracken GH, Loock CA, et al: Pharmacokinetics and bacteriologic efficacy of moxalactam, cefotaxime, cefoperazone and rocephin in experimental bacterial meningitis. J Infect Dis 143:156–163, 1981

30. Kafetzis D, Bruch K, Young J: Cefotaxime in the treatment of purulent meningitis in pediatrics. Presented at the Twenty-first Interscience Conference on Antimicrobial Therapy and Chemotherapy. Chicago, Nov 1981

31. Krasinski K, Kusmiesz H, Nelson JD: Pharmacologic interactions among chloramphenicol, phenytoin and phenobarbital. Pediatr Infect Dis 1:232–235, 1982

32. Weeks JL, Mason EO, Baker CF: Antagonism of ampicillin and chloramphenicol for meningeal isolates of group B streptococci. Antimicrob Agents Chemother 20:281–285, 1981

33. Strausbaugh LJ, Sande MA: Factors influencing the therapy of experimental *Proteus mirabilis* meningitis in rabbits. J Infect Dis 137:251–260, 1978

34. Hoffman HF, Hendrick EB, Hiscox JL: Cerebral abscesses in early infancy. J Neurosurg 33:172–177, 1970

6

Congenital Infections

CONGENITAL SYPHILIS

The rising incidence of veneral disease in the United States has resulted in an increased number of infants with congenital syphilis. Transmission of spirochetes transplacentally to the neonate usually occurs during the last half of pregnancy, and the risk of congenital infection is increased if the mother is in the early stages of disease.

Infants with congenital syphilis may be either asymptomatic at birth or may present with florid manifestations of disease.[1] Classically the infant has petechial and purpuric skin lesions, hepatosplenomegaly, respiratory distress due to pneumonia, and signs of central nervous system involvement. The majority of infected infants, however, manifest a milder form of the disease or no symptoms in the early newborn period.

The dermatologic findings are usually the most striking and most variable feature of congenital syphilis. A maculopapular rash is frequently prominent on the face, palms, and soles. Bullous lesions of the hands and feet that rupture and ooze a clear, highly infectious fluid are particularly characteristic. Lesions around the anus and genitalia may be observed. Rhinitis with a continuous profuse nonpurulent discharge is found in some infants with congenital syphilis. The fluid teems with viable organisms, which causes persistent excoriations of the upper lip that heal with fine scarring (rhagades).

Diminished movement and guarding of one or more extremities (Parrot's paralysis) is common and is due to painful periostitis of the long bones. Metaphyseal erosions are also seen.

Central nervous system syphilis occurs in 30–50 percent of infected infants, the majority of whom have no abnormal neurologic findings during the early months of life.[1] The diagnosis of neurosyphilis in these asymptomatic infants is difficult to document. The cerebrospinal fluid (CSF) cell counts and protein concentrations may be within the range of values observed in healthy neonates,[2] and the fluorescent treponemal antibody absorption (FTA-ABS) test may be positive in spinal fluid of normal infants.[3] This antibody and others are passively transmitted across the blood–brain barrier; the concentration in CSF is related to that in serum.[3] The diagnosis of congenital neurosyphilis is confirmed by the presence of a reactive spinal fluid VDRL.

Mothers with active syphilis have reactive VDRL and FTA-ABS tests. The antibodies are primarily of the IgG class and will be passively acquired by the infant regardless of whether he or she has active disease. Cord serum will therefore have a reactive serology. An infant with active infection manufactures IgM antibody *in utero,* which may be detected by the FTA-ABS–IgM test.[4] There are a number of technical problems with performing and interpreting the FTA-ABS–IgM test that have limited its usefulness.[5] The clinician must therefore depend on the maternal history of adequate treatment, the possibility of reexposure, and family compliance regarding follow-up examinations of the neonate. It is safest to treat the neonate if any uncertainty exists about adequacy of the mother's treatment.

The staphylococcal protein A adsorption test may develop into a useful means of demonstrating IgM antibodies in syphilis and other congenital infections.[6-7] This cell wall protein precipitates IgG of subclasses 1, 2, and 4 by attachment to the Fc fragment of the immunoglobulin molecule. The persistence of 25 percent or more of the original titer after absorption with staphylococcal protein A is considered to indicate presence of IgM antibodies in serum. Further experience is required to confirm the reliability of this test.

Asymptomatic infants with passively acquired IgG antibody will demonstrate a diminution in the VDRL titer over the first several months of life. A sustained or rising titer in a 2- or 3-month-old untreated infant indicates active veneral disease. Treated infants also have a decline in VDRL antibodies to the point of negative test results by 5–6 months of age; serial declines in serum VDRL titers, therefore, do not distinguish between uninfected babies with passively acquired antibodies and successfully treated infected babies. A treponemal antibody test (FTA-ABS or MHA-TP [Microhemagglulination-Treponema Pallidum]) at 9–12 months of age provides this distinction because an infected baby will have persistence of treponemal antibodies in spite of successful therapy.[8]

Penicillin is the drug of choice for all forms of syphilis.[8-9] If the mother's treatment for syphilis was inadequate, unknown, or with drugs other than penicillin G, the infant should be treated regardless of the baby's clinical status. A CSF examination should be performed in all infants who are to be treated for congenital syphilis. In asymptomatic infants with normal CSF, benzathine penicillin G, 50,000 u/kg in a single intramuscular dose, is recommended. This preparation should not be used in any infant with symptomatic disease or in those with subclinical infection and abnormal CSF findings. These patients should be treated either with aqueous crystalline penicillin G, 50,000 u/kg in 2 divided intramuscular or intravenous doses, or with procaine penicillin G, 50,000 u/kg in 1 intramuscular dose daily. Therapy is continued for a minimum of 10–14 days. Taber[8] recommends treating all infants for suspected or proved congenital syphillis with a larger dose of 100,000 u/kg daily for 10 days. It should be pointed out that clinical efficacy data do not exist for these treatment schedules. These recommendations are based primarily on pharmacologic data in neonates[10] and represent conservative therapy in the absence of clinical studies.

CONGENITAL TOXOPLASMOSIS

Considerable information on the epidemiology and pathogenesis of toxoplasmosis has been gained in the past decade. Whereas formerly toxoplasmosis was believed to cause severe morbidity or mortality in most congenitally infected infants, it is now appreciated that up to 90 percent of these infants are asymptomatic at birth.[11-12] Saxon et al,[12] have demonstrated that many of these asymptomatic infants have elevated CSF white blood cell counts and protein concentrations early in life, indicating active central nervous system infection. Because some of these patients will manifest varying degrees of intellectual impairment in late infancy and childhood,[13] it is important to establish the diagnosis early.

Subclinical toxoplasmosis in the neonate is difficult to diagnose because of the presence of transplacentally acquired maternal antibody and the difficulty of interpretating the FTA-ABS–IgM test.[14]

The Sabin-Feldman dye test and complement fixation test[15] have generally been supplanted by immunofluorescent or enzyme-linked immunosorbent assays (ELISA).[16-17] An adaptation of the ELISA test called the immunoglobulin M immunosorbent agglutination assay (IgM-ISAGA)[18] is particularly valuable since it permits discrimination between infected infants and those with passively acquired antibody. The staphylococcal protein A adsorption test has also been used to detect IgM antibodies.[7]

Therapy of congenital toxoplasmosis usually consists of pyrimethamine, 1 mg/kg/day orally in 1 dose, and trisulfapyramidines, 100–150 mg/kg/day orally in 4 doses, given for a total of 30 days. Folinic acid must be supplemented daily to prevent bone marrow suppression. Hospitalization may be necessary to assure compliance, particularly because pyrimethamine and folinic acid are supplied only as tablets and must be pulvarized and put into suspension for administration.

· Pyrimethamine and sulfa are recommended for therapy of toxoplasmosis on the basis of both experimental and clinical data.[19] Sulfadiazine was shown to increase survival in experimentally produced toxoplasmosis in animals, but the organism was recovered from survivors. By contrast, pyrimethamine therapy of murine toxoplasmosis eradicated the parasite and improved survival. When combined, these two agents act synergistically by inhibiting folic acid synthesis at two steps in the metabolic pathway. Although pyrimethamine and a sulfonamide have been used frequently in therapy of congenital toxoplasmosis, there have been no controlled trials to assess the efficacy of this regimen. Saxon et al.[12] treated 3 infants with this drug combination plus folinic acid and compared these patients' 2–4 year follow-up results to those of 5 untreated infants with subclinical toxoplasmosis and to matched control subjects. The 3 treated patients had normal mental and motor development at 34 and 36 months, while the 5 untreated infants showed some degree of intellectual impairment at 20–67 months. These authors emphasized that if chronic central nervous system infection is to be prevented, therapy must be started in early infancy at a time when infection is usually asymptomatic.

Recent studies have shown that trimethoprim is inactive against *Toxoplasma*. The combination of trimethoprim and sulfamethoxazole was no more effective in murine toxoplasmosis than was sulfamethoxazole alone.[20]

Spiramycin, a macrolid antibiotic with antimicrobial activity that is similar to that of erythromycin, has been used in Europe for therapy of acquired toxoplasmosis. The drug is not licensed in the United States, but it is available in Canada. Desmonts and Couvreur[11] treated 98 pregnant women who had recently acquired toxoplasmosis with spiramycin, 2 g/day, for at least 3 weeks. The number of infants with definite and possible congenital toxoplasmosis was significantly fewer than was observed among 82 infants born to infected mothers who received no therapy. The proportion of infants with clinically apparent disease at birth, however, was greater in the treated group. This study suggests that spiramycin may be efficacious during pregnancy, but additional studies are required for confirmation.

CONGENITAL VIRAL INFECTIONS

Viral agents acquired by the fetus during gestation or by the neonate during the intrapartum period may cause inapparent infection or clinical disease ranging in severity from only rash or jaundice to multiple organ involvement. The most common and severe sequelae are consequent to necrotizing encephalitis and include microcephaly, neurologic and intellectual deficits, and behavioral problems.[21-23] With the exception of the herpes simplex viruses, subclinical infection occurs in two-thirds or more of cases. Almost all newborns with herpes simplex infection manifest clinical illness.

Antiviral chemotherapy has been used for treatment of congenital infections with generally disappointing results. These potentially toxic agents should *not* be used in infants with subclinical viral infections. More information is needed on the long-term neurologic sequelae in asymptomatic patients before these agents can be recommended. On the other hand, the mortality and morbidity rates in neonates with disseminated cytomegalovirus or herpes simplex infections are considerable. If a therapeutic agent could be shown to be effective in these patients, its use would be justified despite possible toxicity.

Herpes Simplex Virus Infections

Idoxuridine has been used in an uncontrolled fashion for therapy of neonatal herpes simplex infections. In one study all treated infants had disseminated disease and either died or had evidence of neurologic abnormalities on follow-up examinations.[23-25] Idoxuridine did not reduce the mortality rate or inhibit viral replication within the central nervous system of newborn mice that were experimentally infected with herpes simplex type 2.[26] In a collaborative placebo-controlled study of children and adults with herpes simplex encephalitis, idoxuridine caused serious hematologic toxicity without controlling the central nervous system infection.[27] These observations, plus anecdotal experience with newborns, indicate that this drug has unacceptable toxicity and inadequate efficacy to warrant its use.

Cytosine arabinoside hydrochloride has had limited use in neonatal herpesvirus infections because of its acute toxic effects on bone marrow and the immunologic system. By contrast vidarabine (adenine arabinoside), a purine nucleoside, does not cause significant acute toxicity, is active *in vitro* against the genital strains of herpesviruses, and attains good antiviral activity in CSF.[28] Ch'ien et al. reported preliminary results with vidarabine therapy in 13 neonates with herpes simplex infection.[28] Treatment was started within three days of the first central nervous system signs in 8 babies; all survived and were normal on follow-up at age 6–12 months. Vidarabine therapy was delayed in 5 infants, and only 1 survived; this patient had marked neurologic impairment.

In a larger experience with 56 newborns infected with herpes simplex virus treated with placebo or vidarabine on a randomized, double-blind protocol, a significant benefit of therapy was demonstrated.[29] The case fatality rate was reduced from 78 to 38 percent with vidarabine therapy in infants with central nervous system or disseminated disease; only 14 percent of drug and 8 percent of placebo recipients, however, were neurologically normal at 1 year of age. Results were best with isolated central nervous system infection, in which mortality was reduced from 50 to 10 percent. The dosage of vidarabine was 15 mg/kg/day given intravenously. A larger dosage of 25 mg/kg/day is being tested in a randomized comparison with acyclover therapy (30 mg/kg/day given intravenously). Preliminary analysis suggests an additional benefit of acyclovir, but final evaluation of relative efficacies must await outcome of the clinical trial. In one report, a newborn whose disease progressed during vidarabine therapy showed only temporary improvement with acyclovir treatment.[30] Many unresolved questions remain about therapy of herpesvirus infections at this time.[31]

Cytomegalovirus Infection

Antiviral agents have been used in neonates with congenital cytomegalic inclusion disease without favorable results. Floxuridine and idoxuridine did not significantly alter the clinical illness or viral excretion in 5 patients.[32-34] Cytosine arabinoside and vidarabine produced only transient reduction or eradication of cytomegalovirus urinary excretion during therapy, and there was no appreciable beneficial effect on the clinical course.[35-37] Reversible hematologic and hepatic toxicity was observed in some infants during therapy.[36] Failure of these drugs may be due to inability to inhibit intracellular viral replication.

Varicella-Zoster Virus Infection

Chickenpox is uncommon in pregnancy, occurring at an estimated rate of 0.17 in each 1000 pregnancies,[38] because most women have had chickenpox during childhood. A rare congenital syndrome has been reported when varicella occurs during pregnancy.[38] Of greater concern is the situation of chickenpox occurring near the time of parturition. Epidemiologic evidence suggests that disease in the infant is mild if the mother develops symptoms of varicella 5 days or more before delivery, presumably due to the modifying effects of transplacental antibody. By contrast the infant is at risk for severe, disseminated, and even fatal infection when the mother's rash appears within 4 days of delivery.[38-39] In the latter situation it is recommended that the infant be given zoster immune globulin (0.1 ml/kg) for prophylaxis or modification of disease.[38]

In 1924 Weech[40] reported prevention of varicella in infants by administration of from 3.0 to 4.5 cc of convalescent serum intramuscularly within 6 days of exposure. If zoster immune globulin is not available, convalescent serum can be substituted.

If neonatal varicella is severe or disseminated, vidarabine therapy (15 mg/kg/day given intravenously) should be used in view of its reported success in patients with progressive varicella-zoster virus infection complicating malignancies.[41] As an alternative, plasma transfusion of convalescent serum can be employed. We have had personal experience with severe progressive disseminated varicella in a neonate whose clinical course was dramatically reversed in temporal association with a transfusion of plasma from a convalescent case of varicella.

Other Viral Infections

There is no chemotherapy available for other congenital viral infections such as rubella, lymphocytic choriomeningitis virus infection and enterovirus infections.

CONGENITAL TUBERCULOSIS

Infants can acquire tuberculosis by aspiration of aminiotic fluid or infected material in the birth canal,[42-44] or they can be infected hematogenously while *in utero*. In the latter instance the liver is always involved.[45] In many cases the disease is disseminated and it is difficult to determine the exact mode of acquisition.[46-52]

The tuberculin skin test may be negative in the neonate with tuberculosis.[45,53] Examination of urine or gastric washing can be helpful. It may be necessary to perform a biopsy of the liver or lymph nodes to confirm the disease. It is possible that tuberculin-sensitized lymphocytes may be passed from mother to baby by maternal–fetal transfusion or in breast milk.[54] Thus a positive tuberculin skin test may not always indicate disease in the neonate.

The problem of what to do with a baby newly born to a woman with active, untreated tuberculosis is a knotty one. Several options are open.[53] Observation without treatment is hazardous because by the time the infant develops signs of disease or a positive tuberculin skin test irreparable central nervous system damage may have occurred. Separation from the mother until she has become noncontagious is complicated by the danger that the infant will be sent home to a relative with undiagnosed tuberculosis unless a thorough history of the extended family has been taken. Isoniazid administration to the infant for 2 or 3 months has been recommended, but there are two problems with this course: the proper dosage, safety, and efficacy of isoniazid for the neonate are unknown, and the reliability of administration of the drug cannot always be assured. BCG vaccination means that the tuberculin test will not be useful for differentiating infection with *Mycobacterium tuberculosis* from hypersensitivity to the vaccine.

There is no single best course for managing the asymptomatic infant of a woman with active tuberculosis, but in most situations we feel that the following course is advisable. The infant is separated from the mother temporarily while she is under treatment and acid-fast stains of her sputum are still positive. The infant is treated with isoniazid and immunized with BCG vaccine immediately or after six to eight weeks of drug therapy.[55] The correct dosage of isoniazid for the newborn is unknown, but a dosage between 5–10 mg/kg/day is generally given. Isoniazid does not interfere with successful BCG immunization.[55-56] Skin testing is performed before vaccination and again at 4–6 weeks after vaccination. If hypersensitivity has developed and if there is no indication of tuberculous disease by physical and roentgenographic examination, isoniazid therapy is discontinued. Such infants require frequent, careful follow-up examination.

For the neonate with active tuberculosis, treatment with isoniazid and rifampin probably represents optimal therapy. Streptomycin is optional as a third drug in the regimen. When streptomycin is used, it is given in a dosage of 20 mg/kg daily in 2 divided doses, intramuscularly, for approximately 10 days and then given 2 or 3 times weekly for an additional month. Because of our scanty knowledge of the pharmacology and safety of isoniazid and rifampin in the newborn, the recommended dosages of 5–10 mg/kg/day are based on little more than anecdotal experience. After age 1 month, the usual daily dose is 10 mg/kg. The drugs can be given once daily or in 2 divided doses. For central nervous system involvement the dosages are doubled. Drug therapy is continued for 1 year. Hepatic toxicity from isoniazid is rare in pediatric patients. Short-term triple-drug therapy of 6 months has been proposed for children with active tuberculosis, but there is no experience with this regimen in the neonate. Isoniazid, rifampin, and pyrazinamide would be given for 2 months, followed by isoniazid and rifampin for an additional 4 months.[57]

On rare occasions infants are exposed to nursery personnel with tuberculosis. In Cincinnati several hundred babies were exposed to a nursery aide with cavitary tuberculosis during a three-month period.[58] All infants were recalled for examination and tuberculin testing. None of the tests were positive except in 1 infant who had received BCG vaccine; 139 infants were treated with approximately 10 mg/kg of isoniazid for three months without untoward effects. In view of this experience it appears that brief, casual exposure of the neonate to tuberculosis carries a very low risk of transmission and that routine drug therapy or vaccination is not warranted. Such infants should be followed with tuberculin tests and chest x-rays for three to six months.

CONGENITAL MALARIA

Malaria can be acquired transplacentally, but it usually does not manifest itself in the infant until at least age 2 or 3 months.[59-66] Maternal IgG antibodies temporarily suppress the infection. IgM antibodies have been demonstrated in newborns.[66] Malaria should be suspected as the cause of unexplained recurrent febrile episodes in infants born to mothers from endemic malarial areas.

Little is known of the pharmacology and safety of antimalarial drugs in young infants. The American Academy of Pediatrics' Red Book[67] recommends the following dosage schedule for treatment of an attack. An initial dose of 10 mg/kg of chloroquine phosphate is given orally. (For emergency, a dose of 5 mg/kg of chloroquine dihydrochloride may be given intramuscularly.) Subsequently, doses of 5 mg/kg are given 6 hours, 24 hours, and 48 hours later. Dosage of chloroquine is calculated in terms of the active base. A 250-mg chloroquine phosphate tablet contains an 150-mg chloroquine base. The coated tablets are difficult to break into a dose for infants. Amodiaquine hydrochloride or hydroxychloroquine sulfate tablets each contain 150-mg chloroquine base and are easily broken. For chloroquine-resistant malaria, quinine sulfate is given orally in a dosage of 20–30 mg/kg/day in 3 divided doses for 7–10 days.

For eradication of exoerythrocytic parasites in vivax malaria primaquine phosphate is given in a dosage of 0.3 mg/kg once daily for 14 days.

For chloroquine- and quinine-resistant malaria, experimental drugs are available from the Centers for Disease Control, Atlanta.

> For dosages see Chapter 2 or Abbreviated Guide to Dosage on Inside Covers

REFERENCES

1. Platou RV: Treatment of congenital syphilis. Adv Pediatr 4:39–86, 1949
2. Sarff LD, Platt LH, McCracken GH: Cerebrospinal fluid evaluation in neonates: Comparison of high-risk infants with and without meningitis. J Pediatr 88:473–477, 1976
3. Thorley JD, Holmes RK, Kaplan JM, et al: Passive transfer of antibodies of maternal origin from blood to cerebrospinal fluid in infants. Lancet 1:651–653, 1975
4. Alford CA, Polt SS, Cassady GE, et al: IgM-fluorescent treponemal antibody in the diagnosis of congenital syphilis. N Engl J Med 280:1086–1091, 1969
5. Kaufman RE, Olansky DC, Wiesner PJ: The FTA-ABS (IgM) test for neonatal congenital syphilis: A critical review. J Am Vener Dis Assoc 1:79–84, 1974
6. Tuomanen EJ, Powell KR: Staphylococcal protein A adsorption of neonatal

serum to facilitate early diagnosis of congenital infection. J Pediatr 97:238–243, 1980

7. Chonmaitree T, Powell KR, Menegus MA: Staphylococcal protein A in the serologic diagnosis of congenital rubella and toxoplasmosis. Pediatr Infect Dis 1:228–231, 1982

8. Taber LH: Evaluation and management of syphilis in pregnant women and newborn infants. Pediatr Infect Dis 1:224–227, 1982

9. Centers for Disease Control: Sexually Transmitted Diseases: Treatment Guidelines 1982, Morbid Mortal Weekly Report 31(suppl):35S–60S, August 20, 1982

10. McCracken GH, Kaplan JM: Penicillin treatment for congenital syphilis: A critical reappraisal. JAMA 228:855–858, 1974

11. Desmonts G, Couvreur J: Congenital toxoplasmosis: A prospective study of 378 pregnancies. N Engl J Med 290:1110–1116, 1974

12. Saxon SA, Knight W, Reynolds DW, et al: Intellectual deficits in children born with subclinical toxoplasmosis: A preliminary report. J Pediatr 82:792–797, 1973

13. Wilson CB, Remington JS, Stagno S, et al: Development of adverse sequelae in children born with subclinical congenital Toxoplasma infection. Pediatrics 66:767–774, 1980

14. Remington JS, Desmonts G: Congenital toxoplasmosis: Variability in the IgM fluorescent antibody response and some pitfalls in diagnosis. J Pediatr 83:27–30, 1973

15. Kean BH, Kimball AC: The complement-fixation test in the diagnosis of congenital toxoplasmosis. Am J Dis Child 131:21–28, 1977

16. Walls KW, Bullock SL, English DK: Use of enzyme-linked immunosorbent assay (ELISA) and its microadaptation for the serodiagnosis of toxoplasmosis. J Clin Microbiol 5:273–277, 1977

17. Van Knapen F, Panggabean SO: Detection of circulating antigen during acute infections with Toxoplasma gondii by enzyme-linked immunosorbent assay. J Clin Microbiol 6:545–547, 1977

18. Desmonts G, Naot Y, Remington JS: Immunoglobulin M immunosorbent agglutination assay for diagnosis of infectious diseases: Diagnosis of acute congenital and acquired Toxoplasma infections. J Clin Microbiol 14:486–491, 1981

19. Remington JS, Jacobs L, Kaufman HE: Toxoplasmosis in the adult. N Engl J Med 262:180–186, 237–241, 1960

20. Remington JS: Trimethoprin–sulfamethoxazole in murine toxoplasmosis. Antimicrob Agents Chemother 9:222–223, 1976

21. Nahmias AJ: The torch-syndrome. Hosp Pract 9:65–72, 1974

22. McCracken GH, Shinefield HR, Cobb K, et al: Congenital cytomegalic inclusion disease: A longitudinal study of 20 infants. Am J Dis Child 117:522–539, 1969

23. Hanshaw JB: Herpesvirus hominis infections in the fetus and the newborn. Am J Dis Child 126:546–555, 1973

24. Tuffi GA, Nahmias AJ: Neonatal herpetic infection: Report of two premature infants treated with systemic use of idoxuridine. Am J Dis Child 118:909–914, 1969

25. Golden B, Bell WE, McKee AP: Disseminated herpes simplex with encephalitis in a neonate: Treatment with idoxuridine. JAMA 209:1219–1221, 1969

26. Kern ER, Overall JC, Glasgow LA: Herpesvirus hominis infection in newborn mice. I. An experimental model and therapy with iododeoxyuridine. J Infect Dis 128:290–311, 1973

27. Boston Interhospital Virus Study Group and the NIAID-sponsored Cooperative Antiviral Clinical Study: Failure of high dose 5-iodo-2'-deoxyuridine in the therapy of herpes simplex virus encephalitis. N Engl J Med 292:599–603, 1975

28. Ch'ien LT, Whitley RJ, Nahmias AJ, et al: Antiviral chemotherapy and neonatal herpes simplex virus infection: A pilot study: Experience with adenine arabinoside (ARA-A). Pediatrics 55:678–685, 1975

29. Whitley RJ, Nahmias AJ, Soong S-J, et al: Vidarabine therapy of neonatal herpes simplex virus infection. Pediatrics 66:495–501, 1980

30. Offit PA, Starr SE, Zolnick P, et al: Acyclovir therapy in neonatal herpes simplex virus infection. Pediatr Infect Dis 1:253–255, 1982

31. Whitley RJ, Alford CA Jr: Herpesvirus infections in childhood: Diagnostic dilemmas and therapy. Pediatr Infect Dis 1:81–84, 1982

32. Plotkin SA, Stetler H: Treatment of congenital cytomegalic inclusion disease with antiviral agents. Antimicrob Agents Chemother 1969:372–379, 1970

33. Conchie AF, Barton BW, Tobin J: Congenital cytomegalovirus infection treated with idoxuridine. Br Med J 4:162–163, 1968

34. Feigin RD, Shackelford PG, DeVivo DC, et al: Floxuridine treatment of congenital cytomegalic inclusion disease. Pediatrics 48:318–322, 1971

35. Kohybill EN, Sever JL, Avery TB, et al: Experimental use of cytosine arabinoside in congenital cytomegalovirus infection. J Pediatr 80:485–487, 1972

36. McCracken GH, Luby JP: Cytosine arabinoside in the treatment of congenital cytomegalic inclusion disease. J Pediatr 80:488–495, 1972

37. Ch'ien LT, Cannon NF, Whitley RJ, et al: Effect of adenine arabinoside on cytomegalovirus infection. J Infect Dis 130:32–39, 1974

38. De Nicola LK, Hanshaw JB: Congenital and neonatal varicella. J Pediatr 94:175–176, 1979

39. Meyers JD: Congenital varicella in term infants: Risk considered. J Infect Dis 129:215–217, 1974

40. Weech AA: The prophylaxis of varicella with convalescents' serum. JAMA 82:1245–1246, 1924

41. Whitley R, Hilty M, Haynes R, et al: Vidarabine therapy of varicella in immunosuppressed patients. J Pediatr 101:125–131, 1982

42. Hertzog AJ, Chapman S, Herring J: Congenital pulmonary aspiration-tuberculosis. Am J Clin Pathol 19:1139–1142, 1949

43. Grady RC, Zuelzer WW: Neonatal tuberculosis. Am J Dis Child 90:381–391, 1955

44. Ramos AD, Hibbard LT, Craig JR: Congenital tuberculosis. Obstet Gynecol 43:61–64, 1974

45. Hughesdon MR: Congenital tuberculosis. Arch Dis Child 21:121–138, 1946

46. Harris EA, McCullough GC, Stone JJ, et al: Congenital tuberculosis: A review of the disease with report of a case. J Pediatr 32:311–316, 1948

47. Kendig EL Jr, Angell FL: Streptomycin and promizole in the treatment of widespread pulmonary tuberculosis in a 19-day-old infant. Am Rev Tuberc 61:747–750, 1950

48. Reisinger KS, Evans P, Yost G, et al: Congenital tuberculosis: Report of a case. Pediatrics 54:74–76, 1974

49. Soeiro A: Congenital tuberculosis in a small premature baby. S Afr Med J 45:1025–1028, 1971

50. Meyers JP, Perlstein PH, Light IJ, et al: Tuberculosis in pregnancy with fatal congenital infection. Pediatrics 67:89–94, 1981

51. Hageman J, Shulman S, Schreiber M, et al: Congenital tuberculosis: Critical reappraisal of clinical findings and diagnostic procedures. Pediatrics 66:980–984, 1980

52. Stallworth JR, Brasfield DM, Tiller RE: Congenital miliary tuberculosis proved by open lung biopsy specimen and successfully treated. Am J Dis Child: 134:320–321, 1980

53. Avery ME, Wolfsdorg J: Approaches to newborn infants of tuberculous mothers. Pediatrics 42:519–522, 1968

54. Mohr JA: Lymphocyte sensitization passed to the child from the mother. Lancet 1:688, 1972

55. Podogore JK: Simultaneous administration of isoniazid and BCG to the infant of a tuberculous mother. J Pediatr 89:479, 1976

56. Narain R, Bagga AS, Naganns K, et al: Influence of isoniazid on naturally acquired tuberculin allergy and on induction of allergy by BCG vaccination. Bull WHO 43:53–64, 1970

57. Smith MHD: What about short course and intermittent chemotherapy for tuberculosis in children? Pediatr Infect Dis 1:298–303, 1982

58. Light IJ, Saidelman M, Sutherland JM: Management of newborns after nursery exposure to tuberculosis. Am Rev Respir Dis 109:415–419, 1974

59. McQuay RM, Silberman S, Mudrik P, et al: Congenital malaria in Chicago. Am J Trop Med Hyg 16:258–261, 1967

60. Harvey B, Remington JS, Sulzer AJ: IgM malaria antibodies in case of congenital malaria in the United States. Lancet 1:333–335, 1969

61. Bruce-Chwatt LJ: Acute malaria in newborn infants. Br Med J 3:283–403, 1970

62. Logie DE, McGregor IA: Acute malaria in newborn infants. Br Med J 3:404–406, 1970

63. Wood WG, Mills E, Ferrieri P: Neonatal malaria due to *Plasmodium vivax*. J Pediatr 85:669–670, 1974

64. Ransome-Kuti O: Malaria in childhood. Adv Pediatr 19:319–340, 1969

65. Hendrickse RG, Olumide LO, Akinkunmi A: An investigation of five hundred seriously ill children in whom a "clinical" diagnosis of malaria was made on admission to the Children's Emergency Room at University College Hospital, Ibadan. Ann Trop Med Parasitol 65:1–20, 1971

66. Quinn TC, Jacobs RF, Mertz GJ, et al: Congenital malaria: A report of four cases and a review. J Pediatr 101:229–232, 1982

67. American Academy of Pediatrics: Report of the Committee on Infectious Disease (ed 18). Evanston, Ill., American Academy of Pediatrics, 1982

7

Cardiovascular Infections

BACTERIAL ENDOCARDITIS

Bacterial endocarditis is rare during infancy and extraordinarily rare in the neonate. We have seen only 2 cases of confirmed endocarditis in neonates, so we must turn to the literature to get a perspective on the condition.[1-9]

Most cases occur in babies without underlying heart disease, and the mitral valve is the favored spot for localization of bacteria in the heart. The clinical picture is one of a septic baby who is likely to have focal infection in the lungs, meninges, peritoneum, or elsewhere. The infant may develop congestive heart failure, but usually death supervenes before heart disease is suspected, and endocarditis is a surprise discovery by the pathologist. Given this set of circumstances, recognition is clearly a problem for the physician. If endocarditis is suspected, echocardiography can be helpful in confirming the diagnosis.[5]

Bacterial endocarditis is a rare complication of umbical vein catheters used in intensive care management of respiratory distress syndrome and other conditions.[6-9] In such cases the catheter tip has usually been in the vena cava but sometimes has entered the right atrium or the left atrium through the foramen ovale. Characteristically the thrombi are located on the right atrial wall or tricuspid valve. In a case of *Candida albicans* infection,[9] the elongated fungus mass attached to the site of catheter-induced endothelial injury in the inferior vena cava extended into the right atrium and during diastole prolapsed into the tricuspid orifice. The infant was successfully treated with antifungal drugs and surgical removal of the mass.

Staphylococcus aureus has been the most common pathogen[3-4, 6-7] but streptococci,[4-5] coliform bacilli,[6,8] *Pseudomonas aeruginosa*,[7] and *C. albicans*[9] have also caused endocarditis in the first month of life.

The antimicrobials that are customarily given to neonates after the clinical diagnosis of sepsis—a penicillin and an aminoglycoside—provide adequate initial therapy. Because of the frequency of staphylococcal infection, if endocarditis is suspected a penicillinase-resistant penicillin such as methicillin should be given rather than penicillin or ampicillin.

Unfortunately the condition is almost uniformly and rapidly fatal. If the infant survives the acute phase, antimicrobial therapy is tailored to the culture and susceptibility data and continued for 4–6 weeks.

PERICARDITIS

Pericarditis in newborns is almost always a viral disease. Coxsackie B viruses are the usual agents, and the condition may be part of a syndrome of encephalomyocarditis. Antibiotics are not indicated for viral pericarditis. Whenever the echocardiographic studies demonstrate excessive fluid in the pericardial sac and associated clinical findings cast doubt as to whether one is dealing with bacterial or viral infection, a diagnostic pericardiocentesis should be done.

Bacterial pericarditis is very rare in the newborn period. In a review of the literature in 1967, Gersony and McCracken[10] found 2 cases and added 1 of their own. One was due to S. aureus, another due to Escherichia coli, and the third was of unknown etiology. A case of P. aeruginosa pericarditis in a 5-day-old infant has been reported.[11]

Feldman[12] reviewed 162 evaluable cases of purulent pericarditis in children under 16 years of age that were described in studies published between 1950 and 1977. He does not state the exact number that occurred in the neonatal period, but among the 130 patients with staphylococcal, Haemophilus, pneumococcal, or meningococcal infection, only 6 were neonates. Four neonates had S. aureus and two had Haemophilus influenzae b disease. Group B streptococcal pericarditis has been reported.[13]

For initial antibiotic therapy, a penicillinase-resistant penicillin would be given if gram-positive cocci were seen in the gram-stained specimen of pericardial fluid, and an aminoglycoside given if gram-negative rods were present. Both drugs would be given if no organisms were seen; subsequent treatment would be based on culture and susceptibility testing results.

Surgical drainage is a vital part of treatment. In 50 infants under 2 years old with purulent pericarditis, all 17 infants treated with antibiotics alone died, but the mortality rate was only 18 percent in the 17 treated with antibiotics and pericardial drainage.[10] Interestingly, 3 of 12 babies treated only with drainage in the preantibiotic era survived; 4 untreated infants died. The drainage should be performed with a pericardial window rather than by repeated needle aspirations. It may be necessary to break up loculations of pus behind the heart.

Antibiotic solutions should not be instilled in the pericardial sac. When antibiotics are administered parenterally, concentrations in inflamed pericardial fluid approximate those in the serum.[14]

Antibiotic treatment is continued for a minimum of 10–14 days, depending on the adequacy of surgical drainage and the rate of clinical response. Sequelae such as constrictive pericarditis are unlikely after purulent pericarditis of infancy but should be kept in mind during the follow-up period.

For dosages see Chapter 2 or Abbreviated Guide to Dosage on Inside Covers

---

REFERENCES

1. Lewis IC: Bacterial endocarditis complicating septicaemia in an infant. Arch Dis Child 29:144–146, 1954

2. Macauley D: Acute endocarditis in infancy and early childhood. Am J Dis Child 88:715–731, 1954

3. Blieden LC, Morehead RR, Burke B, et al: Bacterial endocarditis in the neonate. Am J Dis Child 124:747–749, 1972

4. Johnson DH, Rosenthal A, Nadas AS: Bacterial endocarditis in children under 2 years of age. Am J Dis Child 129:183–186, 1975

5. Weinberg AG, Laird WP: Group B streptococcal endocarditis detected by echocardiography. J Pediatr 92:335–336, 1978

6. Edwards K, Ingall D, Czapek E, et al: Bacterial endocarditis in 4 young infants: Is this complication on the increase? Clin Pediatr (Phila) 16:607–609, 1977

7. Symchych PS, Krauss AN, Winchester P: Endocarditis following intracardiac placement of umbilical venous catheters in neonates. J Pediatr 90:287–289, 1977

8. McGuiness GA, Schieken RM, Maguire GF: Endocarditis in the newborn. Am J Dis Child 134:577–580, 1980

9. Johnson DE, Bass JL, Thompson TR, et al: *Candida* septicemia and right atrial mass secondary to umbilical vein catheterization. Am J Dis Child 135:275–277, 1981

10. Gersony WM, McCracken GH: Purulent pericarditis in infancy. Pediatrics 40:224–232, 1967

11. Graham AJP, Martin B: *B. pyocyaneus* pericarditis occurring four days after birth. Cent Afr J Med 1:101–103, 1955

12. Feldman WE: Bacterial etiology and mortality of purulent pericarditis in pediatric patients. Am J Dis Child 133:641–644, 1979

13. Harper IA: The importance of group B streptococci as human pathogens in the British Isles. J Clin Pathol 24:438–441, 1971

14. Tan JS, Holmes JC, Fowler ND, et al: Antibiotic levels in pericardial fluid. J Clin Invest 53:7–12, 1974

8

Lower Respiratory Tract Infections

Neonatal lower respiratory tract infections may be congenitally or post-natally acquired. Perinatal infection results from transplacental transfer of the agent or from aspiration either of infected amniotic fluid (usually associated with prolonged ruptured membranes) or of infected vaginal secretions during delivery. Bacteria, viruses, chlamydia, and spirochetes can produce congenital lower respiratory tract diseases. The common bacterial agents are group B streptococci, *Listeria monocytogenes,* and coliform bacteria. The viral agents include cytomegalovirus, rubellavirus, and herpes simplex virus. *Treponema pallidum* produces a severe, often fatal pneumonia (pneumonia alba), and *Mycoplasma* have caused a rare form of fatal congenital pneumonia. It should be emphasized that in the majority of cases aspiration of meconium stained amniotic fluid or maternal vaginal secretions is not associated with infection. Congenital pneumonia usually manifests itself within the first several days of life, and in many babies clinical illness is apparent at birth. The clinical signs of aspiration are caused by obstruction or chemical pneumonitis, or both.

Postnatally acquired lower respiratory tract diseases can be of viral or bacterial etiology. Viral disease may be sporadic or occur as part of a nosocomial nursery outbreak. The respiratory syncytial virus is the most common pathogen of lower respiratory disease in young infants.[2] The parainfluenza viruses and adenoviruses also cause bronchiolitis and pneumonia during early infancy. An obliterating necrotizing bronchiolitis may be caused by adenoviruses and may result in roentgenographic hyperlucency of a segment or a lobe in later infancy and childhood.

The bacterial pathogens causing postnatally acquired pneumonia are group B streptococcus, *Staphylococcus aureus,* coliforms, and *Pseudomonas.* These infections occur sporadically or in epidemic fashion and are often of nosocomial origin. They may be rapidly progressive necrotic pneumonias that eventuate in pyogenic complications such as empyema and pulmonary abscesses and metastatic disease in bones or meninges.

BRONCHIAL INFECTIONS

Laryngotracheobronchitis and bronchiolitis occur in early infancy but are more common after 1 month of age than in the neonatal period. They are caused by a variety of respiratory viruses, with parainfluenza viruses and respiratory syncytial virus predominating.

Antimicrobial therapy is of no value in uncomplicated laryngotracheobronchitis. Bacterial superinfection is rarely encountered unless broad-spectrum antibiotics are used. An atmosphere of high humidity is provided in order to lessen irritation and drying of secretions. Racemic epinephrine delivered by an intermittent positive-pressure breathing apparatus can cause transient beneficial effect in croup, but should not be used as an outpatient procedure. Steroids are not beneficial for either condition.

PERTUSSIS

The current hypothesis is that pertussis is a toxic disease analogous to diphtheria, tetanus, and botulism.[1] The pertussis toxin is thought to be the protein substance called *lymphocytosis-promoting factor.* In experimental animals this substance is histamine-sensitizing, promotes lymphocytosis, and activates pancreatic islets to release insulin. A toxoid vaccine containing this substance was developed in Japan and in preliminary results appears to be safe and effective. Because the enhanced histamine sensitivity is analogous to the situation of beta blockade in asthma, beta-adrenergic drugs have been tested in patients with pertussis. In a preliminary report[2] salbutamol appeared to decrease the frequency of coughing and whooping episodes, but additional studies are needed to confirm this. The concept has been challenged by animal work that failed to demonstrate beta blockade and showed that all effects could be due to hypersecretion of insulin.[3]

When pertussis occurs in the first month of life, the infection has usually been acquired from one or both parents, whose illnesses had not been correctly diagnosed as whooping cough. In our experience[4] with 11 infants who had pertussis with onset in the neonatal period, the source of infection was an adult in 6 cases, a child in 2 cases, and unknown in 3 cases.

Lapin[5] claims that there have been cases of congenital pertussis, presumably acquired *in utero,* but his literature citations are incomplete, and some are irretrievable. Some cases are described with onset of symptoms as early as age 3 days.[6,7] The earliest onset we have seen is age 7 days,[8] which is compatible with postnatal infection.

Most often very young infants do not whoop. Pertussis should be suspected when an infant has paroxysmal cough with excessive mucus. Fluorescent antibody testing is faster but less sensitive than culture methods.[8] Mucus for examination is obtained from infants with a nasopharyngeal flexible wire swab. If older siblings and parents are tested, expectorated sputum is preferable. After 2–4 weeks of illness, *Bordetella pertussis* organisms disappear spontaneously. An enzyme-linked immunosorbent assay for detection of IgA pertussis antibodies in nasopharyngeal secretions has been reported to be positive after 2–3 weeks and to persist for at least 3 months.[9]

Erythromycin is the most active drug in vitro against *B. pertussis*.[10] Antimicrobial therapy is erythromycin administered orally. If the infant is unable to retain medication because of vomiting after paroxysms, ampicillin is given parenterally. Although others have reported treatment failures with oral ampicillin, in our experience it has promptly eradicated *B. pertussis*.[11] It is questionable whether antibiotic therapy lessens the symptoms of pertussis, but it is valuable for rendering the patient noncontagious. Hyperimmune serum is probably not beneficial.

The greatest hazards to an infant with pertussis are asphyxia and secondary bacterial pneumonias. Of our 11 cases with onset in the neonatal period, 3 (27 percent) were fatal. In a controlled trial[12] hydrocortisone sodium succinate ameliorated the symptoms. The dosage was 30 mg/kg/day given intramuscularly for 2 days with decreasing amounts daily thereafter for a total of 7 or 8 days. The authors recommend that steroids be reserved for severe cases in infants younger than 9 months of age. We concur with their recommendation, although we have no personal experience with the use of corticosteroids in pertussis.

Supportive care is essential. Excessive mucus must be suctioned, and equipment for emergency airway intubation should be at hand. Fluid therapy is necessary, and maintaining adequate nutritional intake may present the greatest challenge.

Infants with pertussis should not be placed in mist tents. Mist therapy provides no substantial amelioration of the paroxysmal coughing episodes, and it increases the risk of secondary infection with *P. aeruginosa* or other "water bugs." Prolonged antimicrobial therapy, particularly with broad-spectrum drugs such as ampicillin, also predisposes to secondary bacterial pneumonias. In most instances, pertussis organisms are eradicated in less than 5 days. Treatment can be stopped and isolation discontinued when 2 successive daily fluorescent antibody examinations and cultures have been negative. If this test is not available, it is recommended that erythromycin and isolation be continued for 10 days.

Atelectasis secondary to mucous plugs is a common complication of pertussis in small babies. Once the infant has passed the stage of severe paroxysms, chest physiotherapy can be employed. In almost all cases the atelectasis will resolve within 2–3 weeks.

PNEUMONIA

Pneumonias of newborn and young infants may be of viral or bacterial origin. It is frequently difficult to distinguish clinically between these two groups of agents. The early clinical symptoms are usually nonspecific. Dyspnea, cyanosis, cough, and grunting are signs that alert the physician to the possibility of lower respiratory tract or cardiac disease. Accentuation of the normal irregularity of breathing is a common finding in the neonate. The physical findings of pneumonia are variable. Flaring of the alae nasi, rapid respirations, and sternal and subcostal retractions are frequently observed. Percussion dullness is difficult to demonstrate but when present signifies consolidation or effusion. Auscultation of the chest may reveal diminished breath sounds over the affected area. Rales or wheezes can usually be heard on deep inspiration but may be absent early in illness, particularly if the infant is dehydrated.

Cultures of blood and material from the trachea are frequently helpful in defining the etiologic agent of neonatal pneumonia. Lung puncture should be considered in severely ill infants with consolidated pneumonia when the cause is unknown or in an infant who fails to respond to conventional antimicrobial therapy.[13] Material obtained by needle aspiration is gram-stained for direct visualization of bacteria, and cultures are done.

A chest roentgenogram should be obtained on all babies with suspected lower respiratory tract disease. Roentgenographic evidence of pneumonia may be present in the absence of specific physical findings. Although it is not usually possible to determine the cause of neonatal pneumonia from a roentgenogram, certain radiologic patterns are associated with specific diseases. With group B streptococcal disease, the roentgenogram may mimic hyaline membrane disease. A consolidating bronchopneumonia with pneumatoceles, with or without emphyema, suggests staphylococcal disease. When a lobar infiltrate is associated with expansion of the lobe, *Klebsiella pneumoniae* infection should be considered. A miliary-type of bronchopneumonia in a septic neonate is characteristic of listeriosis. An interstitial pattern of infiltration suggests the possibility of viral, chlamydial, or *Pneumocystis carinii* infection.

Apnea can be the presenting problem in respiratory syncytial virus infection, and we have also encountered this presentation in chlamydial pneumonia. Although Dworsky and Stagno[14] comment on the similarity of clinical findings in viral, chlamydial, and *P. carinii* pneumonia. Harrison et al.[15] found that chlamydial pneumonia was characterized by radiographic hyperinflation, eosinophilia greater than $400/\mu l$, serum IgG levels greater than 500 mg/dl, and IgM levels greater than 110 mg/dl.

The association of *Chlamydia trachomatis* with pneumonia is well established by convincing circumstantial evidence[14-18] and by recovery of the organism from lung tissue.[19] The situation with *P. carinii* and *Ureaplasma urealyticum* is not as clear.[14,20] It appears that some young infants who are not malnourished or immunocompromised develop *Pneumocystis* infection,[20] but most diagnoses have been based on detection of *Pneumocystis* antigen in blood rather than on histologic demonstration of the organisms, and that is not a well-standardized or easily available test.

Chlamydial cultures are not available in most clinical laboratories. The disease is suspected in afebrile infants between 3 weeks and 3 months of age who have diffuse interstitial or bronchopneumonic infiltrates. Tachypnea is prominent, and the cough is episodic, pseudo-paroxysmal ("staccato"), and nonproductive. Conjunctivitis or eosinophilia is found in fewer than 50 percent of cases but if present would further heighten suspicion of chlamydial pneumonia. Serum antibody levels are elevated at onset of symptoms and are at much higher titers than those found in patients with chlamydial conjunctivitis or genital tract disease.

The clinical course of chlamydial pneumonia is variable, and placebo-controlled prospective evaluations of antibiotic therapy have not been done. General experience and uncontrolled studies[21] nevertheless, indicate that erythromycin or sulfisoxazole therapy for 14 days is beneficial. Ampicillin or amoxicillin treatment probably is efficacious as well. Complete recovery is the rule but one report[22] has implicated chlamydial pneumonia in a syndrome of chronic respiratory disease.

Bacterial pneumonia is suspected on the basis of fever, leukocytosis, and pneumonic infiltrates, although premature infants often have hypothermia and depressed total leukocyte counts with increased numbers of immature forms of leukocytes. Initial therapy for suspected bacterial pneumonia is customarily with a penicillin and an aminoglycoside. The most suitable combination of these drugs is dependent on the clinical features of the illness and the recent historical experience with bacterial diseases in the local nursery or community. For patients in whom the causative agent is never defined and where staphylococcal disease cannot be excluded, therapy with methicillin and gentamicin is indicated. If the organism is identified, the single most effective drug should be used. Penicillin G is most effective against group B streptococci and penicillin-susceptible staphylococci, ampicillin and gentamicin for *Listeria,* and methicillin or another suitable antistaphylococcal penicillin for penicillinase-producing *S. aureus.* For pneumonia caused by coliform bacilli, gentamicin is most often used, but tobramycin or kanamycin are suitable for susceptible strains. Gentamicin-resistant coliform bacilli are usually susceptible to amikacin, and the rare strains resistant to amikacin are usually susceptible to cefotaxime and moxalactam. *Pseudomonas* pneumonia is treated with ticarcillin or mezlocillin in combination with gentamicin for synergistic effect. Therapy is continued for 10–14 days for disease caused by group B streptococci and *Listeria* and for a minimum of 3 weeks for pneumonia caused by gram-negative bacteria and *S. aureus.*

EMPYEMA

Empyema occurring during the first months of life is most frequently associated with pneumonia caused by *S. aureus.*[23-27] Pyothorax associated with group B streptococcal or coliform disease is rarely encountered. *Haemophilus influenzae* infection occurs rarely.[28]

Staphylococci cause a confluent bronchopneumonia characterized by extensive hemorrhagic necrosis and irregular areas of cavitation. The pleural surface is usually covered by a thick layer of fibrinopurulent exudate. Multiple small abscesses are scattered throughout the affected lung. Rupture of a small subpleural abscess may result in a pyopneumothorax. If there is erosion into a large bronchus, a bronchopleural fistula results.

Most patients with staphylococcal pneumonia have roentgenographic evidence of bronchopneumonia early in illness. The infiltrate may be patchy and limited in extent or dense and homogenous involving an entire lobe or hemithorax. Bilateral disease occurs in half the patients. Pleural effusion or empyema is noted in most infants. Pneumatoceles of varying size are common. Although no radiographic picture can be considered absolutely diagnostic, progression over a few hours from bronchopneumonia to empyema or pyopneumothorax, with or without pneumatoceles, is highly suggestive of staphylococcal disease.

All patients with roentgenographic evidence of fluid in the pleural space must have a diagnostic thoracentesis. If serous or milky chylous material is obtained, tube drainage is usually not required and may be contraindicated in chylothorax because of the risk of superinfection. If the aspirate is purulent, gram-and methylene blue–stained smears should be prepared and the material cultured on appropriate media. If gram-positive cocci are observed on stained smears, methicillin should be used until results of the cultures and susceptibility studies are available. If the *S. aureus* is susceptible to penicillin G, this agent should be used. If no organisms are seen, it is appropriate to use methicillin and an aminoglycosidic drug until the causative agent has been defined. Antimicrobial therapy is usually necessary for three weeks or longer. Methicillin-resistant staphylococci are susceptible to vancomycin.

Empyema is best managed with closed drainage using chest tubes of the largest possible caliber. It is generally necessary to place one tube high and anteriorly and a second tube low and posterolaterally for optimal drainage. Pyopneumothorax is another indication for immediate insertion of a catheter into the pleural space. Once the infant's condition has improved and the amount of drainage is minimal, the tubes can be removed. In general, tubes should not remain in the chest for more than five to seven days. The instillation of antimicrobial agents or enzymes into the pleural space does not help to control infection or promote drainage.

Several studies[24-25] have confirmed the excellent long-term prognosis of adequately treated infants with staphylococcal pneumonia. Surgical intervention is rarely indicated for persisting pleural thickening (pleural peel). Follow-up chest roentgenograms are usually normal within several months, and pulmonary function studies are normal when performed 1–16 years after illness.

LUNG ABSCESS

Lung abscesses or infected congenital cysts are rarely encountered during the neonatal period.[29-32] The bacteria involved have been *S. aureus*, *K. pneumoniae*, *Escherichia coli*, and group B streptococcus. Anaerobic bacteria have not been reported, but they have also not been sought by appropriate methodology.

The cause may be difficult to establish. If the roentgenogram reveals an air–fluid level within the abscess cavity, postural drainage and back clapping by trained respiratory therapists should be attempted in order to drain purulent material through the airway. Bronchoscopy with special equipment geared to the infant's size may be necessary if sputum cannot be obtained. Blood cultures are usually sterile.

Drainage and antibiotics are the mainstays of therapy. A penicillin and aminoglycosidic drug are used unless susceptibility studies of the pathogen indicate that a single agent is satisfactory. Respiratory therapists who are familiar with neonates should provide pulmonary toilet to accomplish drainage. Abscess cavities may require weeks or months for complete resolution. Surgical intervention is reserved for patients who show clinical deterioration or for those whose condition is static after several weeks of antibiotic therapy and chest physiotherapy.

For dosages see Chapter 2 or Abbreviated Guide to Dosage on Inside Covers

REFERENCES

1. Pittman M: Pertussis toxin: The cause of the harmful effects and prolonged immunity of whooping cough: A hypothesis. Rev Infect Dis 1:401–412, 1979
2. Pavesio D, Ponzone A: Salbutamol and pertussis. Lancet 1:150–151, 1977
3. Hewlett E, Spiegel A, Wolff J, et al: *Bordetella pertussis* does not induce β-adrenergic blockade. Infect Immun 22:430–434, 1978
4. Nelson JD: The changing epidemiology of pertussis in young infants: The role of adults as reservoirs of infection. Am J Dis Child 132:371–373, 1978
5. Lapin JH: Whooping cough. Springfield, Ill., Charles C Thomas, 1943, p 11
6. Cockayne EA: Whooping-cough in the first days of life. Br J Child Dis 10:534–537, 1913
7. Phillips J: Whooping-cough contracted at the time of birth, with report of two cases. Am J Med Sci 116:163–165, 1921
8. Brooksaler F, Nelson JD: Pertussis: A reappraisal and report of 190 confirmed cases. Am J Dis Child 114:389–396, 1967
9. Goodman YE, Wort AJ, Jackson FL: Enzyme-linked immunosorbent assay for detection of pertussis immunoglobulin A in nasopharyngeal secretions as an indicator of recent infection. J Clin Microbiol 13:286–292, 1981
10. Bannatyne RM, Cheung R: Antimicrobiol susceptibility of *Bordetella pertussis* strains isolated from 1960 to 1981. Antimicrob Agents Chemother 21:666–667, 1982
11. Nelson JD: Antibiotic treatment of pertussis. Pediatrics 44:474–476, 1969
12. Zoumboulakis D, Anagnostakis D, Albanis V, et al: Steroids in treatment of pertussis: A controlled clinical trial. Arch Dis Child 48:51–54, 1973
13. Minicia I, Donoco E, Howard JE, et al: Lung puncture in the etiological diagnosis of pneumonia. Am J Dis Child 122:278–282, 1971
14. Dworsky ME, Stagno S: Newer agents causing pneumonitis in early infancy. Pediatr Infect Dis 1:188–195, 1982
15. Harrison HR, English MG, Lee CK, et al: *Chlamydia trachomatis* infant pneumonitis: Comparison with matched controls and other infant pneumonitis. New Engl J Med 298:702–708, 1978
16. Schachter J, Lum L, Gooding CA, et al: Pneumonitis following inclusion blenorrhea. J Pediatr 87:779–780, 1975
17. Alexander ER: Chlamydia: The organism and neonatal infection. Hosp Pract 14:63–69, 1979
18. Beem MO, Saxon EM: Respiratory-tract colonization and a distinctive pneumonia syndrome in infants infected with *Chlamydia trachomatis*. New Engl J Med 296:306–310, 1977
19. Frommell GT, Bruhn FW, Schwartzman JD: Isolation of *Chlamydia trachomatis* from infant lung tissue. New Engl J Med 296:1150–1152, 1977

20. Stagno S, Pifer LL, Hughes WT, et al: *Pneumocystis carinii* pneumonitis in young immunocompetent infants. Pediatrics 66:56–62, 1980

21. Beem MO, Saxon E, Tipple MA: Treatment of chlamydial pneumonia of infancy. Pediatrics 63:198–203, 1979

22. Harrison HR, Taussig LM, Fulginiti VA. *Chlamydia trachomatis* and chronic respiratory disease in childhood. Pediatr Infect Dis 1:29–33, 1982

23. Pyrles CV: Staphylococcal pneumonia in infancy and childhood. Pediatrics 21:609–621, 1958

24. Wise MB, Beudry PH, Bates DV: Long-term follow-up of staphylococcal pneumonia. Pediatrics 38:398–401, 1966

25. Ceruti E, Contreras J, Neira M: Staphylococcal pneumonia in childhood. Am J Dis Child 122:386–392, 1971

26. Rebhan AW, Edwards HE: Staphylococcal pneumonia: A review of 392 cases. Can Med Assoc J 82:513–517, 1960

27. Chartrand SA, McCracken GH Jr: Staphylococcal pneumonia in infants and children. Pediatr Infect Dis 1:19–23, 1982

28. Ginsburg CM, Howard JB, Nelson JD: Report of 65 cases of *Haemophilus influenzae* b pneumonia. Pediatrics 64:283–286, 1979

29. Mark PH, Turner JAP: Lung abscess in childhood. Thorax 23:216–220, 1968

30. Moor TC, Battersby JS, Stanley J: Pulmonary abscess in infancy and childhood: Report of 18 cases. Ann Surg 151:496–400, 1960

31. Graff DB, Rapkin RH: Primary lung abscess in childhood. J Med Soc NJ 71:649–652, 1974

32. Siegel JD, McCracken GH Jr: Neonatal lung abscess: A report of six cases. Am J Dis Child 133:947–949, 1979

9

Eye, Ear, and Throat Infections

CONJUNCTIVITIS, ENDOPHTHALMITIS, AND ORBITAL CELLULITIS

Eye infections of the newborn may be due to a great variety of micro-organisms. Those of major importance because of frequency or severity are *Neisseria gonorrheae, Chlamydia trachomatis, Staphylococcus aureus,* and *Pseudomonas aeruginosa.* Chlamydial infection is almost always restricted to conjunctivitis, with corneal involvement being very rare.[1] The bacterial agents may progress to endophthalmitis. Orbital cellulitis may be secondary to ethmoid sinusitis or to the syndrome of acute maxillary osteomyelitis (see Chapter 11).

When an infant develops a discharge from the eyes, 3 tests should be performed: (1) gram stain and methylene blue stain of the exudate, (2) culture of the exudate, and (3) Giemsa stain of scrapings made from the lower palpebral conjunctive *after* exudate has been wiped away.

It is almost 100 years since Credé published his report on silver nitrate prophylaxis,[2-3] yet we still see occasional cases of gonococcal ophthalmia in spite of prophylaxis.[4] Some are due to infection *in utero* from prolonged rupture of membranes, some to improper application of silver nitrate or antibiotic, some to omission of the procedure, and some to postnatal exposure.[5]

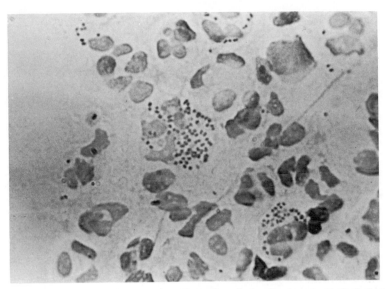

Figure 9-1. *Gram stained specimen of exudate from the eye of a 3-day-old infant with gonococcal conjunctivitis. Numerous intracellular diplococci of* Neisseria gonorrheae *are seen in two polymorphonuclear leukocytes (magnification is 1000).*

From a review of 302 cases of eye infections in newborns at Grady Memorial Hospital in Atlanta,[6] it was determined that 86 were chlamydial, 43 gonococcal, 3 gonococcal and chlamydial, 31 staphylococcal, and 5 chemical. The remaining 134 (44 percent) were of uncertain cause. This frequency distribution of etiologic agents is typical of the experience at large urban general hospitals. Unusual organisms such as *Erwinia*[7] and *Shigella*[8] have been reported to cause conjunctivitis in the newborn.

If gonococci are suspected from examination of gram-stained exudate (see Fig. 9-1), parenteral penicillin therapy is employed. Biochemical identification of *Neisseria* species is important, since meningococci causes conjunctivitis on rare occasions.[9] If staphylococci are seen, methicillin or another penicillinase-resistant penicillin is used. The necessity for topical antibiotics is doubtful. In the presence of acute inflammation, systemic administration results in ample antibiotic in eye secretions to inhibit bacteria. In several patients with gonococcal conjunctivitis, we have demonstrated prompt sterilization of the eye secretions using only intravenously administered penicillin G. The potential hazard of perforation of the globe by the applicator tip of ophthalmic drops or ointment must be considered. If a topical antibiotic is used, chloramphenicol or tetracycline is probably a better choice than penicillin G, although the risk of penicillin sensitization by topical exposure is probably nil in the newborn.

In mid-1976, penicillinase-producing strains of gonococci were imported into the United States from the Far East. These strains remain at a low level of prevalence, but a case of ophthalmia neonatorum due to beta-lactamase–producing N. *gonorrheae* was reported in 1982.[10] The penicillin-resistant gonococcal strains are susceptible to spectinomycin, and most cephalosporin derivatives. There is little experience in treating gonococcal ophthalmia with these drugs. Furthermore, there are no pharmacologic or safety data for spectinomycin in the newborn. Until clinical experience has been accumulated to determine satisfactory therapy for penicillin-resistant gonococcal infections of newborns, cefuroxime, moxalactam, or cefoperazone would probably be the best choice for this difficult problem.

If gram-negative rods are seen in the stained exudate, the greatest concern is *P. aeruginosa* because of the virulent necrotizing endophthalmitis that can result. Parenteral therapy with ticarcillin and gentamicin is given along with topical gentamicin ophthalmic drops. When there is endophthalmitis, subtenon injections of gentamicin are sometimes given daily[11] in addition to parenteral antibiotics.

C. trachomatis is probably the most common cause of neonatal conjunctivitis today.[6] Chlamydial eye infection may begin in the first days of life but usually does not come to the attention of the physician until the second or third week.[1] The diagnostic epithelial inclusion bodies (see Fig. 9-2A, B) are not found in the exudate itself. Scrapings must be made from the palpebral conjunctiva after wiping away all pus. An ophthalmic spud can be used, but we have found an opened paper clip to be a satisfactory and readily available instrument. The material is carefully layered onto a microscope slide and stained by the Giemsa method. (Inclusion bodies can sometimes be discerned with methylene blue stain, but there is better definition with Giemsa stain.) There is a relatively simple tissue culture method for *Chlamydia*,[12] but it is not available in most hospitals.

Chlamydial conjunctivitis can be treated with 1-percent tetracycline or erythromycin ophthalmic solution or ointment applied 3 or 4 times daily for 10–14 days. Sodium sulfacetamide ophthalmic medication is also effective. Oral administration of erythromycin is as effective in curing the eye infection as topical medication and has the added advantage of eradicating *Chlamydia* from the nasopharynx.[13] It is also easier for the parents than trying to apply medication to the eyes. Most cases of chlamydial conjunctivitis heal without scarring.[14]

Prophylaxis for gonococcal and chlamydial conjunctivitis is discussed in Chapter 16.

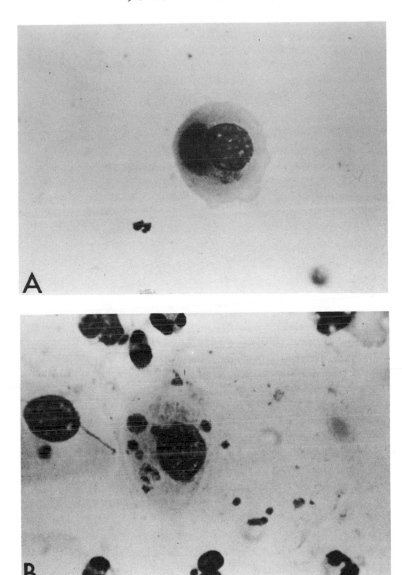

Figure 9-2. (A) The classical caplike cytoplasmic inclusion body in an epithelial cell obtained by scraping the conjunctiva of a 10-day-old infant with inclusion conjunctivitis due to Chlamydia trachomatis. Giemsa stain (magnification is 1000). (B) More commonly, numerous cytoplasmic inclusion bodies of varying size are seen in conjunctival epithelium with chlamydial infection; Giemsa stain (magnification is 1000). (Photographs courtesy of Philip Goscienski, M.D.)

Herpesvirus disease may occur as an isolated eye infection[15] or as part of generalized infection[16]; management is discussed in Chapter 6.

OTITIS MEDIA

Babies with cleft palate commonly develop otitis media in the first month of life,[17] but it also occurs in babies without anatomic abnormalities. Physical examination of the tympanic membrane of neonates is difficult and the principal symptoms are nonspecific ones of low-grade fever, fussiness, and feeding difficulties. Also, these babies occasionally have associated illnesses such as meningitis or pneumonia that may overshadow the otitis media. With the use of pneumatic otoscopy it has become simpler to recognize the presence of fluid in the middle ear cavity.

Babies develop otitis media from bacteria that comprise the oropharyngeal flora. In addition to the *Haemophilus* and pneumococci that also are found in older infants, neonates may be colonized with coliform bacteria and *S. aureus*. Thus it is not surprising that Bland[18] found the latter in middle aspirates from over half the babies under age 6 weeks. In our own experience,[19] coliform organisms were involved in otitis media in approximately 20 percent of neonates. In unselected ambulatory patients 6 weeks of age or less, however, Shurin et al.[20] isolated coliform bacilli from middle ear fluid in only 4 of 70 infants, and *S. aureus* from 4 additional babies. *Streptococcus pneumoniae, Branhamella catarrhalis,* and *Haemophilus influenzae* were the most common bacteria encountered. It is possible that infants with neonatal complications, nasotracheal tubes, prolonged nursery stays, and previous antibiotic therapy are more likely to have disease due to coliform bacilli or staphylococci. These were the most common pathogens in one report of otitis media of infants in an intensive care unit.[21] Prolonged nasotracheal intubation was associated with ipselateral otitis media in those babies.

Group B streptococci can cause otitis media as an isolated entity[20] or as part of generalized sepsis.[22]

The role of *C. trachomatis* in otitis media is not clear because neonates and very young infants have not been extensively studied. Chang et al.[23] isolated *Chlamydia* from middle ear exudate of 3 infants but did not evaluate patients under 5 months of age.

Given these problems, the physician has several courses of action to choose. (Regardless of the antibiotic therapy for otitis, the physician must first convince him- or herself that the baby does not have meningitis, sepsis, or pneumonia.)

One may decide to perform needle aspiration of the middle ear fluid and choose antibiotics on the basis of gram stain, culture, and *in vitro* susceptibility testing. The procedure is technically more difficult in neonates than in older infants but by no means impossible.

Alternatively one may hospitalize the infant and treat him or her with parenteral antibiotics such as methicillin and gentamicin. There are hypothetical disadvantages to this course of action. Methicillin has lesser activity against pneumococci than does penicillin, and although gentamicin is highly effective against *Haemophilus* organisms *in vitro,* there is no clinical experience with it as an anti-*Haemophilus* drug. Cefoperazone or cefotaxime is active against pneumococci, *Haemophilus* organisms, and coliform bacteria.

As a third possible course of action, the physician could treat with the drugs commonly given to older infants with otitis and hope that the patient is among the majority with infection due to the common respiratory pathogens, rather than among the minority with ampicillin or sulfa-resistant coliform bacteria. With 2 or 3 days' observation it should be clear whether the baby is responding to treatment. If there is no improvement, needle aspiration of middle ear fluid should be performed in order to obtain culture and susceptibility information.

The last course of action is appropriate for full-term infants with uncomplicated neonatal courses, providing that there are no clinical signs suggesting sepsis or meningitis. Because the signs of serious illness can be subtle in newborns, we are inclined to be liberal with use of blood cultures and lumbar punctures in very young infants who have otitis media.

MASTOIDITIS

The mastoid portion of the temporal bone is not pneumatized at birth, so although the mastoid antrum may be infected concomitantly with middle ear disease, the clinical syndrome of mastoiditis is rarely seen in the neonatal period. The youngest infant we have seen with mastoiditis was 2 months old.[24] The alerting sign is swelling and redness above and behind the ear because the inflammatory process finds egress through the tympanomastoid fissure. In osteomyelitis of the mastoid bone, which is a very rare condition, surgical treatment is as important as the antibiotic therapy.[25]

An unusual case of *H. influenzae* meningitis and mastoiditis was reported by Lee et al.[26] On the 5th day of life erythema was noted behind the right ear, and later a frank abscess developed. A simple mastoidectomy done at 3 weeks of age was remarkable for revealing infected mesenchymal tissue in the mastoid antrum but a normal middle ear cavity.

SINUSITIS

The maxillary and ethmoid sinuses are present at birth in most infants.[27] Orbital cellulitis secondary to ethmoid sinusitis is occasionally seen in the first month of life, and maxillary sinus infection can be seen as part of the syndrome of maxillary osteomyelitis of the newborn (see Chapter 11). An unusual case of ethmoiditis and conjunctivitis due to *Shigella flexneri* has been reported.[8]

Orbital or periorbital swelling commonly accompanies paranasal sinusitis, particularly ethmoiditis.[28] Computed tomography can be helpful in distinguishing orbital involvement from preseptal cellulitis.[29]

ORAL INFECTIONS

Thrush is the only infection of the oral mucous membranes of practical significance in the newborn. Some infants with congenital *Herpesvirus hominis* infection have oral lesions, and granulomas of the pharynx may be seen in infants with listeriosis.[30]

Thrush is best treated with topical nystatin suspension. One milliliter is dropped into the anterior portion of the mouth and allowed to run back over the oral mucous membranes. This is repeated 4 times daily. Alternatively the drug can be swabbed onto the oral mucous membranes. Most cases will respond within a week. Gentian violet in a 0.5-percent or 1-percent aqueous solution is also effective but undesirable because of the intense blue staining of the mouth and everything else it touches. If thrush is recalcitrant to usual therapy consideration should be given to the possibility that the infant has a T-cell immunodeficiency syndrome.

Diphtheria has occurred in newborns on rare occasions.[31] Treatment is with antitoxin and penicillin G. Goebel and Ströder[32] treated 59 cases in infants under 1 month of age; 26 were fatal.

> For dosages see Chapter 2 or Abbreviated Guide to Dosage on Inside Covers

REFERENCES

1. Goscienski PJ: Inclusion conjunctivitis in the newborn infant. J Pediatr 77:19–26, 1970
2. Credé: Die Verhütung der Augenentzündung der Neugeborenen. Arch Gynaekol 17:50–53, 1881

3. Forbes GB, Forbes GM: Silver nitrate and the eyes of the newborn: Credé's contribution to preventive medicine. (Includes English translation of Credé's original article.) Am J Dis Child 121:1–4, 1971

4. Snowe RJ, Wilfert CM: Epidemic reappearance of gonococcal ophthalmia neonatorum. Pediatrics 51:110–114, 1973

5. Thompson TR, Swanson RE, Wiesner PJ: Gonococcal ophthalmia neonatorum: Relationship of time of infection to relevant control measures. JAMA 228:186–188, 1974

6. Armstrong JF, Zacarias F, Rein MF: Ophthalmia neonatorum: A chart review. Pediatrcs 57:884–892, 1976

7. London R, Bottone E: Erwinia conjunctivitis in children. Pediatrics 49:931–932, 1972

8. Overton ME, Heath JD, Stapleton FB: Conjunctivitis and ethmoiditis due to Shigella flexneri in an infant. Clin Pediatr (Phila) 20:231, 1981

9. Hansman D: Neonatal meningococcal conjunctivitis. Br Med J 1:748, 1972

10. Raucher HS, Newton MJ, Stern RH: Ophthalmia neonatorum caused by penicillinase-producing Neisseria gonorrheae. J Pediatr 100:925–926, 1982

11. Golden B: Sub-tenon injection of gentamicin for bacterial infections of the eye. J Infect Dis 124:S271–S274, 1971

12. Yoder BL, Stamm WE, Koester CM, et al: Microtest procedure for isolation of Chlamydia trachomatis. J Clin Microbiol 13:1036–1039, 1981

13. Patamasucon P, Rettig PJ, Faust KL, et al: Oral v topical erythromycin therapies for chlamydial conjunctivitis. Am J Dis Child 136:817–821, 1982

14. Goscienski PJ, Sexton RR: Follow-up studies in neonatal inclusion conjunctivitis. Am J Dis Child 124:180–182, 1972

15. Berkovich S, Ressel M: Neonatal herpes keratitis. J Pediatr 69:652–653, 1966

16. Ch'ien LT, Whitley RJ, Nahmias AJ, et al: Antiviral chemotherapy and neonatal herpes simplex virus infection: A pilot study—Experience with adenine arabinoside (ARA-A). Pediatrics 55:678–685, 1975

17. Paradise JL, Bluestone CD: Early treatment of the universal otitis media of infants with cleft palate. Pediatrics 53:48–54, 1974

18. Bland RD: Otitis media in the first 6 weeks of life: Diagnosis, bacteriology and management. Pediatrics 49:187–197, 1972

19. Tetzlaff TR, Ashworth C, Nelson JD: Otitis media in children less than twelve weeks of age. Pediatrics 59:827–832, 1977

20. Shurin PA, Howie VM, Pelton SI, et al: Bacterial etiology of otitis media during the first six weeks of life. J Pediatr 92:893–896, 1978

21. Berman SA, Balkany TJ, Simmons MA: Otitis media in the neonatal intensive care unit. Pediatrics 62:198–201, 1978

22. Ellis SS, Johnson A, Austin TL: Group B streptococcal meningitis associated with otitis media. Am J Dis Child 130:1003–1004, 1976

23. Chang MJ, Rodriguez WJ, Mohla C: Chlamydia trachomatis in otitis media in children. Ped Infect Dis 1:95–97, 1982

24. Ginsburg CM, Rudoy R, Nelson JD: Acute mastoiditis in infants and children. Clin Pediatr (Phila) 19:549–553, 1980

25. Ronis BJ, Ronis MS, Liebman EP; Acute mastoiditis as seen today. Eye Ear Nose Throat Mo 47:502–507, 1968

26. Lee TB, Stingle WH, Ombres P, et al: Neonatal meningitis and mastoiditis caused by *Hemophilus influenzae*. JAMA 235:407–409, 1976
27. Maresh MM: Paranasal sinuses from birth to late adolescence. Am J Dis Child 60:55–78, 1940
28. Shapiro ED, Wald ER, Brozanski BA: Periorbital cellulitis and paranasal sinusitis: A reappraisal. Pediatr Infect Dis 1:91–94, 1982
29. Goldberg F, Berne AS, Oski FA: Differentiation of orbital cellulitis from preseptal cellulitis by computed tomography. Pediatrics 62:1000–1005, 1978
30. Seeliger HPR: Listeriosis. New York, Hafner, 1961, pp 148–149
31. Naiditch MJ, Bower AG: Diphtheria: A study of 1,433 cases observed during a ten-year period at the Los Angeles County Hospital. Am J Med 17:229–245, 1954
32. Goebel F, Ströder J: Ueber Die Diphtherie des Säuglings. Dtsch Med Wochenschr 73:389–391, 1948

10

Cutaneous and Glandular Infections

SUPERFICIAL SKIN LESIONS

Superficial pustular staphylococcal disease is the commonest skin infection of neonates. Transient neontal pustular melanosis, a noninfectious congenital skin condition, can be confused with impetigo neonatorum.[1] The lesions of impetigo are generally 3–5 mm in diameter and break easily when rubbed with a povidone-iodine or alcohol sponge. The great minority of such infections do not progress to pyoderma with involvement of the deeper layers of the skin or to staphylococcal disease of other organs. They respond to simple topical measures; systemic antibiotic treatment is not indicated. Hexachlorophene bathing is often done, although the real benefits of this procedure are doubtful.

The greatest problem with impetigo neonatorum in a nursery is not the threat to the majority of the infected infants but is the difficulty in controlling spread of the infection. Rigorous control measures are indicated (see Chap. 15).

Bullous impetigo, in which the lesions may be several centimeters in diameter, is part of the expanded scalded skin syndrome due to phage group II *Staphylococcus aureus*.[2-8] Most affected infants have only localized lesions, but occasionally babies develop Ritter's disease, which is the eponymic equivalent in newborns of scalded skin syndrome of older infants[3 8] (see Fig. 10-1). Most staphylococci that produce exfoliatin belong to phage group II, but some strains of phage group I also produce exfoliatin and have been incriminated in a mild form of Ritter's disease in a nursery epidemic.[8] It is now recognized that there are two distinct types of exfoliatin.[9]

161

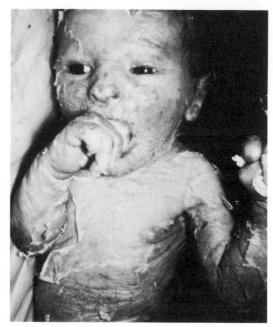

Figure 10-1. *Ritter's disease, or toxic epidermal necrolysis of the newborn. Note the peeling, cracking type of desquamation with fissuring around the mouth.*

Bacteremic complications are more common in neonates than in older infants with the scalded skin syndrome. They should be treated with a systemic penicillinase-resistant penicillin such as methicillin, since most phage group II staphylococci are penicillin-resistant. Steroids are contraindicated.[10] Formerly it was thought that reverse isolation technique was necessary to protect the patient against secondary infection of denuded skin. Actually the cleavage plane is very superficial in the epidermis, and the risk is virtually nil. Maceration may occur in intertrigenous areas. This can be prevented by local soaks with Burow's solution or benzalkonium chloride solution.

On occasion, impetigo is due to Group B streptococci.[11-12]

Vesicular lesions occur with herpesvirus infection and congenital syphilis. A case of congenital vesicular eruption attributed to *Haemophilus influenzae* b has been reported.[13]

Dermatophyte infections of the newborn are rare. The lesions appear similar to tinea lesions in older children. Experience with griseofulvin in the newborn is extremely limited, but cases have been treated with 10 mg/kg/day.[14]

Candida skin lesions acquired postnatally are usually confined to mucous membranes or to skin of the diaper area. Congenital candidiasis, due to ascending infection from the vagina, is distinctly different.[15] Lesions are present at or shortly after birth and are widespread over the head, trunk, and extremities. There is intense erythema and tiny white papules that gradually enlarge. Diagnosis is made from microscopic and culture examination of skin scrapings. The skin lesions respond to topical treatment with nystatin.

PYODERMA AND ECTHYMA

Deep pustular lesions of the skin are almost always due to *S. aureus,* although we have seen such infections caused by coliform bacilli. Incision and drainage should be done, in addition to cultures and gram stain with the purulent material. Methicillin or a related drug is given for staphylococcal infection, and an aminoglycosidic antibiotic is given if gram-negative bacilli are seen in the gram-stained specimen. If the pustular lesion has the characteristic appearance of ecthyma gangrenosa (see Fig. 10-2), *Pseudomonas aeruginosa* infection should be suspected and treatment given with ticarcillin or mezlocillin and an anti-*Pseudomonal* aminoglycoside drug. Most such patients have bacteremia, and the prognosis is grave.

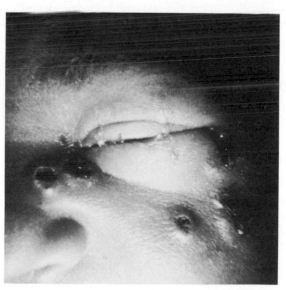

Figure 10-2. *Ecthymatous skin lesions characteristic of Pseudomonas aeruginosa* infection in a 3-week-old premature infant with *Pseudomonas* sepsis secondary to conjunctivitis. Note the elevated border with central necrosis.

CELLULITIS AND FASCIITIS

Group A streptococci are the usual cause of diffuse, well-demarcated cellulitis, or erysipelas. The involved skin is intensely red, hot, and moderately indurated. Occasionally streptococci can be recovered from "tissue juice" aspirated from the border of the lesion (rarely is the blood culture positive) but most often it is a clinical diagnosis without laboratory confirmation. Penicillin G is given, and although the borders continue to advance during the first 12–24 hours, stabilization of body temperature and improvement in general appearance of the infant gives reassurance that the diagnosis and therapy are correct.

Group B streptococcal cellulitis and adenitis[16] differ from most group B streptococcal syndromes in having an older age of onset (mean, 5 weeks). Infants with facial or submaxillary cellulitis had ipselateral otitis media, suggesting that the middle ear was the primary site of infection.

A rare cause of cellulitis of the face secondary to forceps injury was *Gardnerella (Haemophilus) vaginalis.*[17]

A virulent and often disastrous form of cellulitis is necrotizing fasciitis. Initially it resembles uncomplicated cellulitis, but the baby rapidly becomes very toxic, the lesion advances aggressively, and the central portion becomes discolored and anesthetic (Fig. 10-3). The infants always have bacteremia and frequently develop hypocalcemia and hypoproteinemia.[18] Treatment is intensive antibiotic therapy and radical surgical dissection of necrotic skin, fat, muscle, and fascia. Most cases are due to group A streptococci, but neonatal necrotizing fasciitis due to *S. aureus,*[19] *Escherichia coli,*[18] and group B streptococcal infection has been reported.[20-21] Initial antibiotic therapy should be with a penicillinase-resistant penicillin and an aminoglycosidic drug, pending culture results. If the infants survive the first stormy days, extensive skin grafting is generally necessary.

FUNISITIS AND OMPHALITIS

Asymptomatic colonization of the umbilical cord with *S. aureus* is common, although the incidence can be reduced markedly by a single application to the cord of triple dye.[22-25] This colonization has epidemiologic importance, but it is rare to see disease of the cord, or funisitis, due to staphylococci. Group A streptococci also may colonize the umbilical cord and be important as a focal point for epidemic streptococcal disease in a nursery. Unlike staphylococci, they are prone to cause an inflammatory reaction.[25-28] Streptococcal funisitis is mild and consists of slight exudation without frank pus ("wet or weeping cords"), a musty odor, and minimal redness of the umbilical skin. Treatment consists of systemic penicillin and

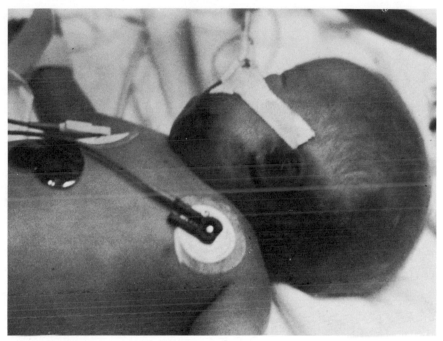

Figure 10 3.   *Neonate with necrotizing fasciitis and sepsis due to Group B streptococcus. The lesion began in the neck and spread rapidly to the cheek, ear, and scalp. The infant died.*

topical therapy with antibiotic ointment or with triple dye. (Topical therapy is mainly given for epidemiologic reasons to eliminate surface colonization, since systemically administered antibiotic does not reach the avascular part of the umbilical cord.) Because the group A streptococci are highly susceptible to penicillin G, a single injection of benzathine penicillin G is satisfactory for mild, superficial infections.[25-28]

Omphalitis, or infection of the umbilicus, can have many causes. Culture and susceptibility test results are necessary to select an appropriate antibiotic. Persistent low-grade infection of an umbilical artery that failed to obliterate spontaneously has been reported to mimic patent urachus.[29]

An unusual form of funisitis of unknown etiology, termed *subacute necrotizing funisitis,* has been reported.[30] This is probably not caused by bacteria, but the necrotic cords easily become infected with a variety of gram-negative organisms. An aminoglycoside antibiotic should be given while awaiting culture and susceptibility test results. A specific etiology has not been established for a variant that is called chronic viral funisitis because of virus-like inclusions in the placenta.[31]

INFECTED CEPHALHEMATOMAS, AND SUBGALEAL AND SCALP ABSCESSES

Cephalhematomas may be infected during ill-advised attempts to aspirate the blood, or they may be seeded with bacteria if a baby has bacteremia. In 4 reports[32-35] including a total of 14 patients, the infecting organisms were *E. coli* in 5 cases and 1 each of "Paracolon" species, *P. aeruginosa*, *S. epidermidis*, and *Bacteroides* (unspecific species). In 5 cases the organism was not known. Associated sepsis, meningitis, and osteomyelitis have occurred in some infants.

Treatment consists of evacuation of pus and antibiotics according to culture and susceptibility. Before definitive etiologic diagnosis is made, the initial choice of antibiotics should be directed against gram-negative enteric organisms, *Pseudomonas* and *S. aureus*. Combinations such as methicillin and gentamicin, or ticarcillin and gentamicin, would be reasonable choices. With the latter combination one would be relying on the antistaphylococcal activity of gentamicin as well as its anti–gram-negative organism spectrum.

A rare condition that we have seen on 4 occasions is infection of the subgaleal space. In three cases the infection was due to *S. aureus* and in the other to *P. aeruginosa*. The fascia under the galea aponeurotica is loosely arranged so that the scalp moves freely over the cranial bones. If infection is introduced into the subgaleal space, it spreads rapidly from the forehead to the occiput, with the top of the head converted into a virtual sac of pus. Such babies are toxic and critically ill. They require immediate surgery and intensive antibiotic therapy after blood and pus have been cultured. Gram stain of pus should be done to aid in selecting antibiotic therapy. Initially methicillin and gentamicin can be given. Duration of treatment is at least 10 days but is continued for 4–6 weeks if there is associated osteomyelitis of the skull, or meningitis. Later surgery may be required to remove necrotic bone.

Scalp abscesses are not uncommon in neonates, secondary to injury by forceps, needles, or fetal monitoring electrodes.[36-43] Most are superficial and managed with incision and drainage. If there is a significant amount of associated cellulitis, a 5–7-day course of antibiotic therapy can be given. Most scalp abscesses are due to staphylococci or gram-negative enteric organisms, but we have seen 1 case due to group B streptococci (without associated sepsis or meningitis), and gonococcal scalp abscess has been reported.[44-47]

SUPPURATIVE MASTITIS

S. aureus used to be thought of as the exclusive cause of neonatal breast abscess. The first cases due to coliform bacteria were reported in 1970,[46] and since then we and others[47-50] have reported additional cases due to *E. coli, Klebsiella* and *Salmonella* species, and *Proteus mirabilis.* We treated 2 infants with breast infection due to group B streptococci.[51] Mixed infections also occur. One of our patients had infection due to *E. coli* and *S. aureus,*[48] and Stetler et al.[46] isolated *E. coli* and *Klebsiella ozenae* from aspirated pus in 1 of their cases.

This varied spectrum should not be surprising. Infants get breast infection with organisms that comprise the skin flora, and this commonly includes coliform bacteria and group B streptococci as well as *S. aureus.* It is only surprising that gram-negative bacilli had never been implicated before 1970. The common nursery practice during the 1960s of bathing infants with hexachlorophene soaps, which decreases *S. aureus* cutaneous colonization, may have contributed to the emergence of gram-negative organisms as more frequent causes of breast abscesses.

It is clear that the physician should never assume that staphylococci are the cause, or there may be a delay in starting the appropriate antimicrobial. When the infant with breast abscess is first examined, the nipple and surrounding skin should be thoroughly cleaned with povidone-iodine solution or soap, and some fluid expressed through the nipple. Gram stain of this material should reveal whether one is dealing with gram-negative or gram-positive bacteria, and culture of it and pus removed during surgical drainage will provide the definitive diagnosis. If gram-positive cocci are seen, methicillin or another penicillinase-resistant penicillin is given. For gram-negative bacilli, an aminoglycosidic antibiotic would be appropriate.

If there is only mild cellulitis and no discernible fluctuance, antibiotic treatment alone may suffice. We have seen this on rare occasions with staphylococcal infection; both of our patients with group B streptococcal infection responded promptly to penicillin treatment without abscess formation. In most instances, however, surgical incision and drainage will be required. When there is extensive inflammation, needle aspiration should be attempted even when to the examining finger there is no obvious fluctuance. On several occasions we have been astounded at the amount of pus obtained from a nonfluctuant breast abscess.

Most neonates with breast infection do not have fever or other constitutional signs of infection, and bacteremia is rare.[48] It is conceivable that incision and drainage alone might suffice. We nevertheless recommend that all infants be given antibiotics. The duration of treatment will depend on the rate of response. Response is generally rapid, and we have found that healing is complete within 5–7 days in most instances.

The frequency of interference with normal breast development in later years is unknown. One case of marked disparity in breast size was reported in 1936.[52] We followed the cases of 5 girls and found that 2 of them had poor development of breast tissue on the affected side.[48]

Breast abscess does not occur in premature infants for the simple reason that they do not have breast tissue.

SUPPURATIVE PAROTITIS

Bacterial infection of the parotid gland in newborns has been reported on many occasions.[53-66] It is easy to recognize and could only be confused with infection of a preauricular lymph node. We have seen 1 instance where there was a delay in initiating therapy because the swelling was at first attributed to trauma from obstetrical forceps.

The infection is more common in low birthweight than full-term infants, and is more common in males than females. Dehydration predisposes to stasis of parotid secretions and subsequent infection. Bilateral infection is rare.

S. aureus causes most cases, but there have been reported infections due to group A streptococci, viridans streptococci, *E. coli, Pseudomonas,* and pneumococci.[60-61] Pus can be expressed through the parotid duct by pressure on the inflamed gland. Gram stain may be difficult to interpret because of contaminating bacteria from mouth microflora. We have cleaned the buccal mucosa with povidone-iodine solution before collecting the specimen for bacteriologic study without apparent harm to the tissues. If there is fluctuance, needle aspiration of pus can be performed.

Antibiotic treatment is started with a penicillinase-resistant penicillin such as methicillin unless there are unusual circumstances suggesting the possibility of gram-negative bacterial infection, in which case an amino-glycosidic antibiotic would be appropriate.

In most cases antibiotic therapy alone suffices, and surgical incision and drainage is not necessary. Extirpation of the gland should not be done. Septic focal complications in other organs are uncommon, as is bacteremia.

Response to therapy generally is quite rapid. In our experience most patients require only 7–10 days of treatment until healing is complete.

> For dosages see Chapter 2 or Abbreviated Guide to Dosage on Inside Covers

REFERENCES

1. Ramamurthy RS, Reveri M, Esterly NB, et al: Transient neonatal pustular melanosis. J Pediatr 88:831–835, 1976
2. Melish ME, Glasgow LA: Staphylococcal scalded skin syndrome: The expanded clinical syndrome. J Pediatr 78:958–967, 1971
3. Light IJ, Brackvogel V, Walton RL, et al: An epidemic of bullous impetigo arising from a central admission–observation nursery. Pediatrics 49:15–21, 1972
4. Albert S, Baldwin R, Czekajewski S, et al: Bullous impetigo due to group II

Staphylococcus aureus: An epidemic in a normal newborn nursery. Am J Dis Child 120:10–13, 1970

5. Florman AL, Holzman RS: Nosocomial scalded skin syndrome: Ritter's disease caused by phage group 3 *Staphylococcus aureus.* Am J Dis Child 134:1043–1045, 1980

6. Curran JP, Al-Salihi FL: Neonatal staphylococcal scalded skin syndrome: Massive outbreak due to an unusual phage type. Pediatrics 66:285–290, 1980

7. Annunziato D, Goldblum LM: Staphylococcal scalded skin syndrome: A complication of circumcision. Am J Dis Child 132:1187–1188, 1978

8. Faden HS, Burke JP, Glasgow LA, et al: Nursery outbreak of scalded skin syndrome: Scarlatiniform rash due to phage group I *Staphylococcus aureus.* Am J Dis Child 130:265–268, 1976

9. Kondo I, Sakurai S, Sarai Y, et al: Two serotypes of exfoliatin and their distribution in staphylococcal strains isolated from patients with scalded skin syndrome. J Clin Microbiol 1:397–400, 1975

10. Rudolph RI, Schwartz W, Leyden JJ: Treatment of staphylococcal toxic epidermal necrolysis. Arch Dermatol 110:559–562, 1974

11. Belgaumkar TK: Impetigo neonatorum congenita due to group B beta-hemolytic streptococcus infection. J Pediatr 86:982–983, 1975

12. Lopez JB, Gross P, Boggs TR: Skin lesions in association with β-hemolytic *Streptococcus* Group B. Pediatrics 58:859–861, 1976

13. Halal F, Delorme L, Brazeau M, et al: Congenital vesicular eruption caused by *Haemophilus influenzae* type b. Pediatrics 62:494–496, 1978

14. Weston WL, Thorne EG: Two cases of tinea in the neonate treated successfully with griseofulvin. Clin Pediatr (Phila) 16:601–602, 1977

15. Kam LA, Giacoia GP: Congenital cutaneous candidiasis. Am J Dis Child 129:1215–1218, 1975

16. Baker CJ: Group B streptococcal cellulitis-adenitis in infants. Am J Dis Child 136:631–633, 1982

17. Leighton PM, Bulleid B, Taylor R: Neonatal cellulitis due to *Gardnerella vaginalis.* Pediatr Infect Dis 1:337–338, 1982

18. Wilson HD, Haltalin KC: Acute necrotizing fasciitis in childhood. Am J Dis Child 125:591–595, 1973

19. Weinberg M, Haynes RE, Morse TS: Necrotizing fasciitis in a neonate. Am J Dis Child 123:591–594, 1972

20. Howard JB, McCracken GH Jr: The spectrum of group B streptococcal infections in infancy. Am J Dis Child 128:815–818, 1974

21. Ramamurthy RS, Srinivasan G, Jacobs NM: Neonatal fasciitis and necrotizing cellulitis due to group B streptococcus. Am J Dis Child 131:1169–1170, 1977

22. Barrett FF, Mason EO, Jr, Fleming D: The effect of three cord-care regimens on bacterial colonization of normal newborn infants. J Pediatr 94:796–799, 1979

23. Speck WT, Driscoll JM, Polin RA, et al: Staphylococcal and streptococcal colonization of the newborn infant: Effect of antiseptic cord care. Am J Dis Child 131:1005–1008, 1977

24. Kornblum R, Wang SF, Hedrick E: Triple dye and staphylococcal infections. Pediatrics 61:501, 1978

25. Nelson JD, Dillon HC Jr, Howard JB: A prolonged nursery epidemic associated with a newly recognized type of group A streptococcus. J Pediatr 89:792–796, 1976

26. Dillon HC Jr: Group A type 12 streptococcal infection in a newborn nursery: Successfully treated neonatal meningitis. Am J Dis Child 112:177–184, 1966

27. Geil CC, Castle WK, Mortimer EA Jr: Group A streptococcal infections in newborn nurseries. Pediatrics 46:849–854, 1970

28. Gezon HM, Schaberg MJ, Klein JO: Concurrent epidemics of *Staphylococcus aureus* and group A streptococcus disease in a newborn nursery: Control with penicillin G and hexachlorophene bathing. Pediatrics 51:383–390, 1973

29. Kenigsberg K: Infection of umbilical artery stimulating [sic] patent urachus. J Pediatr 86:151–152, 1975

30. Navarro C, Blanc WA: Subacute necrotizing funisitis: A variant of cord inflammation with a high rate of perinatal infection. J Pediatr 85:689–697, 1974

31. Navarro C, Blanc WA: Chronic viral funisitis. J Pediatr 91:967–973, 1977

32. Burry VF, Hellerstein S: Septicemia and subperiosteal cephalhematomas. J Pediatr 69:1133–1135, 1966

33. Lee Y-h, Berg RB: Cephalhematoma infected with *Bacteroides*. Am J Dis Child 121:77–78, 1971

34. Ellis SS, Montgomery JR, Wagner M, et al: Osteomyelitis complicating neonatal cephalhematoma. Am J Dis Child 127:100–102, 1974

35. Overturf GD, Balfour G: Osteomyelitis and sepsis: Severe complications of fetal monitoring. Pediatrics 55:244–247, 1975

36. Yadav YC, Khana A: Scalp abscess. J Laryngol Otol 82:945–948, 1968

37. Cordero L Jr, Hon EH: Scalp Abscess: A rare complication of fetal monitoring. J Pediatr 78:533–537, 1971

38. Plavidal FJ, Welch A: Fetal scalp abscess secondary to intrauterine monitoring. Am J Obstet Gynecol 125:65–70, 1976

39. Winkel CA, Snyder DL, Schlaerth JB: Scalp abscess: A complication of the spiral fetal electrode. Am J Obstet Gynecol 126:720–722, 1976

40. Yasunaag S: Complications of fetal monitoring: Scalp abscess and osteomyelitis. IMJ 150:41–43, 1976

41. Feder HM, MacLean WC Jr, Moxon R: Scalp abscess secondary to fetal scalp electrode. J Pediatr 89:808, 1976

42. Balfour HH Jr, Block SR, Bowe ET, et al: Complications of fetal blood sampling. Am J Obstet Gynecol 107:288–294, 1970

43. Turbville DF, Heath RE Jr, Bowen FW Jr, et al: Complications of fetal scalp electrodes: A case report. Am J Obstet Gynecol 122:530–531, 1975

44. Plavidal FJ, Werch A: Gonococcal fetal scalp abscess: A case report. Am J Obstet 127:437–438, 1977

45. Reveri M, Krishnamurthy C: Gonococcal scalp abscess. J Pediatr 94:819–820, 1979

46. Stetler H, Martin E, Plotkin S, et al: Neonatal mastitis due to *Escherichia coli*. J Pediatr 76:611–613, 1970

47. Nelson JD: Suppurative mastitis in infants. Am J Dis Child 125:458–459, 1973

48. Rudoy RC, Nelson JD: Breast abscess during the neonatal period. Am J Dis Child 129:1031–1034, 1975

49. Burry VF, Breezley M: Infant mastitis due to gram-negative organisms. Am J Dis Child 124:736–737, 1972

50. McGuigan MA, Lipman RP: Neonatal mastitis due to *Proteus mirabilis*. Am J Dis Child 130:1296, 1976

51. Nelson JD: Bilateral breast abscess due to group B streptococcus. (letter) Am J Dis Child 130:567, 1976

52. Kalwbow H: Ueber Mastitis neonatorum und ihre Folgen. Zentralbl Gynaekol 60:1821–1824, 1936

53. Elterich TO: Purulent parotitis in the newborn: Case report and review of the literature. J Pediatr 3:761–764, 1933

54. Kugelmass IN: Suppuration of the salivery glands in the newborn. NY state J Med 51:613–614, 1951

55. White RHR: Acute suppurative parotitis in the newborn. Br Med J 1:1232, 1952

56. Burke FG: Suppurative parotitis in an infant. Clin Proc Child Hosp (DC) 4:68–73, 1948

57. Ross S, Guin GH, Jackson C: Bilateral parotid gland abscess in a newborn infant. Clin Proc Child Hosp (DC) 13:172–177, 1957

58. Baxter RH, MacDonald MT: Acute suppurative parotitis in the newborn. New Engl J Med 217:351–353, 1937

59. Reisman HA, Fischer G: Acute suppurative parotitis in a newborn premature infant. Am J Dis Child 71:387–393, 1946

60. Leake D, Leake R: Neonatal suppurative parotitis. Pediatrics 46:203–207, 1970

61. David RB, O'Connel EJ: Suppurative parotitis in children. Am J Dis Child 119:332–335, 1970

62. Haritos NP: Suppurative parotitis in the newborn. Clin Proc Child Hosp (DC) 17:201–207, 1961

63. Campbell WAB: Purulent parotitis in the newborn: Report of a case. Lancet 2:386, 1951

64. Shulman BH: Acute suppurative infections of salivary glands in the newborn. Am J Dis Child 80:413–416, 1950

65. Neuhauser EBD, Ferris BG Jr: The treatment of acute suppurative parotitis in infants. J Pediatr 27:589–590, 1945

66. Sanford HN, Shmigelsky I: Purulent parotitis in the newborn. J Pediatr 26:149–154, 1945

11

Bone and Joint Infections

Bone and joint infections can be extraordinarily difficult to suspect in neonates and young infants. As a generalization one can say that osteomyelitis tends to be a milder, low-grade illness in the neonate than in older children,[1] but this is a deceptive statement in the sense that few illnesses of newborns other than meningitis can have such disastrous long-term effects. The physician should therefore be alert to the earliest signals, such as failure to move spontaneously an extremity or apparent pain on movement. When skeletal infection is suspected, roentgenograms are helpful if they show characteristic changes in the deep tissues or enlargement of a joint space, but whenever one is in doubt the aspirating needle is the final diagnostic instrument and the only one that can confirm the diagnosis. The value of radioisotope bone scans in neonatal osteomyelitis has not been thoroughly explored.

Osteomyelitis and arthritis have been reported consequent to several invasive procedures in newborns: heel puncture,[2-3] femoral venipuncture,[4] other needle punctures,[5] exchange transfusion,[6] fetal monitoring electrodes,[7] intravenous alimentation,[8] and umbilical artery catheters.[9-10] Blumenfeld et al.[11] believe that infection of the os calcis secondary to heel pricks for blood sampling is caused by using an improper site; they present anatomic and histopathologic evidence that the os calcis can be avoided if the stick is made in the extreme lateral or medial plantar surface of the heel. An unusual complication of suprapubic bladder puncture was infection of the symphysis pubis.[12] Osteomyelitis of cranial bones has complicated infected cephalhematomas.[13] In most cases the origin is unknown and presumed to be hematogenous.

The pathology of neonatal osteomyelitis has been studied by Ogden and Lister.[14] Because the neonate has transphyseal blood vessels, infection in the metaphysis can penetrate the physis, destroy that important growth plate, and spread to the epiphysis and joint space. Metaphyseal pus can also break through the thin cortex and enter the joint, subperiosteal space, and soft tissues. Primary infection in a joint can readily penetrate the epiphysis, since a portion of metaphyseal bone is intraarticular in the newborn period. The proclivity for contiguous joint involvement has been recognized clinically in neonatal osteomyelitis.[15]

The infecting organisms in osteomyelitis[15-23] and septic arthritis[24-29] are varied, but the predominant ones are *Staphylococcus aureus* and gram-negative enteric organisms such as *Klebsiella, Proteus,* and *Escherichia.* Group B streptococci can cause both arthritis and osteomyelitis.[30-33] Gonococcal arthritis or tenosynovitis used to be relatively common[27] and is still seen on occasion.[26] *Salmonella* arthritis may occur in the newborn,[25,29] and *Candida* joint infection has been seen in neonates with disseminated candidiasis.[9,34]

The etiology in our personal series of 28 cases of suppurative skeletal infections in neonates consists of 12 cases of *S. aureus,* 3 of group B streptococcus, 2 each of *Haemophilus influenzae* b and *Staphylococcus epidermidis,* and 1 each of *E. coli, Pseudomonas aeruginosa, Neisseria gonorrheae, Klebsiella pneumoniae,* and *Salmonella* infection. In 4 cases the bacterial cause was unknown.

Pyarthrosis and osteomyelitis due to group B streptococcus, especially serotype III, have been recognized with increased frequency during the past decade. Otherwise healthy neonates are most commonly affected.[32] Single bone or joint involvement is characteristic, and the proximal humerus is most often involved.[33] This is thought to be due to minor trauma to the shoulder as it passes beneath the symphysis pubis during delivery.

One particular and peculiar form of osteomyelitis of the newborn has been well documented but is not commonly known: maxillitis, or osteomyelitis of the superior maxilla.[35-37] Initially the infant is likely to be misdiagnosed as having dacryocystitis or orbital cellulitis, but the swollen cheek should make one wary, as should unilateral nasal discharge of pus and swelling of the alveolar ridge. The disease is almost always due to *S. aureus.*

Considering the varied bacteria that can cause bone and joint infections it is imperative to get specimens of bone or joint aspirate for culture. Blood culture should also be done, since it is positive in almost half the cases; it sometimes provides the diagnosis of the cause when the pus cultures are sterile.[22,25] We have found reverse immunoelectrophoresis or latex agglutination testing of joint fluid very useful in *Haemophilus* and group B streptococcal infections.

Gram and methylene blue stain of aspirate helps select initial antimicrobial drugs, but if no microorganisms are seen it is advisable to begin treatment with two drugs—a penicillinase-resistant penicillin such as methicillin, and an aminoglycosidic antibiotic. Definitive treatment is based on culture and susceptibility testing results.

Surgical removal of pus is an integral part of treatment and is equally important to antibiotic therapy. Open drainage is essential for management of septic hip disease. In infants the main blood supply to the head of the femur is via several vessels coursing up the neck. Because the head and neck of the femur are enclosed within the synovial space, these vessels are easily compressed by increased pressure. For other joints repeated daily evacuation of fluid with needle and syringe is usually adequate. In osteomyelitis, surgical drainage of the subperiosteal space and the metaphysis should be done if pus is obtained during diagnostic aspiration. Sometimes metaphyseal pus is effectively decompressed by spontaneous rupture into the adjacent point. If only a small amount of bloody material has been obtained at the diagnostic aspiration, immediate surgery is not necessary, and the patient is observed under antibiotic therapy for resolution of local and systemic signs. Repeat aspirations are done if there is not satisfactory improvement, to determine whether pus has accumulated.

Antibiotics need not be injected into infected synovial spaces. In several studies[38-42] it has been conclusively shown that parenterally administered antibiotics attain concentrations in joint fluid comparable to those in serum, and these are adequate to inhibit susceptible bacteria. Similarly, adequate concentrations are achieved in bone tissue with parenterally administered antibiotics.[43-44] Not only is it unnecessary to inject drugs into joint spaces but it is possibly harmful. Very little is known about adverse effects of very large concentrations of antibiotic on synovial tissue or cartilage. If irrigation is desirable for complete removal of pus, this can be accomplished with sterile normal saline solution.

Antibiotic treatment of staphylococcal and gram-negative enteric infection should be continued by the parenteral route for at least 3 weeks. If response of clinical signs has been slow, it is advisable to prolong therapy for from 4 to 6 weeks. In the case of gonococcal or streptococcal infection, 10 days of antibiotic therapy should be sufficient if surgical treatment has been adequate.

Physical therapy to ensure full range of motion should be started as soon as pain has abated. In infants it is frequently difficult to assess residual joint abnormalities and abnormal bone growth patterns until many months have passed so it is important to have long-term follow-up after treatment has been concluded to determine whether additional surgical or physical medicine treatment is necessary.

For dosages see Chapter 2 or Abbreviated Guide to Dosage on Inside Covers

REFERENCES

1. Weissberg ED, Smith AL, Smith DH: Clinical features of neonatal osteomyelitis. Pediatrics 53:505–510, 1974
2. Lilien LD, Harris VJ, Ramamurthy RH, et al: Neonatal osteomyelitis of the calcaneus: Complication of heel puncture. J Pediatr 88:478–480, 1976
3. Goldberg I, Shauer I., Klier I, et al: Neonatal osteomyelitis of the calcaneus following heel pad puncture. A case report. Clin Orthop 158:195–197, 1981
4. Asnes RS, Arendar GM: Septic arthritis of the hip: A complication of femoral venipuncture. Pediatrics 38:837–841, 1966
5. Nelson DI., Hable KA, Matsen JM: *Proteus mirabilis* osteomyelitis in two neonates following needle puncture. Am J Dis Child 125:109–110, 1973
6. Qureshi ME, Puri SP: Osteomyelitis after exchange transfusion. Br Med J 2:28–29, 1971
7. Overturf GD, Balfour G: Osteomyelitis and sepsis: Severe complications of fetal monitoring. Pediatrics 55:244–247, 1975
8. Groff DB: Complications of intravenous hyperalimentation in newborns and infants. J Pediatr Surg 4:460–464, 1969
9. Pittard WB III, Thullen JD, Fanaroff AA: Neonatal septic arthritis. J Pediatr 88:621–624, 1976
10. Lim MO, Gresham EL, Franken EA, et al: Osteomyelitis as a complication of umbilical artery catheterization. Am J Dis Child 131:142–144, 1977
11. Blumenfeld TA, Turi GK, Blank WA: Recommended site and depth of newborn heelskin punctures based on anatomic measurements and histopathology. Lancet 1:230–233, 1979
12. Kalager T, Digrames A: Unusual complication after suprapubic puncture. Br Med J 1:91–92, 1979
13. Ellis SS, Montgomery JR, Wagner M, et al: Osteomyelitis complicating neonatal cephalhematoma. Am J Dis Child 127:100–102, 1974
14. Ogden JA, Lister G: The pathology of neonatal osteomyelitis. Pediatrics 55:474–478, 1975
15. Fox L, Sprunt K: Neonatal osteomyelitis. Pediatrics 62:535–542, 1978
16. Blockey NJ, Watson JT: Acute osteomyelitis in children. J Bone Joint Surg [BR] 52:77–87, 1970
17. Berant M, Kahana D: *Klebsiella* osteomyelitis in a newborn. Am J Dis Child 118:634–637, 1969
18. Levy HL, O'Connor JF, Ingall D: Neonatal osteomyelitis due to *Proteus mirabilis,* JAMA 202:582–586, 1967
19. Upmalis IH: Osteomyelitis in infancy. Can J Surg 10:75–78, 1967
20. Dennison WM: Haematogenous osteitis in the newborn. Lancet 2:474–476, 1955
21. Blanche DW: Osteomyelitis in infants. J Bone Joint Surg [AM] 34:71–84, 1952
22. Dich VQ, Nelson JD, Haltalin KC: Osteomyelitis in infants and children: A review of 163 cases. Am J Dis Child 129:1273–1278, 1975
23. Rhodes PG, Hall RT, Burry VF, et al: Sepsis and osteomyelitis due to *Staphy-*

lococcus aureus phage type 94 in a neonatal intensive care unit. J Pediatr 88:1063–1064, 1976

24. Weisgerber G, Boureau M, Bensahel H: L'arthrite aigüe de la hance chez le nouveau-né et le nourrisson. Arch Fr Pediatr 30:83–94, 1973

25. Nelson JD: The bacterial etiology and antibiotic management of septic arthritis in infants and children. Pediatrics 50:437–440, 1972

26. Kohen DP: Neonatal gonococcal arthritis: Three cases and review of the literature. Pediatrics 53:436–440, 1974

27. Cooperman MB: Gonococcal arthritis in infancy. Am J Dis Child 33:932–948, 1927

28. Granoff DM, Nankervis GA: Infectious arthritis in the neonate caused by *Haemophilus influenzae*. Am J Dis Child 129:730–733, 1975

29. David JR, Black RL; *Salmonella* arthritis. Medicine 39:385–403, 1960

30. Howard JB, McCracken GH: The spectrum of group B streptococcal infections. Am J Dis Child 128:815–818, 1974

31. Memon IA, Jacobs NM, Yeh TF, et al: Group B streptococcal osteomyelitis and septic arthritis. Am J Dis Child 133:921–923, 1979

32. Ancona RJ, McAuliffe J, Thompson TR, et al: Group B streptococcal sepsis with osteomyelitis and arthritis. Am J Dis Child 133:919–923, 1979

33. Edwards MS, Baker CJ, Wagner ML, et al: An etiologic shift in infantile osteomyelitis: The emergence of the group B streptococcus. J Pediatr 93:579–583, 1978

34. Yousefzadeh DK, Jackson JH: Neonatal and infantile candidal arthritis with or without osteomyelitis: A clinical and radiographical review of 21 cases. Skeletal Radiol 5:77–90, 1980

35. Hitchin AD, Naylor MN: Acute maxillitis of infancy. Oral Surg 10:715–724, 1957

36. Lieberman H, Brem J: Syndrome of acute osteomyelitis of the superior maxilla in early infancy. N Engl J Med 260:318–322, 1959

37. Cavanagh F: Osteomyelitis of the superior maxilla in infants: A report on 24 personally treated cases. Br Med J 1:468–472, 1960

38. Nelson JD: Antibiotic concentrations in septic joint effusions. N Engl J Med 284:349–353, 1971

39. Chow A, Hecht R, Winters R: Gentamicin and carbenicillin penetration into the septic joint. (letter) N Engl J Med 285:178–179, 1971

40. Drutz DJ, Schaffner W, Hillman JW, et al: The penetration of penicillin and other antimicrobials into joint fluid. J Bone Joint Surg [AM] 49a:1415–1421, 1967

41. Baciocco EA, Iles RL: Ampicillin and kanamycin concentrations in joint fluid. Clin Pharmacol Ther 12:858–863, 1971

42. Parker RH, Schmid FR: Antibacterial activity of synovial fluid during therapy of septic arthritis. Arthritis Rheum 14:96–104, 1971

43. Smilack JD, Flittie WH, Williams TW Jr: Bone concentrations of antimicrobial agents after parenteral administration. Antimicrob Agents Chemother 9:169–171, 1976

44. Tetzlaff TR, Howard JB, McCracken GH Jr, et al: Antibiotic concentrations in pus and bone of children with osteomyelitis. J Pediatr 92:135–140, 1978

12

Gastrointestinal and Liver Infections

INFECTIOUS DIARRHEAL DISEASE

In modern society, gastrointestinal infections of neonates are far less common than they once were, and intravenous fluid and electrolyte therapy and antibiotics have essentially erased mortality from this former scourge of nurseries. Nevertheless outbreaks of infectious diarrhea still occur, and because of their potential for rapid spread within a nursery constant vigilance is required.

Bacterial Infections

Most outbreaks of infecttious diarrhea in nurseries are due to *Escherichia coli*[1-2] or *Salmonella* species.[3-7] Enterococci were reported to cause diarrhea in neonates,[8] but this has not been confirmed by other investigators. *Shigella* infection is uncommon,[9-10] and for unknown reasons shigellosis in neonates is episodic and does not spread in nurseries in spite of the highly infectious nature of shigellae. Campylobacter infections have occurred in neonates.[11-12]

For many years after Bray's original association of certain serotypes of *E. coli* with diarrhea in infancy,[13] the pathogenetic mechanism was a mystery. It is now known that phenomena of adherence, toxigenicity, and invasiveness can be involved. Most *E. coli* strains that are epidemiologically related to outbreaks of diarrhea in nurseries do not produce enterotoxin and are not invasive by the Sereny test.[14] One epidemic of nursery infection due to enterotoxigenic *E. coli* 0142 has been reported.[15] This is not a traditional enteropathogenic serotype, although it was first recognized in a

177

premature nursery outbreak of diarrhea.[16] The frequency of strains with the property of adherence to epithelial cells is not known because it has not been thoroughly investigated. In 1982, Rothbaum et al.[17] reported several cases of protracted diarrhea beginning in neonates or young infants due to E. coli 0119:B4, an organism that was not toxigenic or invasive but had the property of adherence to enterocytes.

When an index case of enteropathogenic E. coli diarrhea is recognized in a nursery, secondary cases are very likely to ensue. If a cohort system is used, all other babies in the cohort should have samples taken by rectal swabs tested by culture and preferably by fluorescent antibody technique, which is more sensitive for identifying asymptomatic carriers.[2] If cohorting is not used, all infants in the nursery should be tested. Ill and healthy colonized infants should be segregated and treated with orally administered neomycin (100 mg/kg/day in 3 divided doses) or with colistin sulfate (15 mg/kg/day in 3 divided doses) for 5 days. Neomycin causes rapid disappearance of the organism and abbreviates the period of diarrhea, but approximately 20 percent of infants revert to the asymptomatic carrier state.[18] Repeated surveillance of infants is necessary until it has been shown that the pathogenic strain has been eliminated from the nursery.

Antimicrobial therapy for Salmonella gastroenteritis has always been a controversial topic, but most experts agree that newborns should be treated. This is based on anecdotal experience that many young infants have a protracted course of illness and may be more susceptible to metastatic focal infections from Salmonella.[19] We recommend treatment with ampicillin or, in the case of ampicillin-resistant salmonellae, with chloramphenicol. In retrospective studies,[3-4] antibiotic therapy appeared to increase the likelihood that an infant would become an asymptomatic carrier of salmonellae for a prolonged time, but that has not been the case in 2 prospective studies.[20-21] For acute gastroenteritis, five to seven days of therapy should be sufficient. Asymptomatic carriers should not be given antibiotic therapy; they should be carefully followed, however, to ensure that they are growing and developing normally. We have seen several infants whose acute diarrhea subsided promptly but who failed to gain weight because of a low-grade enteritis manifested only by somewhat abnormally formed stools that on microscopic examination contained polymorphonuclear leukocytes.

Shigellosis in the newborn may present as a diarrheic or dysenteric syndrome or may be evidenced only by a septic or toxic infant.[9] Ampicillin was formerly the drug of choice, but many strains have become resistant. Most are susceptible to trimethoprim–sulfamethoxazole in a daily dose of 10 mg trimethoprim–50 mg sulfamethoxazole/kg/day in 2 divided doses. Sulfa drugs are contraindicated in jaundiced newborns.

The effectiveness of antibiotics for campylobacter infection is not established. Two treatment trials[22-23] of erythromycin verus placebo failed to demonstrate a significant benefit on clinical signs but, in each study treatment was begun rather late in the course of illness, and in 1 study the authors stated that some patients with severe disease appeared to have improvement coincident with administration of antibiotics.[22] Until the status of antibiotics is resolved, we recommend erythromycin therapy.[24]

Viral Infections

Infection with rotavirus[25-30] and other noncultivatable viruses[31] is common in many nursery infants and appears to be spread from infant to infant. It is often asymptomatic infection. There is no specific antiviral agent for therapy. In 1 trial,[32] human gammaglobulin or placebo was given to low birthweight infants with each feeding during the first week of life. Rotavirus-associated diarrhea developed in 6 of 11 babies given placebo and in 1 of 14 babies given gammaglobulin.

NECROTIZING ENTEROCOLITIS

Bacteria play a critical role in both the pathogenesis of necrotizing enterocolitis and the complications of bacteremia and peritonitis.[33-34] The gas responsible for the x-ray appearance of pneumatosis intestinalis, which is characteristic of well-developed cases of necrotizing enterocolitis, is mainly hydrogen produced by intestinal bacteria.[35]

No specific bacteria or viruses have been implicated as essential pathogens for the syndrome. In 1982 an interesting association between coronavirus infection and necrotizing enterocolitis was reported;[36] this needs further investigation. Claims that clostridial strains were causative in the disorder[37-39] were dispelled when appropriately controlled studies were done demonstrating that *Clostridium difficile* and its toxin are commonly present in stools of neonates and bear no relationship to necrotizing enterocolitis.[40-42]

The status of antibiotic prophylaxis for necrotizing enterocolitis is discussed in Chapter 15.

Bacteremia and peritonitis are common complications of necrotizing enterocolitis. Combining the data from 10 series of cases, blood cultures were positive in 52 of 156 patients, or 33.3 percent.[43] Most were *E. coli,* *Klebsiella,* or *Enterobacter* species, but there have been instances of *Staphylococcus aureus* and *Pseudomonas* bacteremia. Similar bacteria are encountered in peritoneal fluid.[43]

In addition to parenteral antibiotic treatment, intragastric administration of kanamycin or gentamicin has been widely used. Although the benefits of local intestinal treatment with these nonabsorbable drugs have not been critically tested,[43] Martin[44] feels that morbidity and mortality have been substantially decreased by the combined parenteral–intragastric antibiotic regimen. He administers 15 mg/kg/day of gentamicin or 30 mg/kg/day of kanamycin through the nasogastric tube every 4 hours and clamps the tube for one hour after each dose.

Significant absorption of orally administered gentamicin occurs in babies with necrotizing enterocolitis and, added to the serum content of gentamicin from parenteral administration, can cause potentially toxic amounts of drug in serum.[45] In a controlled study, furthermore, oral gentamicin did not favorably affect the clinical course.[45] For these reasons we do not use or recommend oral aminoglycosides as adjunctive therapy.

The duration of antimicrobial therapy depends upon the rate of response, but generally is from 10–14 days in those who do not develop intestinal perforation and 21 days or longer in those complicated cases requiring surgery. Treatment is continued until there is clinical and radiographic resolution of all symptoms and the infant is tolerating feedings.

The classical triad of necrotizing enterocolitis is abdominal distension, gastrointestinal bleeding, and pneumatosis intestinalis. It is not unusual for premature infants to have episodes of distension, vomiting, and loose stools. Such babies are customarily treated as if they had incipient necrotizing enterocolitis by the regimen outlined above. Most do not progress further and have resolution of symptoms within a few days. Whether these represent aborted cases of necrotizing enterocolitis or another entity is a moot point.

PERITONITIS

Peritoneal infection in neonates is most often secondary to perforation of the stomach or intestines. The microorganisms that are encountered reflect the microflora of the gastrointestinal tract. The best available study of acquisition of gut flora in the first hours and days of life is that of Mata and Urrutia[46] who investigated breast-fed Guatemalan infants. Anaerobic streptococci appeared in the first 12 hours of life. From 12–24 hours, *Bifidobacteria, Clostridia,* and anaerobic streptococci were present in large quantities. *Bacteroides* and veillonellae appeared on subsequent days. *E. coli* also appeared early but in far fewer numbers. The unpublished studies done in Houston by Yow and coworkers (personal communication, November 1974) suggest that a similar sequence occurs in babies born in the United States and that colonization with aerobic gram-negative bacilli is greater in formula-fed than in breat-fed infants.

Bell et al.[47] studied the aerobic and anaerobic flora of peritoneal fluid from 31 neonates with gastrointestinal perforation. Twenty-three percent had mixed aerobic and anerobic bacteria, and 55 isolates were obtained. The organisms were the expected coliform and gram-positive coccal flora of the gut. Seven babies had *Bacteroides* species.

Thus in early life secondary peritonitis is likely to be due to penicillin-susceptible anaerobes and to a lesser extent to coliform bacteria. The use of penicillin, or ampicillin, and an aminoglycoside antibiotic is indicated. If perforation occurs later in the newborn period, *Bacteroides fragilis* may be present in the gut flora. Gram stain of peritoneal fluid is useful, since *Bacteroides* organisms have a characteristic appearance.

Virtually all strains of *B. fragilis* are susceptible to metronidazole and chloramphenicol, and most are susceptible to clindamycin, mezlocillin, and ticarcillin. Chloramphenicol is best avoided in neonates, and there is little experience with clindamycin or metronidazole in the newborn. Mezlocillin or ticarcillin along with an aminoglycoside can be used pending culture and susceptibility test results.

The case fatality rate in secondary peritonitis was 77 percent in 1 review of 172 cases spanning 15 years.[48] Mortality was 35 percent in the more recent report of Bell et al.[47]

Peritonitis secondary to appendicitis has also been observed on rare occasions. In a review of the literature in 1970, Parsons, Miscal, and McSherry[49] found 31 patients under 1 month old and added a case of their own.

Primary peritonitis is rare in neonates.[50-51] Fowler, in his review,[50] states that male neonates are twice as likely as female newborns to have the condition, but exact figures are not given, nor are there details regarding the causative bacteria. We have treated a neonate with primary peritonitis due to group A streptococci.[52] That patient had cellulitis of the abdominal wall, which has been previously noted as a sign in neonates with peritonitis of any cause.[49] If roentgenograms demonstrate findings of peritonitis without free air in the abdominal cavity, one is likely to be dealing with primary peritonitis, and surgery is not indicated.[50] Needle aspiration of peritoneal fluid should be done, and antibiotics selected according to the types of microorganisms seen and cultured.

PERIRECTAL ABSCESS

Perirectal abscess is uncommon in children and very rare in the newborn. In 1 series of cases of the disease in pediatric patients, 10 patients were less than 1 year old, but it is not specifically stated whether any were newborns.[53] In the only other report of which we are aware, 13 of the 29 patients were less than 1 year of age, but again it is not stated whether any were newborns.[54] There were 28 patients with fistula-in-ano, 20 of whom were in the abscess state, in Arminski and McLean's[55] review of proctologic problems in children. The comments infer that some were neonates, but no details are presented.

The mechanism of production is unknown. There is no obvious trauma or other predisposing factor in most cases, and there is usually no fistulous tract to the rectum or anus.

S. aureus or coliform bacteria are most often involved, and there may be mixed infection.

The principal therapy is surgical drainage. Enberg et al.[53] concluded that antibiotics were of no apparent benefit or harm, but most of their patients did receive antibiotic therapy based upon culture and susceptibility testing results. Nine of Krieger and Chusid's[54] patients were treated with incision and drainage alone, and of the 20 who were given antibiotics none was treated for longer than 6 days.

BACTERIAL HEPATITIS, CHOLANGITIS AND LIVER ABSCESS

Bacterial hepatitis can occur in infants with sepsis,[56] and pyogenic liver abscesses are occasionally seen in newborns.[57-60] In 1981 Moss and Pysher[59] reviewed the subject. They uncovered 24 cases of liver abscess in the newborn and added 13 cases. Sepsis, vessel cannulation, and abdominal surgery were associated factors. Abscesses are usually multiple. Solitary liver abscesses occur rarely[60] and require surgical drainage. Amebic liver abscess has not been reported in the newborn; the youngest case on record occurred in an infant 6 weeks of age.[61]

Various bacteria cause these conditions, but coliform bacilli and staphylococci are usually involved.[59] Initial antibiotic therapy with methicillin in combination with an aminoglycoside or cephalosporin would therefore be appropriate. If radionuclide scans of the liver demonstrate large abscesses, surgical drainage or percutaneous needle aspiration is done.

Suppurative cholangitis is rare but has been reported in an infant who became ill at 7 weeks of age with infection due to *Enterobacter agglomerans*.[62]

INFANT BOTULISM

Infants can develop botulism from intestinal colonization with *Clostridium botulinum* rather than from ingestion of preformed botulinal toxin in food.[63-64] Botulism is a rare cause of sudden infant death.[65] More commonly the infant has a gradual progression of symptoms from constipation to serious neurologic impairment. The source of *C. botulinum* to the infant is not known in most circumstances, but honey added to milk or infant formula has been epidemiologically incriminated in some cases.[66]

The relation of breast feeding to botulism presents an interesting paradox.[67] Infant botulism is more common in breast-fed than formula-fed babies, but the onset is later, and the disease is milder.

Therapy is supportive. There is no evidence that antitoxin or antibiotic therapy is beneficial. In fact, aminoglycoside therapy may be detrimental and may augment neuromuscular blockade.[64]

> For dosages see Chapter 2 or Abbreviated Guide to Dosage on Inside Covers

REFERENCES

1. Kaslow RA, Taylor A Jr, Dwoeck HS, et al: Enteropathogenic *Escherichia coli* infection in a newborn nursery. Am J Dis Child 128:797–801, 1974
2. Nelson JD, Whitaker JA, Hempstead B, et al: Epidemiological application of the fluorescent antibody technique: Study of a diarrhea outbreak in a premature nursery. JAMA 176:26–30, 1961
3. Szanton VL: Epidemic salmonellosis: A 30-month study of 80 cases of *Salmonella oranionburg* infection. Pediatrics 20:794–808, 1957
4. Abroms IF, Cochran WD, Holmes LB, et al: A *Salmonella newport* outbreak in a premature nursery with a one-year follow-up. Pediatrics 37:616–623, 1966
5. Rice PA, Craven PC, Wells JG: *Salmonella heidelberg* enteritis and bacteremia: An epidemic on two pediatric wards. Am J Med 60:509–516, 1976
6. Ip HMH, Sin WK, Chau PY, et al: Neonatal infection due to *Salmonella worthington* transmitted by a delivery-room suction apparatus. J Hyg 77:307–314, 1976
7. Ryder RW, Crosby-Ritchie A, McDonough B, et al: Human milk contaminated with *Salmonella kottbus:* A cause of nosocomial illness in infants. JAMA 238:1533–1534, 1977
8. Erwa HH: Enterococci in diarrhoea of neonates. Trans R Soc Trop Med Hyg 66:359–361, 1972
9. Haltalin KC: Neonatal shigellosis: Report of 16 cases and review of the literature. Am J Dis Child 114:603–611, 1967
10. Kraybill EN, Controni G: Septicemia and enterocolitis due to *Shigella sonnei* in a newborn infant. Pediatrics 42:530–531, 1968
11. Anders BJ, Lauer BA, Paisley JW: *Campylobacter* gastroenteritis in neonates. Am J Dis Child 135:900–902, 1981
12. Buck GE, Kelly MT, Pichanick AM, et al: *Campylobacter jejuni* in newborns: A cause of asymptomatic bloody diarrhea. Am J Dis Child 136:744, 1982
13. Bray JSB: Bray's discovery of pathogenic *Esch. coli* as a cause of infantile gastroenteritis. Arch Dis Child 48:923–926, 1973

14. Goldschmidt MC, DuPont HL: Enteropathogenic *Escherichia coli:* Lack of correlation of serotype with pathogenicity. J Infect Dis 133:153–156, 1976

15. Boyer KM, Petersen NJ, Farazneh I, et al: An outbreak of gastroenteritis due to *E. coli* 0142 in a neonatal nursery. J Pediatr 86:919–927, 1975

16. Olarte J: Epidemic diarrhea in premature infants: Etiologic significance of a newly recognized type of *Escherichia coli* (0142:K86nBm:H6). Am J Dis Child 109:436–438, 1965

17. Rothbaum R, McAdams AJ, Gianella R, et al: A clinicopathologic study of enterocyte-adherent *Escherichia coli:* A cause of protracted diarrhea in infants. Gastroenterology 83:441–454, 1982

18. Nelson JD: Duration of neomycin therapy for enteropathogenic *Escherichia coli* diarrheal disease: A comparative study of 113 cases. Pediatrics 48:248–258, 1971

19. Davis RC: *Salmonella* sepsis in infancy. Am J Dis Child 135:1096–1099, 1981

20. Kazemi M, Gumpert TG, Marks MI: A controlled trial comparing sulfamethoxazole–trimethoprim, ampicillin and no therapy in the treatment of *Salmonella* gastroenteritis in children. J Pediatr 83:646–650, 1973

21. Nelson JD, Kusmiesz H, Jackson LH, et al: Treatment of *Salmonella* gastroenteritis with ampicillin, amoxicillin or placebo. Pediatrics 65:1125–1130, 1980

22. Pitkänen T, Pettersson T, Pönkä A, et al: Effect of erythromycin on the fecal excretion of *Campylobacter fetus* subspecies jejuni. J Infect Dis 145:128, 1982

23. Anders BJ, Lauer BA, Paisley JW, et al: Double-blind placebo controlled trial of erythromycin for treatment of campylobacter enteritis. Lancet 1:131–132, 1982

24. Patamasucon P, Kaojarern S, Kusmiesz H, et al: Pharmacokinetics of erythromycin ethylsuccinate and estolate in infants under 4 months of age. Antimicrob Agents Chemother 19:736–739, 1981

25. Murphy AM, Albrey MB, Crewe EB: Rotavirus infections of neonates. Lancet 2:1149–1150, 1977

26. Cameron DJS, Bishop RF, Veenstra AA, et al: Noncultivable viruses and neonatal diarrhea: Fifteen-month survey in a newborn special care nursery. J Clin Microbiol 8:93–98, 1978

27. Rodriguez WJ, Kim HW, Brandt CD, et al: Rotavirus: A cause of nosocomial infection in the nursery. J Pediatr 101:274–277, 1982

28. Soenarto Y, Sebodo T, Ridho R, et al: Acute diarrhea and rotavirus infection in newborn babies and children in Yogyakarta, Indonesia, from June 1978 to June 1979. J Clin Microbiol 14:123–129, 1981

29. Chrystie IL, Totterdell BM, Banatvala JE: Asymptomatic endemic rotavirus infections in the newborn. Lancet 1:1176–1178, 1978

30. Bishop RF, Cameron DJS, Veenstra AA, et al: Diarrhea and rotavirus infection associated with differing regimens for postnatal care of newborn babies. J Clin Microbiol 9:525–529, 1979

31. Vaucher YE, Ray CG, Minnich LL, et al: Pleomorphic, enveloped, virus-like particles associated with gastrointestinal illness in neonates. J Infect Dis 145:27–36, 1982

32. Barnes GL, Doyle LW, Hewson PH, et al: A randomized trial of oral gammaglobulin in low-birth-weight infants infected with rotavirus. Lancet

1:1371–1373, 1982

33. Mizrahi A, Barlow O, Berdon W, et al: Necrotizing enterocolitis in premature infants. J Pediatr 66:697–706, 1965

34. Santulli TV: Acute necrotizing enterocolitis: Recognition and management. Hosp Pract 11:129–135, 1974

35. Engel RR: Studies of the gastrointestinal flora in necrotizing enterocolitis. Report of the sixty-eighth Ross Conference on Pediatric Research: Necrotizing Enterocolitis in the Newborn Infant. Ross Laboratories, Columbus, Ohio, 1975, pp 65–70

36. Chany C, Moscovici O, Lebon P, et al: Association of coronavirus infection with neonatal necrotizing enterocolitis. Pediatrics 69:209–214, 1982

37. Howard FM, Flynn DM, Bradley JM, et al: Outbreak of necrotizing enterocolitis caused by *Clostridium butyricum*. Lancet 2:1099–1102, 1977

38. Sturm R, Staneck JL, Stauffer LR, et al. Neonatal necrotizing enterocolitis associated with penicillin-resistant, toxigenic *Clostridium butyricum*. Pediatrics 66:928–931, 1980

39. Kliegman RM, Fanaroff AA, Izant R, et al. Clostridia as pathogens in neonatal necrotizing enterocolitis. J Pediatr 95:287–289, 1979

40. Sherertz RJ, Sarubbi FA: The prevalence of *Clostridium difficile* and toxin in a nursery population: A comparison between patients with necrotizing enterocolitis and an asymptomatic group. J Pediatr 100:435–439, 1982

41. Stark PL, Lee A: Clostridia isolated from the feces of infants during the first year of life. J Pediatr 100:362–365, 1982

42. Donta ST, Myers MG: *Clostridium difficile* toxin in asymptomatic neonates. J Pediatr 100:431–434, 1982

43. Nelson JD: The role of oral and parenteral antibiotics in necrotizing enterocolitis. Report of the sixty-eighth Ross Conference on Pediatric Research: Necrotizing Enterocolitis in the Newborn Infant. Ross Laboratories, Columbus, Ohio, 1975, pp 80–85

44. Martin LW: Neonatal necrotizing enterocolitis: Surgical considerations. Report of the Sixty-eight Ross Conference on Pediatric Research: Necrotizing Enterocolitis in the Newborn Infant. Ross Laboratories, Columbus, Ohio, 1975, pp 90–94

45. Hansen TN, Ritter DA, Speer ME, et al: A randomized, controlled study of oral gentamicin in the treatment of neonatal necrotizing enterocolitis. J Pediatr 97:836–839, 1980

46. Mata LJ, Urrutia JJ: Intestinal colonization of breast-fed children in a rural area of low socioeconomic level. Ann NY Acad Sci 176:93–109, 1971

47. Bell MJ, Ternberg JL, Bower RJ: The microbial flora and antimicrobial therapy of neonatal peritonitis. J Pediatr Surg 15:569–573, 1980

48. Fonkalsrud EW, Ellis DG, Clatworthy HW Jr: Neonatal peritonitis. J Pediatr Surg 1:227–239, 1966

49. Parsons JM, Miscal BG, McSherry CK: Appendicitis in the newborn infant. Surgery 67:841–843, 1970

50. Fowler R: Primary peritonitis: Changing aspects 1956–1970. Aust Paediatr J 7:73–83, 1971

51. Blumberg L: Primary peritonitis. S Afr Med J 36:638–641, 1962

52. Nelson JD, Dillon HC Jr, Howard JB: A prolonged nursery epidemic associated with a newly recognized type of group A streptococcus. J Pediatr 89:792–796, 1976

53. Enberg RN, Cox RH, Burry VF: Perirectal abscess in children. Am J Dis Child 128:360–361, 1974

54. Krieger RW, Chusid MJ: Perirectal abscess in childhood: A review of 29 cases. Am J Dis Child 133:411–412, 1979

55. Arminski TC, McLean DW: Proctologic problems in children. JAMA 194:1195–1197, 1965

56. Parker RGF: Jaundice and infantile diarrhea. Arch Dis Child 33:330–334, 1958

57. Dehner LP, Kissane JM: Pyogenic hepatic abscesses in infancy and childhood. J Pediatr 74:763–773, 1969

58. Chusid MJ: Pyogenic hepatic abscess in infancy and childhood. Pediatrics 62:554–559, 1978

59. Moss TJ, Pysher TJ: Hepatic abscess in neonates. Am J Dis Child 135:726–728, 1981

60. Madsen CM, Secouris N: Solitary liver abscess in a newborn. Surgery 47:1005–1009, 1960

61. Haffar A, Boland FJ, Edwards MS: Amebic liver abscess in children. Pediatr Infect Dis 1:322–327, 1982

62. Wyllie R, Fitzgerald JF: Bacterial cholangitis in a 10-week-old infant with fever of undetermined origin. Pediatrics 65:164–167, 1980

63. Arnon SS, Midura TF, Clay SA, et al: Infant botulism: Epidemiological, clinical and laboratory aspects. JAMA 237:1946–1951, 1977

64. Wilson R, Morris JG, Snyder JD, et al: Clinical characteristics of infant botulism in the United States: A study of the non-California cases. Pediatr Infect Dis 1:148–150, 1982

65. Arnon SS, Midura TF, Damus K, et al: Intestinal infection and toxin production by *Clostridium botulinum* as one cause of sudden infant death syndrome. Lancet 1:1273–1277, 1978

66. Arnon SS, Midura TF, Damus K, et al: Honey and other environmental risk factors for infant botulism. J Pediatr 94:331–336, 1979

67. Arnon SS, Damus K, Thompson B, et al: Protective role of human milk against sudden death from infant bolutism. J Pediatr 100:568–573, 1982

13

Genitourinary Infections

URINARY TRACT INFECTIONS

Incidence

Urinary tract infections occur in approximately 1 percent of full term neonates and in 2.4–3.5 percent of premature infants.[1-3] The clinical symptoms of urinary tract infection in infants are nonspecific.[1,4] The neonate may appear septic or may have decreased activity, feeding problems, and the other constitutional signs that can be seen with infections of other organ systems. In a study of 100 young infants with urinary tract infections, 63 percent had fever (more than half had temperatures over 39°C), 55 percent were irritable, 38 percent refused one or more feedings, and approximately one-third had vomiting or diarrhea.[4] Male infants accounted for 75 percent of patients in the first 3 months of life compared with 11 percent of patients who were 3–8 months old. Of 41 infants who were less than 30 days of age, 33 (81 percent) were males. Physical examination usually reveals few or no abnormalities other than fever. We noted abdominal distension and jaundice in 8 percent and 7 percent of patients, respectively.[4] Occasionally, enlarged kidneys can be palpated in an infant with bilateral vesicoureteral reflux and hydronephrosis.

Diagnosis

Collection of a urine specimen for microscopic examination and culture is indicated as part of the routine examination in all babies thought to have infection. It is difficult to get a satisfactory specimen by bag, and catheter specimens are easily contaminated, especially in uncircumcised males. In most situations it is preferable to perform percutaneous needle aspiration of the urinary bladder.[5-6] This should not be done in infants who are dehydrated or who have a bleeding problem. Minor, transient hematuria is uncommon, and serious problems from hemorrhage[7] or perforation of the colon[8] have been exceedingly rare. (If the colon is inadvertently punctured, there are usually no untoward consequences except that the urine specimen is contaminated.) Many hundreds of suprapubic bladder punctures have been performed in newborns at our hospital over the past decade with only one potentially serious complication. A baby with respiratory distress syndrome, who did not have a bleeding or clotting disorder, had gross hematuria after needle aspiration of the urinary bladder. Roentgenographic studies demonstrated a large clot in the bladder measuring 2 × 3 cm. The clot lysed spontaneously, and the infant passed fragments of it over several days, so that surgical intervention was not necessary.

If an infant is not acutely ill and immediate antimicrobial therapy is not needed, one can obtain a "clean-catch" bag specimen of urine for culture. If the specimen has bacterial growth, the finding should be confirmed or refuted by suprapubic bladder aspiration. In most circumstances, however, one does not have time for such a leisurely approach to diagnosis, so the initial urine should be the best possible specimen for culture.

Although pyuria commonly accompanies significant bacteria, results of urinalysis can be falsely positive or falsely negative.[9-10] We found pyuria (greater than or equal to 10 WBC/HPF) in 70 percent of urine specimens from infants with documented infection.[4] Direct microscopic examination of uncentrifuged fresh urine for bacteria is useful. If bacteria are seen, there are generally greater than 10^5 colony-forming units CFU/ml. In our experience, approximately 85 percent of infants with documented infection have bacteria seen on direct examination of the urine.

The quantitative urine culture will most often contain more than 50,000 colonies/ml, but occasionally one finds a small number of organisms.[3] Any number of bacteria in a urine specimen obtained by percutaneous needle puncture of the bladder should be considered significant. If several bacterial species are present in the culture growth, it is likely that the specimen has been contaminated by inadvertent bowel puncture.

Etiology

The spectrum of bacteria that cause urinary tract infections in neonates is similar to that encountered in older infants,[3-4,6,11] namely coliform bacteria and, rarely, gram-positive cocci. Of 100 infants managed in our center, 88 percent had *E. coli* as the pathogen.[4] Other organisms encountered were nonenterococcal group D streptococci, enterococci, *S. aureus,* and *Enterobacter cloacae.* Group B streptococci,[12] *Citrobacter diverus,*[13] and other microorganisms have also been implicated. Because coliform bacteria are likely to be hospital-acquired, particularly when they are recovered from infants in intensive care units, many will be resistant to the sulfonamides and some to the aminoglycosides as well.

Evaluation

Blood cultures should be obtained before initiation of therapy. Of 91 infants who had blood cultures drawn in our study, 20 (21.9 percent) had bacteremia with *E. coli,* the same organism recovered from urine cultures of each of these infants.[4] The rate of positive blood cultures was inversely correlated with age: 31 percent in the 1st month, 21 percent in the 2nd month, 14 percent in the 3rd month, and 6 percent in the 3rd through 8th month of age. Cerebrospinal fluid (CSF) examination should be performed if the infant appears septic. In our series cultures of all 88 CSF specimens obtained were sterile.[4]

In cases of bacteremia and urinary infection, it is uncertain how often bacteremia is the primary event and seeding of the kidney or bladder is a secondary event or vice versa. The follow-up studies of Bergström et al.[9] suggest that the former situation is likely if the illness occurs in the first 10 days of life, since such patients are unlikely to have recurrences, and the laboratory evaluation generally fails to demonstrate an anatomic or functional abnormality of the urinary tract. The likelihood of obstructive uropathy is greater if the first infection occurs after age 10 days. We feel nevertheless, that radiographic studies are indicated in all neonates with urinary tract infection.

The roentgenographic examinations are an intravenous pyelogram and voiding cystourethrogram. It is advisable to perform the pyelogram during hospitalization, particularly in the infant with suspected upper tract involvement. Sonography is a useful initial tool to evaluate size and integrity of the kidneys and ureters. In our experience, 20 percent of infants have roentgenographic abnormalities, including vesicoureteral reflux, hydronephrosis, duplication of the collecting systems, and uteropelvic obstruction.[4] Maherzi and associates[14] found radiographic abnormalities in 44 percent of symptomatic infants who were in the neonatal intensive care unit.

Therapy

Therapy is initiated with an aminoglycoside and ampicillin to provide broad antimicrobial coverage. Until the results of blood cultures are known, dosages suitable for sepsis are used. If the blood cultures are sterile, the usual dosage for sepsis can be reduced by half because these antibiotics are concentrated in urine. Repeat urine cultures show eradication of bacteriuria within 24–48 hours of initiation of appropriate therapy. Delayed sterilization may be caused by resistance of the pathogen to the drugs given, inappropriately low doses, or obstruction of the urinary system with abscess formation. In uncomplicated cases treatment is continued 10 days, the last 3–5 days of which may be with drugs like amoxicillin or cephalexin given orally. A sulfonamide is inappropriate for the young infant because of displacement of bilirubin from albumin in the jaundiced patient and possible hepatic toxicity.

All neonates and young infants should be followed for many years for recurrence of infection that occurs in approximately 30–35 percent of patients.

Renal abscess is rare. It occurred in only 1 of 80 patients with urinary tract infection in the series of Bergström et al.[11] In patients with disseminated staphylococcal infection, multiple renal abscesses occur, but this syndrome is exceedingly rare in neonates. Perinephric abscess is an extreme rarity; it would require surgical drainage as well as antimicrobial therapy.

VAGINITIS

From the influence of transplacental maternal hormones, bloody or mucoid vaginal discharge is common during the first week or two of life. If the discharge persists, *Trichomonas vaginalis* infection should be suspected. Maternal hormones provide the proper milieu for supporting this parasite: low pH, abundant glycogen, and a thick epithelium. The discharge is whitish and mucoid.

A swab specimen of vaginal discharge is placed in approximately 0.5 ml of normal saline solution and examined immediately or kept in a water bath at 37°C. A drop of the specimen is placed on a slide under a cover slip for microscopic examination. A Giemsa stain can be done to study the morphology of the trichomonads. In heavy infections the distinctive parasites can be readily seen by direct examination. In lighter infections it may be necessary to culture the specimen on Diamond's medium (available from Eaton Laboratories) for 2–3 days. A wet-mount preparation is then made from the culture medium.

Trichmonas infection of newborn females is probably more common than generally realized. It was first reported by Trussel et al.[15] in 1942 and reviewed recently by Al-Salihi, Curran, and Wang.[16] We have seen several cases in premature infants. The symptoms are generally ignored for some time because of the frequency of "normal" vaginal discharge in the newborn. Sometimes the diagnosis is stumbled on by an alert technician who sees the flagellates during microscopic examination of the urine. Although *T. vaginalis* has been reported to cause urinary tract infection in the newborn[17] it is likely that the urine specimen was contaminated by vaginal secretions. In 1 case reported by Al-Salihi, Curran, and Wang,[16] many trichomonads were present in voided urine, but none were found in urine obtained by suprapubic needle aspiration of the bladder. We had a similar experience in 1 case.

Treatment with metronidazole results in rapid cure.[18] The dosage is approximately 15 mg/kg/day given orally in 3 divided doses. Treatment is continued for 5–10 days. Although there have been warnings regarding unnecessary use of metronidazole because of its carcinogenic potential in rats and its mutagenic effect on bacteria, there is no suitable alternative treatment for trichomoniasis in the newborn.

Candida vaginitis or vulvitis occurs occasionally. Treatment is with topical 1-percent aqueous genitian violet, or nystatin cream or ointment. Such infants usually have oral thrush as well, which is treated with oral nystatin suspension.

Bacterial vaginitis is extremely rare in the neonate. Stark and Glode[19] described a 25-day-old infant with gonococcal vaginitis. They speculated that silver nitrate eye prophylaxis prevented neonatal ophthalmia but did not alter mucosal colonization with *Neisseria gonorrhoeae* that the baby obtained at delivery from the mother, who had a positive cervical culture. Vaginitis developed at the approximate time of estrogen withdrawal; estrogen protects the vaginal mucosa from gonococcal infection.

FOURNIER'S SYNDROME

Fournier's syndrome is a malignant gangrenous infection of the scrotum, penis, and perineum. It can rarely occur in newborn infants, as described by Sussman and coworkers.[20] They reported 2 neonates, one 9 days old and one 3 weeks old, with gangrenous ulcerations of the scrotum with extension to the penis and perineum in one patient and to the thigh in the other. *E. coli* was cultured from the lesions. Debridement and aminoglycoside therapy was successful, and regeneration of affected areas was rapid.

For dosages see Chapter 2 or Abbreviated Guide to Dosage on Inside Covers

REFERENCES

1. Littlewood JM: Sixty-six infants with urinary tract infection in the first month of life. Arch Dis Child 47:218–222, 1972
2. Edelmann CM, Jr, Ogwo JE, Fine BP, et al: The prevalence of bacteriuria in full-term and premature newborn infants. J Pediatr 82:125–132, 1973
3. Hellerstein S: Recurrent urinary tract infections in children. Pediatr Infect Dis 1:271–281, 1982
4. Ginsburg CM, McCracken GH: Urinary tract infections in young infants. Pediatrics 69:409–412, 1982
5. Nelson JD, Peters PC: Suprapubic aspiration of urine in premature and term infants. Pediatrics 36:132–134, 1965
6. Saccharow L, Pryles CV: Further experience with the use of percutaneous suprapubic aspiration of the urinary bladder: Bacteriologic studies in 654 infants and children. Pediatrics 43:1018–1024, 1969
7. Lanier B, Daeschner CW: Serious complication of suprapubic aspiration of the urinary bladder. (letter) J Pediatr 79:711, 1971
8. Weathers WT, Wenzl JE: Suprapubic aspiration of the bladder: Perforation of a viscus other than the bladder. Am J Dis Child 117:590–592, 1969
9. Aronson AS, Svenningsen NW: Screening for urinary tract infection in newborn infants. (letter) J Pediatr 83:508, 1973
10. Edelmann CM Jr: (reply to letter) J Pediatr 83:509–510, 1973
11. Bergström T, Larson H, Lincoln K, et al: Studies of urinary tract infection in infancy and childhood. XII. Eighty consecutive patients with neonatal infection. J Pediatr 80:848–866, 1972
12. St-Laurent-Gagnon T, Weber ML: Urinary tract streptococcus group B infection in a 6-week-old infant. JAMA 240:1269, 1978
13. Barton LL, Walentik C: *Citrobacter diversus* urinary tract infection. Am J Dis Child 136:467–468, 1982
14. Maherzi M, Gugnard J-P, Torrado A: Urinary tract infection in high-risk newborn infants. Pediatrics 62:521–523, 1978
15. Trussel RE, Wilson ME, Longwell FH, et al: Vaginal trichomoniasis, complement fixation, puerperal morbidity and early infection of newborn infants. Am J Obstet Gynecol 44:292–296, 1942
16. Al-Salihi FL, Curran JP, Wang J-S: Neonatal *Trichomonas vaginalis:* Report of three cases and review of the literature. Pediatrics 53:196–200, 1974
17. Littlewood JM, Kohler MG: Urinary tract infection by *Trichomonas vaginalis* in a newborn baby. Arch Dis Child 41:693–695, 1966
18. Crowther IA: *Trichomonas* vaginitis in infancy. Lancet 1:1074–1075, 1962
19. Stark AR, Glode MP: Gonococcal vaginitis in a neonate. J Pediatr 94:298–299, 1979
20. Sussman SJ, Schiller RP, Shashikumar VL: Fournier's syndrome. Am J Dis Child 132:1189–1190, 1978

14

Disseminated Fungal Infections

CANDIDIASIS

All fungal infections with the exception of candidiasis are rare in neonates. Premature infants, infants undergoing parenteral alimentation therapy, those who have received broad-spectrum antibiotics, and immunocompromised neonates are at risk for hematogenous dissemination of *Candida albicans* from superficial colonization sites. (see Chap. 15).[1-13] Fungemia can lead to localized disease in virtually any organ of the body. Meningitis,[9-12] arthritis,[2,6,8-9] osteomyelitis,[2,5] endophthalmitis,[3,13] and pneumonia[1,4,11] are common. Fungus balls in the urine can cause acute urinary tract obstruction[7] that may necessitate surgical intervention.

Standard antimicrobial therapy for disseminated fungus infection is with amphotericin B, but there are no pharmacokinetic data in newborns and very little information on its use in infants and children.[10,12-14] In most reports of its use in infants, the standard adult dosages have been employed. Customarily the initial dose is 0.25 mg/kg. Daily doses are increased by 0.25 mg/kg increments every other day until the maximum daily dose of 0.75–1mg/kg is reached. Each dose is diluted in 5-percent dextrose solution (saline solution should not be used) and infused intravenously over a 4–6 hour period. The bottle and tubing should be protected against light by wrapping them in aluminum foil. After satisfactory response the drug dose intervals may be increased to every other day. A total dose of 30–35 mg/kg is usually given over a 4–6 week period.

It would seem appropriate to use smaller daily doses in neonates because of delayed excretion of the drug, but in the absence of sufficient data or experience with them it is not possible to make such a recommendation. It has also been argued that the dosage of amphotericin B should be tailored to fit the *in vitro* susceptibility of the organism being treated,[14] but most laboratories cannot perform reliable and reproducible susceptibility testing. Amphotericin B has been administered intrathecally for fungal meningitis. When a dose of 0.3 mg is injected intrathecally into an adult, fungistatic concentrations are achieved, but arachnoiditis results unless the dose is infused slowly over a 1-hour period.[15] The appropriate intrathecal or intraventricular dosage for neonates is unknown.

The patient being treated with amphotericin B should be carefully monitored for evidence of renal or hematologic toxicity.

Flucytosine (formerly 5-fluorocytosine) has been used to treat systemic candidiasis. Some *Candida* strains are resistant to this drug, so *in vitro* susceptibility testing should be done. There is also a propensity for resistant strains to emerge during therapy with flucytosine. Hill et al.[4] successfully treated a premature infant with disseminated candidiasis. They initially gave 100 mg/kg/day orally in 4 divided doses. Two hours after a 25-mg/kg/dose, the serum concentration was 40 µg/ml. This decreased to 27 µg/ml at 4 and 6 hours. The cerebrospinal fluid (CSF) concentration 6 hours after a dose was 40 µg/ml. Flucytosine is one of the rare drugs that diffuses well into CSF and gives roughly equivalent serum and CSF concentrations.[16]

There is *in vitro* synergism between amphotericin B and flucytosine against *Candida* species.[17] It is possible that combined drug therapy may be beneficial *in vivo* as well, and Lilien et al.[12] have successfully treated *Candida meningitis* with the combination.

There is no reported experience with miconazole in the neonate, and ketoconazole therapy is not feasible, since a parenteral formulation is not available at this time.

In summary, our knowledge about systemic antifungal drugs in neonates is abysmally meager, and it is difficult to make valid recommendations for their use.

OTHER DISSEMINATED FUNGAL DISEASES

Aspergillosis. Aspergillosis has been reported in 3 neonates,[18-20] with onsets of illness at 2, 13, and 14 days of age. Prematurity and antibiotic therapy may have been predisposing factors. All were autopsy diagnoses. Multiple organs were infected, principally the lungs, heart, liver, and spleen. Therapy for aspergillosis is amphotericin B.

Coccidioioidomycosis. In spite of the prevalence of coccidioidomycosis in certain geographic areas, infection in the neonatal period is rare.[21-25] Until 1981, no case of maternal–fetal transmission had been reported. Bernstein et al.[26] presented strong circumstantial evidence that disease that developed at 6 days of age was acquired from the mother's genital tract. The disease usually becomes disseminated in neonates and is fatal. Amphotericin B, miconazole, and ketaconozole—alone or in combinations—have been successfully used to treat coccidioidomycosis in older infants and children.

Cryptococcosis. Only 6 cases of neonatal cryptococcosis have been reported, and all were fatal.[27-30] The route of infection is not clear, but *in utero* transmission was possible in 1 infant who was symptomatic at birth. *Cryptococcus neoformans* has been identified in brain, liver, spleen, eyes, and skin of affected newborns. In older patients, combination therapy with amphotericin B and flucytosine is used, but there is no reported experience with therapy in neonates.

Histoplasmosis. Although histoplasmosis of infancy is common in endemic areas and has been seen in babies as young as 2 months of age,[31 32] we are not aware of its occurrence in neonates.

Malasseziosis. *Malessezia furfur (Pityrosporum orbiculare)* is a dermatophyte of low pathogenicity. A case of pulmonary vasculitis was reported[33] in an infant who weighed 740 g at birth. Because of progressive pulmonary deterioration, a lung biopsy was performed when the baby was 1 month of age. The specimen demonstrated vasculitis, and the organism was isolated by culture. The infant died in spite of amphotericin B and flucytosine therapy.

Nocardiosis. *Nocardia asteroides* is not a fungus, but the clinical expressions of nocardiosis are similar to those of deep fungal infection. Nocardiosis in a 28-day-old infant was reported in 1904.[34] We are not aware of its occurrence in neonates since that time. If it were encountered, sulfonamides remain the drugs of choice, but aminoglycosides are also effective.[35] In the murine experimental model of nocardiosis, amikacin is more effective than sulfadiazine.[36]

Phycomycosis. Phycomycosis (formerly mucormycosis) is deep tissue infection due to species of *Mucor, Rhizopus,* or *Absidia.* Only a few cases have been reported in neonates,[37-41] and in most the infection originated in the gastrointestinal tract. Prematurity and antibiotic therapy were thought to be predisposing factors. Necrosis due to these invasive organisms is prominent, and as a result peritonitis ensues from gut perforation. One infant had isolated central nervous system infection.[40] Therapy with amphotericin B is sometimes supplemented with griseofulvin, nystatin, or iodides. All reported neonatal cases were autopsy diagnoses, so there is no experience with treating the disease in newborns.

> For dosages see Chapter 2 or Abbreviated Guide to Dosage on Inside Covers

REFERENCES

1. Gherardi J: Systemic moniliasis in infancy. JAMA 193:67–69, 1965
2. Adler S, Randall J, Plotkin SA: *Candida* osteomyelitis and arthritis in a neonate. Am J Dis Child 123:595–596, 1972
3. Meyers BR, Lieberman TW, Ferry AP: *Candida* endophthalmitis complicating candidemia. Ann Intern Med 79:647–653, 1973
4. Hill HR, Mitchell TG, Matsen JM, et al: Recovery from disseminated candidiasis in a premature neonate. Pediatrics 53:748–752, 1974
5. Freeman JB, Wlenke JW, Saper RT: *Candida* osteomyelitis associated with intravenous alimentation. J Pediatr Surg 9:783–784, 1974
6. Pittard WB, Thullen JD, Faranoff AA: Neonatal septic arthritis. J Pediatr 88:621–624, 1976
7. Hill JT: Candidiasis of the urinary tract. Proc R Soc Med 67:1155–1156, 1974
8. Yousefzadeh DK, Jackson JH: Neonatal and infantile candidal arthritis with or without osteomyelitis: A clinical and radiographical review of 21 cases. Skeletal Radiol 5:77–90, 1980
9. Klein JD, Yamauchi T, Horlick SP: Neonatal candidiasis, meningitis and arthritis: Observations and a review of the literature. J Pediatr 81:31–34, 1972
10. Kozinn PJ, Taschdjian CL, Pishvazadeh P, et al: *Candida* meningitis successfully treated with amphotericin B. New Engl J Med 268:881–884, 1963
11. Bayer AS, Edwards JE Jr, Seidel JS, et al: *Candida* meningitis: Report of seven cases and review of the English literature. Medicine 55:477–486, 1976
12. Lilien LD, Ramamurthy RS, Pildes RS: *Candida albicans* meningitis in a premature neonate successfully treated with 5-fluorocytosine and amphotericin B: A case report and review of the literature. Pediatrics 61:57–61, 1978
13. Stern GA, Fetkenhour CL, O'Grady RB: Intravitreal amphotericin B treatment of *Candida* endophthalmitis. Arch Ophthalmol 95:89–93, 1977
14. Cherry JD, Lloyd CA, Quilty JF, et al: Amphotericin B therapy in children: A review of the literature and a case report. J Pediatr 75:1063–1069, 1969
15. Atkinson AJ Jr, Binschadler DD: Pharmacokinetics of intrathecally administered amphotericin B. Am Rev Respir Dis 99:917–924, 1969
16. Shadomy S: *In vitro* studies with 5-fluorocytosine. Appl Microbiol 17:871–877, 1969
17. Montgomerie JZ, Edward JE Jr, Guze LB: Synergism of amphotericin B and 5-fluorocytosine for *Candida* species. J Infect Dis 132:82–86, 1975
18. Zimmerman LE: Fatal fungus infections complicating other diseases. Am J

Clin Pathol 25:46–65, 1955

19. Allan GW, Andersen DH: Generalized aspergillosis in an infant 18 days of age. Pediatrics 26:432–440, 1960

20. Akkoyunlu A, Yücell FA: Aspergillose bronchopulmonaire et encephalomeningei chez un nouveau-ne de 20 jours. Arch Fr Pediatr 14:615, 1957

21. Cohen R: Coccidiodomycosis: Case report in children. Arch Pediatr 66:241–265, 1949

22. Hyatt HW: Coccidiodomycosis in a three week old infant. Am J Dis Child 105:93–98, 1963

23. Townsend TE, McKey RW: Coccidioidomycosis in infants. A.M.A. J Dis Child 86:51–53, 1953

24. Christian JR, Sarre SG, Peers JH, et al: Pulmonary coccidioidomycosis in a 21 day old infant. A.M.A. J Dis Child 92:66–74, 1956

25. Shafai T: Neonatal coccidoidomycosis in premature twins. Am J Dis Child 132:634, 1978

26. Bernstein DL, Tipton JR, Schott SF, et al: Coccidioidomycosis in a neonate: Maternal–infant transmission. J Pediatr 99:752–754, 1981

27. Oliverio-Campos J: Congenital meningoencephalitis due to torulosis neoformans. Preliminary report. Bol Clin Hopit Civis (Lisbon) 18:609, 1954

28. Neuhauser EBD, Tucker A: The roentgen changes produced by diffuse torulosis in the newborn. Am J Roentgenol 59:805–815, 1948

29. Nassau E, Weinberg-Heiruti C: Torulosis of the newborn. Harefuah 35:50, 1948

30. Heath P: Massive separation of retina in full-term infants and juveniles. JAMA 144:1148–1154, 1950

31. Holland P, Holland NH: Histoplasmosis in early infancy. Am J Dis Child 112:412–421, 1966

32. Nelson JD, Bates R, Pitchford A: Histoplasma meningitis: Recovery following amphotericin B therapy. Am J Dis Child 102:218–223, 1961

33. Redline RW, Dahms BB: Malassezia pulmonary vasculitis in an infant on long-term intralipid therapy. New Engl J Med 305:1395–1398, 1981

34. Idriss ZH, Cunningham RJ, Wiltert CM: Nocardiosis in children: Report of three cases and review of the literature. Pediatrics 55:479–484, 1975

35. Yogev R, Greenslade T, Firlit CF, et al: Successful treatment of Nocardia asteroides infection with amikacin. J Pediatr 96:771–773, 1980

36. Wallace RJ, Septimus EJ, Musher DM, et al: Treatment of experimental nocardiosis in mice: Comparison of amikacin and sulfonamide. J Infect Dis 140:244–248, 1979

37. Levin SF, Isaacson C: Spontaneous perforation of the colon in the newborn. Arch Dis Child 35:378–382, 1960

38. Gatling RR: Gastric mucormycosis in a newborn infant. Arch Pathol 67:249–255, 1959

39. Neame P, Rayner D: Mucormycosis. Arch Pathol 70:261–268, 1960

40. Jackson JR, Karnauchow PN: Mucormycosis of the central nervous system. Can Med Assoc J 76:130–133, 1957

41. Isaacson C, Levin SF: Gastrointestinal mucormycosis in infancy. S Afr Med J 35:581–584, 1961

15

Nosocomial Infections

In this chapter the word *colonization* is used to denote superficial residence of microoganisms on skin or mucous membranes; *disease* indicates tissue invasion and signs of illness; and *infection* in a general term expressing a relation between a parasite and host and carries a connotation of communicability. The word *nosocomial* in its literal sense means "of or related to a hospital," but by common usage it has come to mean "hospital-acquired," so that a nosocomial infection is an infection acquired in a hospital.

INCIDENCE

The 79 hospitals in 31 states that comprise the National Nosocomial Infections Study Group of the Centers for Disease Control reported a nosocomial infection rate in newborn nurseries of 1.4 percent.[1] The rates varied from a low of 0.6 percent in community hospitals to a high of 2.7 percent in university hospitals, and infections in neonates accounted for 4.2 percent of all nosocomial infections. Nosocomial infection rates as high as 25 percent have been reported from neonatal intensive care units (NNICU),[2] and infection rates are significantly greater in babies with birthweights less than 1500 g. In epidemic situations virtually all infants in an NNICU can become colonized with an antibiotic-resistant coliform or

198

staphylococcal organism. Overcrowding and understaffing are significantly associated with outbreaks of illness.[3]

MICROORGANISMS

Bacteria, viruses, fungi, and parasites can cause nosocomial infections in nurseries. The greatest attention has focused on bacterial infections because of their numerical predominance and because the organisms are easy to cultivate and identify. Respiratory and enteric viruses may well be more prominent than the periodical literature suggests.

The bacteria of greatest importance vary from time to time in an individual nursery, from decade to decade nationwide in the United States, and from country to country. By and large these shifts in etiologic agents have defied explanation. The national problem with phage group 80/81 *Staphylococcus aureus* that began in the 1950s disappeared in the 1960s independent of many unsuccessful attempts at control. Coliform bacilli and group B streptococci were the principal etiologic bacteria in the 1970s, but phage group II staphylococci causing superficial cutaneous infections were major problems in some nurseries. The reasons underlying the importance of group B streptococci as pathogens in the United States and their lesser frequency in most of the rest of the world remain unexplained. Group B streptococci are most often vertically transmitted from mother to infant, but nosocomial spread has been a serious problem in some nurseries.[4-6]

Generalizations can be made about the proclivities of certain organisms to cause certain types of diseases. *S. aureus* is likely to cause pneumonia and infections of skin or surgical wounds. Bacteremia and meningitis are typical of aerobic and anaerobic gram-negative enteric bacilli. Viruses cause respiratory, enteric, or central nervous system infection. *Candida* species cause superficial skin and mucous membrane infection or, rarely, disseminated sepsis with endocarditis or endarteritis. *Pseudomonas aeruginosa* causes conjunctivitus, pneumonia, sepsis with ecthymatous skin lesions, and occasionally noma neonatorum.[7]

Nosocomial diarrheal outbreaks in nurseries due to toxigenic coliform bacilli,[8] enteropathogenic *Escherichia coli*,[9-11] *shigellae*,[11] *salmonellae*,[13] enterococci,[14] and rotaviruses[15] have been reported.

Group A streptococci, unlike group B streptococci, have a high disease-to-colonization ratio and occur in epidemic form in nurseries.[16-21] In preantibiotic times gonococci[22] were important nosocomial pathogens.

The list of microorganisms involved in nosocomial infections encompasses virtually all human pathogens and commensal organisms.

MODES OF TRANSMISSION

Neonates can develop infection endogenously from invasion of acquired flora of the skin, respiratory tract, and gut, or from exogenously acquired microorganisms.

Among 23 reported outbreaks[22-44] of gram-negative infection, resuscitation equipment was responsible for transmission of *P. aeruginosa* infection in 3 outbreaks, and nonfermenters contaminated eyewash solution in 2 outbreaks. In all other outbreaks of bacillary infections, hands of nursery personnel were the proved or suspected mode of transmission.

Because disposable equipment and gas sterilization are readily available in modern nurseries, outbreaks of disease from contaminated equipment are rare events, but in isolated cases they remain a potential hazard for infection that demands constant attention to aseptic technique. Intravenous fluids may become contaminated in preparation or by means of defective seals. Homemade intravenous fluids for total parenteral alimentation are especially hazardous. Faucet aerators, table and sink surfaces, and humidification equipment may serve as fomites for spread of infection, particularly with *Pseudomonas* organisms and other "water bugs."

Respiratory syncytial virus[45] and echovirus 11[46] pulmonary infections are spread in nurseries by droplet inhalation and by touching and cuddling babies, with resultant hand contamination by infected secretions.[47] Coxsackievirus infection[48-50] is spread by the fecal–oral route, presumably by hands of personnel. The mode of transmission of rotavirus infection in neonates is not clear but may involve fecal–oral and respiratory routes as well as vertical transmission.[51-53]

Disseminated disease due to *Candida* organisms may arise endogenously or from contaminated intravenous lines. An unusual mode of infection was *Rhizopus* contamination of elastic surgical bandages, with resultant wound infection.[54]

Acquisition of Flora, and Antibiotic Pressure

In the absence of intrauterine infection, the newborn infant's first exposure to microorganisms is to those of the maternal cervix and vagina. The microflora of the maternal cervix during labor consists in 75 percent of mothers of a mixture of aerobes and anaerobes, and in 25 percent of only aerobes.[55] Aerobic bacteria are chiefly *Staphylococcus epidermidis,* diphtheroids, and *Gardnerella (Haemophilus) vaginalis,* and, although *Bacteroides* species are found, *Bacteroides fragilis* is rare.[55-56]

In the 1950s *S. aureus* colonization of the umbilicus,[57] skin, and nares developed rapidly in most babies; more recently, however, *S. aureus* colonization has been uncommon except at times of outbreaks. Evans and coworkers[58] cultured nares and umbilical stumps sequentially during the first week of life and found fewer than 10 percent of babies colonized with *S. aureus*. *S. epidermidis* and nonhemolytic streptococci were found in the nares, and the same bacterial species plus *Klebsiella-Enterobacter* species on the umbilicus. *E. coli* colonization has been shown to increase during summer months, and increased humidity has been associated with both *E. coli* and *Pseudomonas* colonization.[59]

Anaerobic fecal flora develop rapidly during the first days of life.[60-61] By 1 week of age the frequency of colonization with *B. fragilis* and other anaerobes in vaginally delivered, formula-fed infants is comparable to that in adults.[60] Breast feeding or caesarean section significantly decreases *Bacteroides* colonization.[60]

In the intensive care environment the neonate's flora is altered.[61-62] *Klebsiella, Enterobacter,* or *Citrobacter* organisms are predominant in the flora of the skin, mucous membranes, and gut,[61] and antibiotic therapy is significantly associated with this alteration from normal flora and with antibiotic-resistant bacteria.[61-64] Sprunt and coworkers found that infants in intensive care units who maintained normal flora did not become infected; disease occurred only in those with altered respiratory flora.[65]

Nasojejunal feeding tube placement rapidly leads to abnormal colonization of the jejunum with coliform bacilli.[66] Endotracheal tubes result in colonization of the trachea with organisms that would otherwise be implanted in the nasopharynx.[67]

Antibiotics are generally used sparingly in nurseries for full-term infants, but in intensive care units as many as two-thirds of infants receive antibiotic therapy for three or more days.[61-62] Most commonly a beta-lactam antibiotic (penicillin G or ampicillin) and an aminoglycoside are given to sick neonates. The intense antibiotic pressure in the environment encourages emergence of resistant mutants. Colonization with aminoglycoside-resistant coliform bacilli sets the stage for possible outbreaks of disease. Many such outbreaks have been reported, first with kanamycin-resistant bacilli,[28,33,36,39] later with coliforms resistant to kanamycin and gentamicin,[38,40,43] and finally with *Klebsiella* organisms resistant to kanamycin, gentamicin, and amikacin.[41] Resistance is usually due to transferable plasmids. As of 1983, coliforms resistant to third-generation cephalosporin derivatives such as moxolactam, cefotaxime, and cefoperazone have not produced outbreaks in nurseries, but with increasing use resistant mutants can be anticipated.

Risk Factors and High-Risk Procedures

With the advent of intensive care nurseries in the 1960s, the sick newborn became exposed to new risks of infections due to invasive procedures.

Umbilical Catheters

Some infants develop sepsis, omphalitis, and liver abscesses as a result of catheters in umbilical vessels.[68-69]

Introduction of a catheter may permit organisms to ascend along the catheter–umbilical vessel interface and also may release contaminated thrombi present in the lumen of the vessel.[70-71] Thrombi that result from mechanical injury to the endothelial lining of the vein or artery following catheterization provide a nidus for multiplication of microorganisms.[72-74] Organisms resident in the umbilical cord and trough have been cultured from the blood and from the catheter tip on its removal.[68,70-71,75]

Contamination of catheter tips cultured after removal has varied from less than 10 percent[76-77] to more than 50 percent.[68,74,78] The incidence of bacteremia in infants with umbilical catheters, as determined by cultures of blood obtained from a peripheral vein, was approximately the same in infants who received antimicrobial agents as in those who did not.[68,79,80] The frequency with which catheter tips become colonized or produce bacteremia does not appear to be related to duration of catheterization, birthweight, age at the time of insertion, or local care at the site of insertion of a catheter for intravenous infusion.[68,74,78]

Infectious complications following catheterization of the umbilical artery occurred in only 1.2 percent of 1503 cases, but such complications occurred in 3.7 percent of 187 cases following catheterization of the umbilical vein.[66,72,76-77,79-89] This may be due to slower blood flow and ease of propagation of thrombi in the umbilical vein and to its direct access to the portal vein and liver parenchyma.

Radial Artery Catheters

Percutaneous catheterization of the radial artery may be a safer and more effective alternative to catheterization of the umbilical vessels for monitoring critically ill newborn infants. In a series of 147 radial artery catheterizations, there was only 1 instance of catheter-related bacteremia, although 25 percent of catheter tip cultures were positive.[90] Risk of bacteremia due to scalp vein needles is very low; no cases occurred in 2 series involving 361 babies.[91-92]

Indwelling Peripheral or Central Venous Catheters

Indwelling polyethylene catheters are sometimes used for prolonged intravenous therapy. In 4 reported series[92-95] involving 893 patients, 1.2 percent developed bacteremia attributed to the catheter. Most patients were adults, however, and in the pediatric series by Peter et al.[92] the bacteremia rate was 8 percent. As in the case of umbilical vessel catheters, there appears to be no advantage to use of topical antibiotic ointments at the catheter-skin junction compared with sterile gauze dressings.

Central venous catheters are often used for total parenteral nutrition infusions. In spite of the use of in-line filters, bacterial and fungal contamination has been a problem. In 13 reported series including a total of 2727 patients, the frequency of bacteremia was 2.5 percent and that of candidemia was 3.4 percent.[93-105] Pore size of the filter may be a critical factor. Holmes et al.[106] found that *Pseudomonas* organisms penetrated 0.45-μ filters within 12 hours and *Klebsiella* or *Serratia* penetrated within 48 and 72 hours, respectively. No bacteria penetrated the 0.22-μ–pore size filter under the test conditions.

Other Procedures

The temporary insertion of an umbilical vein catheter for the purpose of performing an exchange transfusion induces a transient bacteremia in 10 percent of patients,[71,107] but this is cleared spontaneously by the infant. Prophylactic systemic antibiotics have no effect on the rate of bacteremia. Blood withdrawn through the umbilical vein catheter is not suitable for culture, since in approximately half the specimens it is contaminated and does not accurately reflect bacteremia as determined by culture of peripheral vein blood.

Scalp electrodes used for intrapartum fetal monitoring have been associated with scalp abscesses due to *Haemophilus influenzae* b and to group A and B streptococci, gonococci, and anaerobic bacteria.[108-109] In some cases there was bacteremia or extension to bone. During the period in which 9 cases occurred at the Johns Hopkins Hospital, spiral scalp electrodes were used in 1030 infants of a total 2061 live births, giving an incidence of 0.9 percent infectious complication rate for the procedure.[109]

Respiratory therapy equipment, humidifiers, and any equipment containing water are potential nosocomial infection hazards.

INFECTION CONTROL AND SURVEILLANCE

Information on diseases in infants and personnel in the nursery should be maintained on a continuous basis to provide an early warning system for nursery epidemics. In most situations surveillance cultures of personnel, infants, and fomites are not cost-effective and are not recommended.[110]

Sick infants transferred to intensive care units from other hospitals may introduce new, potentially dangerous microorganisms. It is policy in some units to perform surveillance cultures from the anterior nares, rectum, and umbilical cord on such infants and to isolate the new patient until it is known that the infant is not colonized with aminoglycoside-resistant coliforms, *Pseudomonas* organisms, or methicillin-resistant staphylococci.

Detailed information regarding routine procedures for infection control in nurseries is available from several sources.[111-114] Nursery-acquired infections may become apparent days to weeks after discharge of the infant. A surveillance system that not only provides information about infections within the nursery but also follows up infants after discharge is therefore desirable. Various techniques can be used, including postcards, telephone calls, and records of visits to physicians' offices.

Several cases of infection occurring within a brief period or in close physical proximity, or disease caused by an unusual pathogen, should be cause for concern. An epidemiologic survey may be sufficient to identify the source. Nursery practices should be reviewed for possible laxity or use of poor technique. Personnel with any suppurative lesion must be excluded from the nursery. Guidelines for management of a nursery epidemic are provided in a publication of the American Academy of Pediatrics.[112] In complex situations specific recommendations can be sought from the hospital epidemiologist or from the Hospital Infectious Branch of the Centers for Disease Control in Atlanta, Georgia. The latter group provides significant resources for the investigation and control of hospital infections; their advice is available by invitation from the local state health department.

The identity of similar bacterial isolates from multiple cases can be suggested by antibiogram patterns. Bacteriophage susceptibility profiles are useful for establishing identity of *S. aureus* isolates, and serotyping can be used for bacteria such as *E. coli* and group A or B streptococci. DNA fingerprinting has been applied to study of herpes simplex viruses in situations of nosocomial spread of that virus.[115-116]

Frequent use of antibiotics in intermediate and intensive care nurseries is a selective pressure that encourages emergence of resistant variants. Such changes generally occur slowly over months or years[117] but rarely may take place within a few weeks.[63] These shifts in antibiotic susceptibility are usually plasmid-mediated and have occurred notably with the aminoglycoside antibiotics. Because resistance is usually due to specific bacterial enzymes, those enzymes that attack kanamycin may not be operative against gentamicin and vice versa.[118] Outbreaks due to multiply-resistant coliform bacilli have occurred, however.[40] Amikacin is a poor substrate for these bacterial enzymes and is usually effective against kanamycin- and gentamicin-resistant bacteria; an outbreak due to amikacin resistant-coliforms has however, been reported.[41]

Because of these considerations, some intensive care units have employed a strategy of changing the aminoglycoside used routinely from one to another on a regular schedule, such as every 6 or 12 months, hoping thereby to diminish the selective antibiotic pressure. Data on antibiotic susceptibility patterns of clinically important bacterial isolates should be reviewed periodically to detect emergence of resistance. In nurseries that make heavy use of antibiotics, it may be useful to perform periodically rectal cultures of randomly selected infants as surveillance for shifts in resistance patterns, since endogenous coliform bacilli are responsible for most disease.

MANAGEMENT OF OUTBREAKS

Staphylococcal Infections

Routine daily bathing of infants with hexachlorophene decreases colonization rates with *S. aureus* on skin and mucous membranes.[119] Daily bathing for three weeks decreased disease rates in 1 study,[120] but hexachlorophene bathing was not reliable in controlling outbreaks.[121] Colonization rates do not correlate consistently with outbreaks of disease.[122]

Because of the rare but serious systemic toxicity from absorbed hexachlorophene,[123] in December 1971 the Food and Drug Administration recommended that routine bathing of neonates with hexachlorophene soaps be discontinued. Since that time outbreaks of severe invasive staphylococcal disease due to phage group I or II organisms have occurred periodically.[124-125]

When multiple cases of staphylococcal disease occur within a limited period in a nursery and it is determined by antibiograms or bacteriophage testing that a single strain is involved, the following steps can be undertaken sequentially to control the outbreak.

1. Surveillance cultures (anterior nasal swab cultures, and skin or umbilical cord swab cultures) of all infants in the nursery will define the extent of colonization. Strict adherence to hand washing and other aseptic techniques should be enforced. Colonized babies who will not be discharged at 2 or 3 days of age should be segregated. Epidemiologic surveillance for new cases of disease is carried out. Investigation for a specific environmental source of the outbreak should be undertaken but will usually be unrevealing. In the majority of cases these measures suffice for control of the outbreak.

2. If after 1 or 2 weeks of the above measures new cases of disease continue to occur, a cohorting program should be implemented if physical facilities permit. The value of performing nasal cultures of hospital personnel is debatable. Some physicians recommend restricting colonized personnel to work only with colonized infants, but the value of this tactic has not been proved, and it creates logistic difficulties. In almost all cases the cohort system and strict enforcement of aseptic technique terminate the outbreak.

3. Only in the most prolonged and persistent staphylococcal outbreak would one consider implementation of a bacterial interference regimen with *S. aureus* 502A.[126] The methods and results of bacterial interference pro-

grams have been reviewed by Shinefield et al.[127] An alpha-hemolytic strep-tococcus designated strain 215 has also been used for bacterial interfer-ence.[128] Passing an umbilical catheter through a stump colonized with *S. aureus* 502A is potentially hazardous.[129]

Diarrheal Disease

Outbreaks of diarrheal disease are almost always of infectious origin and are caused by bacteria such as toxigenic or "enteropathogenic" *E. Coli,*[8,10] *Shigella,*[12] *Salmonella,*[13] or viruses.[15,51]

When outbreaks occur, all infants with diarrhea should be segregated from other infants. Strict enteric precautions for handling soiled diapers and hand washing should be stressed. Rectal swab or stool cultures for bacterial pathogens should be performed on sick infants and other infants cared for by the same personnel. If pathogens cannot be identified in the fecal cultures and if the diarrhea is of the secretory type, aspiration of small bowel contents for culture can be valuable. If the technology for identifying noncultivatable viruses is available, such studies should be undertaken.[51] When enteropathogenic serotypes of *E. coli* are involved, specific fluores-cent antibody study of rectal swab specimens rapidly identifies asympto-matic carriers that could serve as reservoirs for perpetuation of the out-break.[130]

When a bacterial pathogen is responsible for the outbreak, appropriate antibiotic therapy is instituted. The exception is *Salmonella* infection, in which antibiotic therapy is not effective or desirable in routine cases[131] but is reserved for those with bacteremic complications, acute colitis, or pro-tracted diarrhea and failure to thrive. Oral colonization has been implicated as epidemiologically important in nosocomial spread of *Salmonella* infec-tion in a nursery outbreak;[132] in such cases care must be taken with formula bottles and other objects contaminated with oral secretions.

Formerly it was recommended that nurseries for low birthweight in-fants be closed to admissions and new units opened when a substantial outbreak of diarrheal disease occurred.[133] With the measures outlined above, this disruptive, impractical, extreme solution should never be necessary.

Respiratory Infections

Aside from pertussis,[134] lower respiratory infections in nurseries are almost always due to viruses but increasing attention has focused on re-spiratory syncytial virus infection[45,47,135] and echovirus 11 infection.[46] Type A Influenza virus has also caused nosocomial infection in nurseries.[136-137]

If a specific immunofluorescent technique is employed, nasopharyngeal suction smears or anterior nasal swab smears can be used for rapid identification of respiratory syncytial virus and influenza infection.[45,138-139]

Infants with respiratory symptoms should be housed in separate nurseries from asymptomatic babies. In the intensive care unit, separate isolation facilities should be available. The major hazard is airborne transmission of virus to other infants and personnel; transmission of infected secretions by hands or fomites can also occur,[47] however, so it is recommended that gowns be worn when handling babies, and hand washing is important. In controlled trials,[140-141] gowning and masking was not significantly better than hand washing alone in preventing nosocomial transmission of respiratory viruses; nevertheless, these procedures are generally employed during an outbreak for whatever minimal benefit might accrue from their use. Masks should be changed frequently.

In pertussis outbreaks affected infants and personnel are treated with erythromycin to reduce their infectivity. The dose for newborns is 10 mg/kg given 2 or 3 times daily.[142] In large and persistent outbreaks widespread antibiotic prophylaxis and vaccination programs for personnel may be necessary.[134]

Resistant Enteric Gram-negative Bacilli

Once entrenched in special care units, antibiotic-resistant gram-negative enteric bacteria can be exceedingly difficult to eliminate from the environment. The principal reservoirs of infection are the fecal flora of infants and the tracheas of intubated infants. Antibiotic therapy does not effectively eradicate colonization.

The following approaches can be employed in an attempt to control an outbreak.

1. Rectal swab cultures are obtained from all infants and cultures of tracheal secretions are obtained from intubated babies. (The aminoglycoside to which the organism is resistant can be incorporated into the culture medium to facilitate isolation of resistant strains). All colonized infants, sick or well, are isolated. Body secretions are considered infected and hand washing before and after handling of infants is strictly enforced. An aminoglycoside to which the organism is susceptible (usually amikacin) or a new cephalosporin (moxalactam or cefotaxime) is given to babies with disease. No antibiotic is given to asymptomatically colonized infants. In one reported experience,[143] moxalactam proved useful in an outbreak of infection due to an organism resistant to all aminoglycosides.

Investigation of possible unusual modes of transmission should be undertaken by careful review of all procedures that carry an infection hazard. In most circumstances, cultures of nursery personnel are not productive.

2. If the above measures fail to contain the outbreak, and if there is substantial morbidity and mortality, the unit should be closed to further admissions until all colonized infants have been discharged.

> For dosages see Chapter 2 or Abbreviated Guide to Dosage on Inside Covers

REFERENCES

1. Center for Disease Control: National Nosocomial Infection Study Report, 1977. (6-month summaries) Atlanta, Center for Disease Control, Nov 1979
2. Hemming VG, Overall JC Jr, Britt MR: Nosocomial infections in a newborn intensive-care unit: Results of forty-one months of surveillance. N Engl J Med 294:1310–1316, 1976
3. Haley RW, Bregman DA: The role of understaffing and overcrowding in recurrent outbreaks of staphylococcal infection in a neonatal special-care unit. J Infect Dis 145:875–885, 1982
4. Boyer KM, Vogel LC, Gotoff SP, et al: Nosocomial transmission of bacteriophage type 7/11/12 group B streptococci in a special care nursery. Am J Dis Child 134:964–966, 1980
5. Anthony BF, Okada DM, Hobel CJ: Epidemiology of the group B streptococcus: Maternal and nosocomial sources for infant acquisitions. J Pediatr 95:431–436, 1979
6. Paredes A, Wong P, Mason EO Jr, et al: Nosocomial transmission of group B streptococci in a newborn nursery. Pediatrics 59:679–682, 1977
7. Ghosal SP, Sen Gupta PC, Mukherjee AK, et al: Noma neonatorum: Its aetiopathogenesis. Lancet 2:289–290, 1978
8. Guerrant RL, Dickens MD, Wenzel RP, et al: Toxigenic bacterial diarrhea: Nursery outbreak involving multiple bacterial strains. J Pediatr 89:885–891, 1976
9. Olarte J, Ramos-Alvarez M: Epidemic diarrhea in premature infants. Am J Dis Child 109:436–438, 1965
10. Kaslow RA, Taylor A Jr, Dweck HS, et al: Enteropathogenic *Escherichia coli* infection in a newborn nursery. Am J Dis Child 128:797–801, 1974
11. Boyer KM, Petersen NJ, Farzaneh I, et al: An outbreak of gastroenteritis due to *E. coli* 0142 in a neonatal nursery. J Pediatr 86:919–927, 1975
12. Salzman TC, Scher CD, Moss R: Shigellae with transferable drug resistance: Outbreak in a nursery for premature infants. J Pediatr 71:21–26, 1967
13. Schroeder SA, Aserkoff B, Brachman, PS: Epidemic salmonellosis in hospitals and institutions: A five-year review. New Engl J Med 279:674–678, 1968
14. Erwa HH; Enterococci in diarrhoea of neonates. Trans R Soc Trop Med Hyg 66:359–361, 1972
15. Cameron DJS, Bishop RF, Veenstra AA, et al: Noncultivable viruses and neonatal diarrhea: Fifteen-month survey in a newborn special care nursery. J Clin Microbiol 8:93–98, 1978

16. Nelson JD, Dillon HC Jr, Howard JB: A prolonged nursery epidemic associated with a newly recognized type of group A streptococcus. J Pediatr 89:792–796, 1976

17. Gezon HM, Schaberg MJ, Klein JO: Concurrent epidemics of *Staphylococcus aureus* and group A streptococcus disease in a newborn nursery: Control with penicillin G and hexachloraphene bathing. Pediatrics 51:383–390, 1973

18. Geil CC, Castle WK, Mortimer EA Jr: Group A streptococcal infections in newborn nurseries. Pediatrics 46:849–854, 1970

19. Tancer ML, McManus JE, Belotti G: Group A, type 33, β-hemolytic streptococcal outbreak on a maternity and newborn service. Am J Obstet Gynecol 103:1028–1033, 1969

20. Dillon HC Jr: Group A type 12 streptococcal infection in a newborn nursery. Am J Dis Child 112:117–123, 1966

21. Langewisch WH: An epidemic of group A, type 1 streptococcal infections in newborn infants. Pediatrics 18:438–447, 1956

22. Cooperman MB: Gonococcus arthritis in infancy. Am J Dis Child 33:932–948, 1927

23. Brody JA, Moore H, King EO: Meningitis caused by an unclassified gram-negative bacterium in newborn infants. J Dis Child 96:1–5, 1958

24. Foley JF, Gravelle CR, Englehard WE, et al: *Achromobacter* septicemia: Fatalities in prematures. Am J Dis Child 101:279–288, 1961

25. Plotkin SA, McKitrick JC: Nosocomial meningitis of the newborn caused by a flavobacterium. JAMA 198:662–664, 1966

26. McCormack RC, Kunin CM: Control of a single source nursery epidemic due to *Serratia marcescens*. Pediatrics 37:750–755, 1966

27. Fierer J, Taylor PM, Gezon HM: *Pseudomonas aeruginosa* epidemic traced to delivery-room resuscitators. New Engl J Med 276:991–996, 1967

28. Adler JL, Shulman JA, Terry PM, et al: Nosocomial colonization with kanamycin-resistant *Klebsiella pneumoniae,* types 2 and 11, in a premature nursery. J Pediatr 77:376–385, 1970

29. Becroft DMO, Farmer K, Seddon RJ, et al: Epidemic listeriosis in the newborn. Br Med J 3:747–751, 1971

30. Burke JP, Ingall D, Klein JO, et al: *Proteus mirabilis* infections in a hospital nursery traced to a human carrier. New Engl J Med 284:115–121, 1971

31. Drewett SE, Payne DJH, Tuke W, et al: Eradication of *Pseudomonas aeruginosa* infection from a special-care nursery. Lancet 1:946–948, 1972

32. Morehead CD, Houck PW: Epidemiology of *Pseudomonas* infections in a pediatric intensive care unit. Am J Dis Child 124:564–570, 1972

33. Hable KA, Matsen JM, Wheeler DJ, et al: *Klebsiella* type 33 septicemia in an infant intensive care unit. J Pediatr 80:920–924, 1972

34. Kayyali MZ, Nicholson DP, Smith IM: A *Klebsiella* outbreak in a pediatric nursery: Emergency action and preventive surveillance. Clin Pediatr (Phila) 11:442–426, 1972

35. Bobo RA, Newton EJ, Jones LF, et al: Nursery outbreak of *Pseudomonas aeruginosa:* Epidemiological conclusions from five different typing methods. Appl Microbiol 25:414–420, 1973

36. Hill HR, Hunt CE, Matsen JM: Nosocomial colonization with *Klebsiella,*

type 26, in a neonatal intensive care unit associated with an outbreak of sepsis, meningitis, and necrotizing enterocolitis. J Pediatr 85:415–419, 1974

37. Armstrong-Ressy CT: Epidemiologic notes and reports of nosocomial *Serratia marcescens* infections in neonates—Puerto Rico. Morbid Mortal Wkly Rep, May 18, 1974

38. Arbeter AM, Aff C, Dill P et al: Experiences with a multiple-resistant *Klebsiella pneumoniae* in an infant intensive care unit. (abstract) Pediatr Res 11:433, 1977

39. Cichon MJ, Craig CP, Sargent J, et al: Nosocomial *Klebsiella* infections in an intensive care nursery. South Med J 70:33–35, 1977

40. Eidelman AI, Reynolds J: Gentamicin-resistant *Klebsiella* infections in a neonatal intensive care unit. Am J Dis Child 132:421–422, 1978

41. Cook LN, Davis RS, Stover BH: Outbreak of amikacin-resistant enterobacteriaceae in an intensive care nursery. Pediatrics 65:264–268, 1980

42. Parry MF, Hutchinson JH, Brown NA, et al: Gram-negative sepsis in neonates: A nursery outbreak due to hand carriage of *Citrobacter diversus*. Pediatrics 65:1105–1109, 1980

43. Markowitz SM, Veazey JM Jr, Macrina FL, et al: Sequential outbreaks of infection due to *Klebsiella pneumoniae* in a neonatal intensive care unit: Implication of a conjugative R plasmid. J Infect Dis 142:106–112, 1980

44. Anagostakis D, Fitsialos J, Koretsia C, et al: A nursery outbreak of *Serratia marcescens* infection. Am J Dis Child 135:413–414, 1981

45. Mintz L, Ballard RA, Sniderman SH, et al: Nosocomial respiratory syncytial virus infections in an intensive care nursery: Rapid diagnosis by direct immunofluorescence. Pediatrics 64:149–153, 1979

46. Nagington J, Wreghitt TG, Gandy G, et al: Fatal echovirus 11 infections in outbreak in special-care baby unit. Lancet 2:725–728, 1978

47. Hall CB, Douglas RG, Jr: Modes of transmission of respiratory syncytial virus. J Pediatr 99:100–103, 1981

48. Swender PT, Shott RJ, Williams ML: A community and intensive care nursery outbreak of coxsackievirus B5 meningitis. Am J Dis Child 127:42–45, 1974

49. Farmer K, Patten PT: An outbreak of coxsackie B5 infection in a special care unit for newborn infants. NZ Med J 68:86–89, 1968

50. Farmer K, MacArthur BA, Clay MM: A follow-up study of 15 cases of neonatal meningo-encephalitis due to coxsackie virus B5. J Pediatr 87:568–571, 1975

51. Murphy AM, Albrey MB, Crewe EB: Rotavirus infections of neonates. Lancet 2:1149–1150, 1977

52. Zissis G, Lambert JP, Fonteyne J, et al: Child-mother transmission of rotavirus? (letter) Lancet 1:96, 1976

53. Lewis HM, Parry JV, Davies, HA, et al: A year's experience of the rotavirus syndrome and its association with respiratory illness. Arch Dis Child 54:339–346, 1979

54. Dennis JE, Rhodes KH, Cooney DB, et al: Nosocomial *Rhizopus* infection (zygomycosis) in children. J Pediatr 96:824–828, 1980

55. Thadepalli H, Chan WH, Maidman JE, et al: Microflora of the cervix during normal labor and the puerperium. J Infect Dis 137:568–572, 1978

56. Brook I, Barrett CT, Brinkman CR, et al: Aerobic and anaerobic bacterial flora of the maternal cervix and newborn gastric fluid and conjunctiva: A prospective study. Pediatrics 63:451–455, 1979

57. Fairchild JP, Graber CD, Vogel EH Jr, et al: Flora of the umbilical stump: 2,479 cultures. J Pediatr 53:538–546, 1958

58. Evans HE, Akpata SO, Baki A: Factors influencing the establishment of the neonatal bacterial flora. I. The role of host factors. Arch Environ Health 21:514–519, 1970

59. Evans HE, Akpata SO, Baki A: Factors influencing the establishment of the neonatal bacterial flora. II. The role of environmental factors. Arch Environ Health 21:643–648, 1970

60. Long SS, Swenson RM: Development of anaerobic fecal flora in healthy newborn infants. J Pediatr 91:298–301, 1977

61. Goldman DA, Leclair J, Macone A: Bacterial colonization of neonates admitted to an intensive care environment, J Pediatr 93:288–293, 1978

62. Farmer K: The influence of hospital environment and antibiotics on the bacterial flora of the upper respiratory tract of the newborn. NZ Med J 67:541–544, 1968

63. Franco JA, Eitzman DV, Baer H: Antibiotic usage and microbial resistance in an intensive care nursery. Am J Dis Child 126:318–321, 1973

64. Grylack L, Neugebauer D, Scanlon JW: Effects of oral antibiotics on stool flora and overall sensitivity patterns in an intensive care nursery. Pediatr Res 16:509–511, 1982

65. Sprunt K, Leidy G, Redman W: Abnormal colonization of neonates in an intensive care unit: Means of identifying neonates at risk of infection. Pediatr Res 12:998–1002, 1978

66. Challacombe D: Bacterial microflora in infants receiving nasojejunal tube feeding. J Pediatr 85:113, 1974

67. Harris H, Wirtschafter D, Cassady G: Endotracheal intubation and its relationship to bacterial colonization and systemic infection of newborn infants. Pediatrics 56:816–823, 1976

68. Balagtas RC, Bell CE, Edwards LD, et al: Risk of local and systemic infections associated with umbilical vein catheterization: A prospective study in 86 newborn patients. Pediatrics 48:359–367, 1971

69. Brans YW, Ceballos R, Cassady G: Umbilical catheters and hepatic abscesses. Pediatrics 53:264–266, 1974

70. Lipsitz PJ, Cornet JM: Blood cultures from the umbilical vein in the newborn infant. Pediatrics 26:657–660, 1960

71. Nelson JD, Richardson J, Shelton S: The significance of bacteremia with exchange transfusion. J Pediatr 66:291–299, 1965

72. Neal WA, Reynolds JW, Jarvis CW, et al: Umbilical artery catheterization: Demonstration of arterial thrombosis by aortography. Pediatrics 50:6–13, 1972

73. Larroche JC: Umbilical catheterization: Its complications. Anatomical study. Biol Neonate 16:101–116, 1970

74. Krauss AN, Albert RF, Kannan MM: Contamination of umbilical catheters in the newborn infant. J Pediatr 77:965–969, 1970

75. Houck PW, Nelson JD, Kay JL: Fatal septicemia due to *Staphylococcus aureus* 502A. Am J Dis Child 123:45–48, 1972

76. Casalino MB, Lipsitz PJ: Contamination of umbilical catheters. (letter to the editor) J Pediatr 78:1077, 1971

77. Powers WF, Tooley WH: Contamination of umbilical vessel catheters: Encouraging information. (letter to the editor) Pediatrics 49:470, 1972

78. VanVliet PKJ, Gupta JM: Prophylactic antibiotics in umbilical artery catheterization in the newborn. Arch Dis Child 48:296–300, 1973

79. Bard H, Albert G, Teasdale F, et al: Prophylactic antibiotics in chronic umbilical artery catheterization in respiratory distress syndrome. Arch Dis Child 48:630–635, 1973

80. Krauss AN, Caliendo TJ, Kannan MM: Bacteremia in newborn infants. NY State J Med 72:1136–1137, 1972

81. Cochran WD, Davis HT, Smith CA: Advantages and complications of umbilical artery catheterization in the newborn. Pediatrics 42:769–777, 1968

82. Sarrut S, Alain J, Alison F: Les complications précoces de la perfusion par la veine ombilicale chez le premature. Arch Fr Pediatr 26:651–667, 1969

83. Symansky MW, Fox HA: Umbilical vessel catheterization: Indications, management, and evaluation of the technique. J Pediatr 80:820–826, 1972

84. Vidyasagar D, Downes JJ, Boggs TR Jr: Respiratory distress syndrome of newborn infants. 11.Technic of catheterization of umbilical artery and clinical results of treatment of 124 patients. Clin Pediatr (Phila) 9:332–337, 1970

85. Wigger HJ, Bransilver BR, Blanc WA: Thromboses due to catheterization in infants and children. J Pediatr 76:1–11, 1970

86. Egan EA, Eitzman DV: Umbilical vessel catheterization. Am J Dis Child 121:213–218, 1971

87. Gupta JM, Roberton NRC, Wigglesworth JS: Umbilical artery catheterization in the newborn. Arch Dis Child 43:382–387, 1968

88. Banks DC, Yates DB, Cawdrey HM, et al: Infection from intravenous catheters. Lancet 1:443–445, 1970

89. Fuchs PC: Indwelling intravenous polyethylene catheters. JAMA 216:1447–1450, 1971

90. Adams JM, Speer ME, Rudolph AJ: Bacterial colonization of radial artery catheters. Pediatrics 65:94–97, 1980

91. Crossley KM, Matsen JM: The scalp-vein needle: A prospective study of complications. JAMA 220:985–987, 1972

92. Peter G, Lloyd-Still JD, Lovejoy FH, Jr: Local infection and bacteremia from scalp vein needles and polyethylene catheters in children. J Pediatr 80:78–83, 1972

93. Dudrick SJ, Groff DB, Wilmore DW: Long-term venous catheterization in infants. Surg Gynecol Obstet 129:805–808, 1969

94. Wilmore DW, Dudrick SJ: Safe long-term hyperalimentation. Arch Surg 98:256–258, 1969

95. Filler RM, Eraklis AJ: Care of the critically ill child: Intravenous alimentation. Pediatrics 46:456–461, 1970

96. Ashcraft KW, Leape LL: *Candida* sepsis complicating parenteral feeding. JAMA 212:454–456, 1970

97. McGovern B: Intravenous hyperalimentation. Milit Med 135:1137–1145, 1970.

98. Curry CR, Quie PG: Fungal septicemia in patients receiving parenteral hyperalimentation. N Engl J Med 285:1221–1224, 1971

99. Winters RW, Santulli TV, Heird WC, et al: Hyperalimentation without sepsis. (letter to the editor) N Engl J Med 286:321–322, 1972

100. Peden VH, Karpel JT: Total parenteral nutrition in premature infants. J Pediatr 81:137–144, 1972

101. Driscoll JM Jr, Heird WC, Schullinger JN, et al: Total intravenous alimentation in low-birth-weight infants: A preliminary report. J Pediatr 81:145–153, 1972

102. Goldmann DA, Maki DG: Infection control in total parenteral nutrition. JAMA 223:1360–1364, 1973

103. Dillon JD Jr, Schaffner W, Van Way CW III, et al: Septicemia and total parenteral nutrition. JAMA 223:1341–1344, 1973

104. Ryan JA Jr, Abel RM, Abbott WM, et al: Catheter complications in total parenteral nutrition: A prospective study of 200 consecutive patients. New Engl J Med 290:757–761, 1974

105. Montgomerie JZ, Edwards JE Jr: Association of infection due to *Candida albicans* with intravenous hyperalimentation. J Infect Dis 137:197–201, 1978

106. Holmes CJ, Kunksin RB, Ausman RK, et al: Potential hazards associated with microbial contamination of in-line filters during intravenous therapy. J Clin Microbiol 12:725–731, 1980

107. Risk of infection associated with umbilical vein catheterization: A prospective study in 75 newborn infants. J Pediatr 86:759–765, 1975

108. Reveri M, Kirshnamurthy C: Gonococcal scalp abscess. J Pediatr 94:819–820, 1979

109. Feder HM, Maclean WC, Moxon R: Scalp abscess secondary to fetal scalp electrode. J Pediatr 89:808–809, 1976

110. Allen JR, Oliver TK Jr: The newborn nursery. In Bennett JV, Brachman PR (eds): Hospital Infections (ed 1). Boston, Little Brown, 1979

111. Recommended Standards for Maternity and Newborn Care (ed 2). Ottawa, Information Canada, 1975

112. American Academy of Pediatrics: Standards and Recommendations for Hospital Care of Newborn Infants (ed 6). Evanston, Ill., American Academy of Pediatrics, 1977

113. Planning and Design for Perinatal and Pediatric Facilities. Columbus, Ohio, Ross Laboratories, 1977

114. Centers for Disease Control: Isolation Techniques for Use in Hospitals (ed 3). Springfield, Va., National Technical Information Service, 1982

115. Halperin SA, Hendley JO, Nosal C, et al: DNA fingerprinting in investigation of apparent nosocomial acquisition of neonatal herpes simplex. J Pediatr 97:91–93, 1980

116. Linnemann CC, Buchmann TH, Light IJ, et al: Transmission of herpes simplex virus type 1 in a nursery for the newborn: Identification of viral isolates by DNA "fingerprinting." Lancet 1:964–966, 1978

117. Howard JB, McCracken GH, Jr: Reappraisal of kanamycin usage in neonates. J Pediatr 86:949–956, 1975

118. Benveniste R, Davies J: Structure-activity relationship among the aminoglycoside antibiotics: Role of hydroxyl and amino groups. Antimicrob Agents Chemother 4:402–409, 1973

119. Hargiss C, Larson E: The epidemiology of *Staphylococcus aureus* in a newborn nursery from 1970 through 1976. Pediatrics 61:348–353, 1978

120. Gezon HM, Schaberg MJ, Klein JO: Concurrent epidemics of *Staphylococcus aureus* and group A streptococcus disease in a newborn nursery: Control with penicillin G and hexachlorophene bathing. Pediatrics 51:383–390, 1973

121. Gehlbach SH, Gutman LT, Wilfert CM, et al: Recurrence of skin disease in a nursery: Ineffectuality of hexachlorophene bathing. Pediatrics 55:422–424, 1975

122. Gooch JJ, Britt EM: *Staphylococcus aureus* colonization and infection in newborn nursery patients. Am J Dis Child 132:893–896, 1978

123. Tyrala EE, Hillman LS, Hillman RE, et al: Clinical pharmacology of hexachlorophene in newborn infants. J Pediatr 91:481–486, 1977

124. Light IJ, Brackvogel V, Watton RL, et al: An epidemic of bullous impetigo arising from a central admission–observation nursery. Pediatrics 49:15–21, 1972

125. Faden HS, Burke JP, Glasgow LA, et al: Nursery outbreak of scalded-skin syndrome: Scarlatiniform rash due to phage group I *Staphylococcus aureus*. Am J Dis Child 130:265–268, 1976

126. Eichenwald HF, Shinefield HR, Boris M, et al: "Bacterial interference" and staphylococcic colonization in infants and adults. Ann NY Acad Sci 128:365–380, 1965

127. Shinefield HR, Ribble JD, Boris M: Bacterial interference between strains of *Staphylococcus aureus*, 1960 to 1970. Am J Dis Child 121:148–152, 1971

128. Sprunt K, Leidy G, Redman W: Abnormal colonization of neonates in an ICU: Conversion to normal colonization by pharyngeal implantation of alpha hemolytic streptococcus strain 215. Pediatr Res 14:308–313, 1980

129. Houck PW, Nelson JD, Kay JL: Fatal septicemia due to *Staphyloccus aureus* 502A: Report of a case and review of the infectious complications of bacterial interference programs. Am J Dis Child 123:45–48, 1972

130. Nelson JD, Whitaker JA, Hempstead B, et al: Epidemiological application of the fluorescent antibody technique: Study of a diarrhea outbreak in a premature nursery. JAMA 176:26–30, 1961

131. Nelson JD, Kusmiesz H, Jackson LH, et al: Treatment of *Salmonella* gastroenteritis with ampicillin, amoxicillin, or placebo. Pediatrics 65:1125–1130, 1980

132. Sanborn WR, Lesmana M, Koesno: Oral infection in pediatric salmonellosis. Lancet 2:478, 1976

133. Wheeler WE: Spread and control of *Escherchia coli* diarrheal disease. Ann NY Acad Sci 66:112–117, 1956

134. Linnemann CC Jr, Ramundo N, Perlstein PH, et al: Use of pertussis vaccine in an epidemic involving hospital staff. Lancet 2:540–543, 1975

135. Hall CB, Kopelman AE, Douglas RG Jr, et al: Neonatal respiratory syncytial virus infection. New Engl J Med 300:393–396, 1979

136. Bauer CR, Elie K, Spence L, et al: Hong Kong influenza in a neonatal unit. JAMA 223:1233–1235, 1973

137. Meibalane R, Sedmak GV, Sasidharan P, et al: Outbreak of influenza in a neonatal intensive care unit, J Pediatr 91:974–976, 1977

138. Kaul A, Scott R, Gallagher M, et al: Respiratory syncytial virus infection: Rapid diagnosis in children by use of indirect immunofluorescence. Am J Dis Child 132:1088–1090, 1978

139. Minnich L, Ray CG: Comparison of direct immunofluorescent staining of clinical specimens for respiratory virus antigens with conventional isolation techniques. J Clin Microbiol 12:391–394, 1980

140. Murphy D, Todd JK, Chao RK, et al: The use of gowns and masks to control respiratory illness in pediatric hospital personnel. J Pediatr 99:746–750, 1981

141. Hall CB, Douglas RG Jr: Nosocomial respiratory syncytial viral infections: Should gowns and masks be used? Am J Dis Child 135:512–515, 1981

142. Patamasucon P, Kaojarern J, Kusmiesz H, et al: Pharmacokinetics of erythromycin ethylsuccinate and estolate in infants under 4 months of age. Antimicrob Agents Chemother 19:736–739, 1981

143. McKee K Jr, Stratton C, Cotton R, et al: Nursery outbreak of multiply-resistant *K. pneumoniae:* Control and follow-up. (abstract 531) Twentieth Interscience Conference on Antimicrobial Agents and Chemotherapy New Orleans, La., September 22–24, 1980

16

Prophylactic Antibiotics

OPHTHALMIA NEONATORUM

Gonococcal Ophthalmia

So few modern physicians have seen full-blown gonococcal ophthalmia that it may be worthwhile to quote a description penned a half century before Credé's reports on silver nitrate prophylaxis[1-2] at a time when gonorrhea was the leading cause of blindness.

> An inflammation not unfrequently attacks the eyes of newborn children, which is speedily followed by a copious secretion of pus from the conjunctivia, and, when neglected, often terminates in sloughing of the cornea, or permanent opacity. This disease commonly sets in the second or third day after birth, and commences with increased vascularity of the conjunctiva, lining the eyelids, which later becomes swollen and permanently closed. The inflammation soon extends to the conjunctiva of the eye-ball—the swelling of the lids increases very much, and a copious discharge of thick, white, purulent matter ensues. If we attempt to open the eye at this period, a gush of matter takes place, and frequently the lower lid is everted, exhibiting its interior surface highly inflamed and of a bright red colour. In some severe instances, the tumefaction of the lids is so great as to cause eversion without its being the result of an attempt at opening the eye. We can seldom get a view of the cornea, as the intolerance of light is so great as to cause a turning upwards of the eye-ball upon every attempt at opening the lids.[3]

Gonorrhea is more prevalent nowadays than at any time in the past, and although we still encounter occasional cases of gonococcal conjunctivitis in the newborn, we rarely see the invasive, destructive ophthalmitis described so vividly in the preceding quotation.

Credé's discovery of silver nitrate solution prophylaxis had a monumental and lasting impact on this devastating disease of newborns. It is worthwhile to read his original report of 1881,[1] which has been translated into English by Forbes and Forbes.[2] Credé was chief of the obstetrical clinic in Leipzig, and either his renown or his arrogance was such that the article is signed only with his surname, an affectation that most journal editors would not tolerate nowadays, but Credé also happened to be editor of the journal. After trying a number of prophylactic methods, he settled on irrigation of newborn's eyes with 2-percent salicylic acid, followed by instillation of 2.5-percent silver nitrate solution. This prevented eye infection in babies born to mothers with gonorrheal discharge, but infection still occurred in some unprophylaxed infants whose mothers had no vaginal discharge. On June 1, 1880, therefore, he began treating the eyes of all newborns in his clinic and virtually eliminated gonococcal ophthalmia. He modified the method as follows: the eyes were washed with plain water, and a single drop of 2-percent silver nitrate solution was applied with a small glass rod. A linen eye patch soaked in 2-percent salicylic water was applied for 24 hours. Credé later abandoned the eye patch, and in later years it was found that a 1-percent silver nitrate solution was effective and caused less chemical irritation.

To the present day silver nitrate remains the universal standard, although it is difficult to ascertain a precise efficacy figure because of the uncontrolled nature of most studies. The largest series is that of Greenberg and Vandow.[4] Among over 250,000 infants treated with 1-percent silver nitrate, there were 17 cases of gonococcal conjunctivitis—a failure rate of 6.6/100,000 patients compared with 22.5/100,000 patients in a sample of over 86,000 infants who received no prophylaxis. It is interesting to note that there was only 1 case of gonococcal conjunctivitis in 14,042 babies who had only saline washing of the eyes, giving an attack rate of 7.3/100,000, which is very close to the 6.6 rate with silver nitrate. No one suggests reliance on saline irrigation, but it seems likely that the physical act of washing provides substantial protection against gonorrheal infection. Greenberg and Vandow[4] and others[5-11] have investigated topical antimicrobial agents and systemic penicillin. Tetracycline or erythromycin ointment appears to be comparable in efficacy to silver nitrate and has the advantage of causing less chemical conjunctivitis. Bactracin ointment is ineffective. Penicillin ointment or a single intramuscular injection of 50,000 U of penicillin G is also effective, but penicillin ointment is no longer available commercially, and concerns have been expressed about the sensitizing potential consequent to exposing entire population groups to penicillin on the first day of life. It should be pointed out that there are no data to indicate that newborns become sensitized to penicillin.

Several possible explanations come to mind for the occasional failures encountered with silver nitrate or antibiotics. Almost surely the most common reason would be failure to apply the drops or ointment at all or failure to get the medication into the conjunctival sac: it can be quite difficult to hold the eyes of a newborn open unless the slippery vernix caseosa is thoroughly removed. It is common practice in many places to irrigate the eyes immediately after the silver nitrate solution is applied, in what is probably a vain attempt to decrease the severity of chemical conjunctivitis. The period of exposure of the chemical to bacteria may be too brief, particularly if the "dose" of gonococci is large. If saline solution is used for irrigation, a black precipitate of silver chloride is formed. It has been suggested that this decreases the effectiveness of Credé's prophylaxis, but no firm data support that supposition. In a study of 3 methods of irrigation immediately after instillation of silver nitrate solution (using normal saline solution, sterile water, or boric acid–sodium borate solution), sterile water was reported to reduce the prevalence of chemical conjunctivitis.[12] Nevertheless, because the benefits of irrigation are minimal and because irrigation conceivably diminishes the efficacy of silver nitrate, we do not recommend irrigation after Credé prophylaxis.

With premature rupture of fetal membranes, gonococcal infection may occur *in utero,* and a single dose of prophylaxis may be too little to abort the established infection. Infection is usually acquired during birth.

Infected mothers can conceivably infect their babies several days after birth via the genital-to-hand-to-eyes route. It is also possible that babies are colonized at other sites such as the mouth and anus and can autoinoculate the eyes. It has been suggested[13] that all infants born to mothers with active gonococcal infection should have cultures taken from the eye, pharynx, and rectum and be treated with parenteral penicillin if *Neisseria gonorrheae* is recovered from any site, even if the infant remains asymptomatic. We believe that this is sound advice, although it is based on armchair reasoning rather than established fact.

It should be remembered by physicians and nursery personnel that gonorrheal secretions are highly contagious. If aseptic technique has not been used and there has been definite exposure to infected secretions, at a minimum appropriate cultures should be taken from the exposeé; it probably would also be advisable to give standard treatment for gonorrhea immediately.

It is unlikely that we will ever have data from large-scale, well-controlled studies comparing antibiotics with silver nitrate for efficacy and adverse effects, so we must make our choices based on the information at hand. In many states the decision is made for us by statute law that dictates 1-percent silver nitrate solution and allows no substitute. When a choice is possible, the physician's decision lies between the tradition, low cost, safety, and effectiveness of silver nitrate solution and the greater cost, lesser side effects, and probable equal efficacy of 1-percent tetracycline or 0.5-percent erythromycin ointment. In 1965 we opted for tetracycline ointment, and it has proved highly effective in approximately 150,000 babies born in our hospital since then. The principal reason that we chose antibiotic over silver nitrate was that we had several instances in which the recognition and treatment of nongonococcal eye infections were delayed because the conjunctival inflammation was mistakenly attributed to unusually prolonged chemical conjunctivitis. This is not a problem with tetracycline prophylaxis; we have not seen conjunctival irritation that we could clearly ascribe to the antibiotic ointment. If an antibiotic is used, an individual tube should be used for each infant. A multidose tube used repeatedly would carry the hazard of contamination with *Pseudomonas* or other potentially pathogenic bacteria that could be inadvertently inoculated into the eyes of babies.

Chlamydial Conjunctivitis

Efficacy of prophylaxis for chlamydial conjunctivitis is not entirely clear at this time. In a well-controlled study comparing silver nitrate (which is ineffective against *Chlamydia trachomatis*) with a single application of 0.5-percent erythromycin ophthalmic ointment in a small number of babies born to colonized mothers, Hammerslag et al.[14] found a statistically significant benefit of erythromycin prophylaxis. On the other hand, in a much larger but less well-controlled experience Rettig et al.[15] found no benefit from a single application of tetracycline ointment to the eyes of newborns for prevention of chlamydial conjunctivitis.

On the basis of unpublished information available to its Expert Committee, the Centers for Disease Control recommended in 1982 that either 1-percent tetracycline ointment or 0.5-percent erythromycin ointment be the prophylactic method of choice for neonatal gonococcal and chlamydial conjunctivitis.[16]

INFECTION RELATED TO EXCHANGE TRANSFUSION AND INDWELLING UMBILICAL VESSEL CATHETERS

Very soon after birth the umbilical cord stump is colonized by microorganisms from the infant's environment,[17] and they progress up the umbilical vessels. If there has been premature rupture of the fetal membranes, the cord may be contaminated antepartum, and there is often an inflammatory reaction.[18] Years ago it was common practice in some nurseries to draw blood samples for culture from the umbilical vessels because of their easy accessibility. It was shown that such cultures were worthless because they reflected the microbial flora of the cord rather than bacteremia.[19]

Similarly, if one cultures the first blood aspirated after insertion of an umbilical vein catheter for exchange transfusion, there will be bacterial growth in 40-45 percent of the specimens.[20-21] The same bacterial species are found in swab cultures of the umbilical stump. When the catheter is inserted into the umbilical vein through a small supraumbilical incision, there is a lower frequency of positive cultures.[22] At the termination of the transfusion, the umbilical vein catheter blood specimen is positive for bacteremia in only 10 percent of instances, and with rare exceptions the infants clear this transient bacteremia spontaneously; no benefit from prophylactic antibiotics can be demonstrated.[20-21]

Bacteremic illness or local disease of the umbilicus is very rare after exchange blood transfusion, and available information suggests that prophylactically administered antibiotics have no beneficial effect. It is therefore recommended that cultures should not be taken routinely and that antibiotics should not be given routinely as a precautionary measure. Infants should be closely observed after the procedure. If there are clinical signs of infection, blood for culture should be obtained through a peripheral vein and treatment started with a penicillinase-resistant penicillin and an aminoglycosidic antibiotic.

When indwelling umbilical artery catheters were first employed for monitoring purposes in infants with respiratory distress syndrome, it soon became apparent that they could be associated with serious thrombotic and infectious consequences. It is difficult to assess the exact risk factor for infection secondary to arterial catheters because some authors consider positive cultures of the catheter tip as indicative of infection, but these tips are easily contaminated with umbilical bacteria during removal. Bacteremia or infected aortic thrombi probably occur in no more than 8 percent of patients[23] and in as few as 1 percent.[24] In several studies the role of prophylactic antibiotics has been evaluated, but in none that we are aware of was there a rigid protocol with strict randomization and control of multiple variables. The consensus of the reports is nonetheless that prophylactic antibiotics do not decrease the frequency of infectious complications of indwelling umbilical vessel catheters (see chap. 15).[23-27]

PREMATURE AND PROLONGED RUPTURE OF THE MEMBRANES, AND AMNIONITIS

The risks to the mother and the infant from premature and prolonged rupture of the fetal membrane have been extensively evaluated.[18,28-31] There is no standard definition of what the word *premature* means in this context.

Various authors have defined premature rupture as rupture that occurs 1 hour, 6 hours, or even longer before onset of labor, and some have considered it to apply to rupture of the fetal membranes at any time before onset of labor.

Premature rupture of membranes is associated with an increased incidence of prematurity in the newborn and exposes the mother and fetus to the hazards of amnionitis. The incidence of amnionitis ranges from 5–25 percent depending on the duration of the latent period before onset of labor.[29]

In the series by Pryles et al.,[28] clinical signs suggesting sepsis were present in 31 percent of infants born after premature and prolonged rupture of membranes, compared with only 5 percent of the control group, and there was bacteriologic confirmation of infection in 8 percent and 1 percent of the two groups, respectively.

Attempts to decrease the frequency of amnionitis and fetal infection by administration of antibiotics to the mothers before labor and delivery have met with little success. A double-blind study comparing demeclocycline and placebo in almost 2000 cases failed to demonstrate any advantage of the antibiotic,[30] although one could argue that the choice of antibiotic was a poor one considering the susceptibilities of the types of bacteria involved in perinatal infection.

Prophylactic antibiotics given to infants born after premature rupture of membranes have not demonstrated any conclusive benefit.[18,28-29] Attempts have been made to correlate histologic evidence of infection of the cord with infection in the infant, but there are false positives and false negatives.[18,28] Similarly, gastric aspirate studies for polymorphonuclear cells and culture of the fluid have not been helpful prognosticators.[18]

When an infant is born with these high-risk factors, it is not advisable to administer antibiotics routinely. There is an increased risk of infection, but it is a small one. Rather, the baby should be carefully observed, and if clinical signs of illness develop appropriate cultures should be taken and antibiotic therapy instituted.

STAPHYLOCOCCAL INFECTION

Nosocomial disease due to *Staphylococcus aureus*, phage type 80/81, was a terrible problem in nurseries during the later 1950s and early 1960s. There was great controversy concerning which was the primary cause—fomites, nasal colonization, umbilical cord colonization, or the hands of nursery personnel, or other factors. This was never resolved to the satisfaction of all the warriors involved in the battle, probably because all epidemiologic factors were important and their relative influences varied with time and setting.

It was the general impression that staphylococcal *colonization rates* were decreased by bathing infants with hexachlorophene soaps, but there was never solid documentation that this had a substantial impact on the rates of staphylococcal *disease*. Indeed, it was suggested[32] that the decreased staphylococcal skin colonization due to hexachlorophene bathing resulted in increased colonization of the skin of babies with *Pseudomonas* and gram-negative coliform organisms. The implication was that the widespread use of hexachlorophene bathing had been responsible for the shift in the 1960s from gram-positive to gram-negative bacteria as the predominant pathogens of neonates. The same authors, however, in a later review of their experience in Cincinnati, determined that the decline of *S. aureus* had actually preceded the adoption of hexachlorophene bathing in their nursery. It appears in retrospect that the shift in pathogens was a natural phenomenon that had been influenced very little by the vigorous attempts at staphylococcal control. Measures for control of nosocomial staphylococcal infection are discussed in Chapter 15.

STREPTOCOCCAL INFECTION

The use of benzathine penicillin G as a prophylactic agent in nursery epidemics of group A streptococcal infection is discussed in Chapter 15.

Attempts have been made to prevent group B streptococcal disease by treating carriers during pregnancy, and newborns. Franciosi, Knostman, and Zimmerman[34] treated women with group B streptococci isolated from vaginal cultures with an injection of benzathine penicillin G and reported that they were successful in eradicating the organisms in most women, although they found it necessary in some cases to treat some of the male consorts who were asymptomatic urethral carriers. Steere et al.,[35] in a similar uncontrolled study, were less successful in eradicating the vaginal carrier state with benzathine penicillin G or with oral penicillin V given for 7 days. A controlled study was conducted by Hall et al.[36] They found that they temporarily suppressed vaginal carriage of group B streptococci in pregnant women by giving ampicillin for one week. On follow-up examination at the time of delivery, however, the previously treated women had a comparable carrier rate to the control group and, most important, there was no difference in the infection rates of the newborn offspring in the treated or control groups. Paredes, Wong, and Yow[37] used several antibiotic regimens to treat a small number of sick and well newborns colonized with group B streptococci and were unsuccessful in eradicating the organisms from mucosal surfaces.

Attempts to identify colonized pregnant women in order to treat their offspring prophylactically are impractical because all women would have to have culture examinations performed on several occasions during pregnancy. Many infants, furthermore, are ill at the time of birth as a result of intrauterine infection from ascending bacteria, so penicillin given to the babies after delivery would represent treatment rather than prophylaxis. Yow et al.[38] treated 34 colonized women with intrapartum ampicillin. None of their offspring was colonized with group B streptococcus within 48 hours after birth, compared with a colonization rate of 58 percent in babies born to 24 untreated women. No baby in either group developed disease.

Another approach that has been evaluated is to treat all babies at birth with 1 dose of penicillin G. This strategem evolved from the observation of Steigman et al.[39] that group B streptococcal disease was not encountered at Mt. Sinai Hospital in New York during a 22-year period in which intramuscular penicillin was used as gonococcal prophylaxis. They hypothesized that prevention of streptococcal disease might have been an unplanned benefit of their gonococcal prophylaxis program.

A controlled study of penicillin prophylaxis was carried out by Siegel et al.[40-41] On a randomized schedule, 16,082 infants received a single intramuscular dose of penicillin G (50,000 U to full-term babies and 20,000 U to babies weighing less than 2,000 g), while 15,976 infants treated with tetracycline ophthalmic ointment served as the control group. The conclusions of the study were that penicillin significantly decreased the rates of disease and of asymptomatic colonization with group B streptococci in neonates without causing a significant increase in the incidence of disease due to penicillin-resistant bacteria. Late-onset streptococcal disease was equally common in the two groups. However, in a similar study at Cook County Hospital in Chicago in which only infants weighing less than 2,000 g were evaluated, no benefit of penicillin prophylaxis was found.[42] The apparent explanation for the discrepancy in results lies in the differing patterns of disease seen in the two institutions. Most infants in the Chicago study were ill at birth, while in the study of Siegel et al. illness generally developed several hours after birth in control babies.

We recommend the following approach to prophylaxis against group B streptococcal disease. If the incidence of disease is less than 2–3 cases/1000 liveborn infants, no prophylactic measure would be cost-efficient or likely to cause benefit to significant numbers of patients. If the disease rate is greater than 2–3/1000 live births, prophylaxis can be considered. The approach would depend on the pattern of disease. If illness developed after birth in most babies, the method of Siegel et al.[40-41] might have merit. If, on the other hand, most babies were ill at birth, earlier intervention with culturing of women during the third trimester to identify carriers could be undertaken. Carriers would be treated intrapartum with penicillin or ampicillin and their offspring treated immediately after birth. This approach is being evaluated,[43] but final results are not available at this time.

NECROTIZING ENTEROCOLITIS

The exact pathogenesis of necrotizing enterocolitis is not known, but experimental animal work and clinical observations suggest that it is caused by a complex set of circumstances involving host factors and bacterial factors. Efforts at prophylaxis have focused primarily on the bacterial factors. Results have been contradictory and confusing.

Because the disease occurs mainly in low birthweight infants, studies have been performed only in that group. Egan et al.[44] were the first to report a beneficial effect of oral kanamycin prophylaxis, but there were flaws in the study design.[45] Since that time some studies have reported a beneficial effect of orally administered aminoglycoside antibiotics,[46] and other similarly designed studies have failed to find a beneficial effect.[47-49] It is likely that these contradictory results stem from the fact that necrotizing enterocolitis is a multifactorial disorder and that it is very difficult to control the many variables in clinical studies.

The potential hazards of oral aminoglycoside therapy for treatment of infants with necrotizing enterocolitis were pointed out by Hansen et al.,[49] who measured potentially toxic amounts of aminoglycoside in serum from intestinal absorption superimposed on the amount of drug in serum from parenteral gentamicin therapy.

General use of oral aminoglycoside prophylaxis in nurseries for low birthweight babies can result in emergence of a population of aminoglycoside-resistant bacteria in the nurseries.[47,50]

In view of the uncertainties of beneficial effects of antibiotic prophylaxis for necrotizing enterocolitis and the potential for adverse effects, we believe that routine antimicrobial prophylaxis is not advisable for low birthweight infants who are at risk for this disorder.

For dosages see Chapter 2 or Abbreviated Guide to Dosage on Inside Covers

---

REFERENCES

1. Credé: Die Verhütung der Augenentzündung der Neugeborenen. Arch Gynaekol 17:50–53, 1881; 18:367–370, 1881; 21:179–195, 1883
2. Forbes GB, Forbes GM: Silver nitrate and the eyes of the newborn: Credé's contribution to preventive medicine. Am J Dis Child 121:1–4, 1971
3. Evanson RT, Maunsell H: A Practical Treatise on the Management and Diseases of Children. (first American edition from the first Irish edition of 1836). Philadelphia, Haswell, Barrington, & Haswell, 1838, p 115
4. Greenberg M, Vandow JE: Ophthalmia neonatorum: Evaluation of different

methods of prophylaxis in New York City. Am J Public Health 51:836–845, 1961

5. Watcher HE, Bernager MM: Prophylaxis in eyes of newborn infants: Comparison of silver nitrate and erythromycin. Mo Med 53:187–190, 1956

6. Christian JH: Comparison of ocular reactions with the use of silver nitrate and erythromycin ointment in ophthalmia neonatorum prophylaxis. J Pediatr 57:55–60, 1960

7. Davidson HH, Hill JH, Eastman NJ: Penicillin in the prophylaxis of opthalmia neonatorum. JAMA 145:1052–1055, 1951

8. Allen JH, Barrere LE: Prophylaxis of gonorrheal ophthalmia of the newborn. JAMA 141:522–526, 1949

9. Barsam PC: Specific prophylaxis of gonorrheal ophthalmia neonatorum: A review. N Engl J Med 274:731–734, 1966

10. Mathieu PL: Comparison study: Silver nitrate and tetracycline in newborn eyes: Comparison of incidence of conjunctivitis following instillation of silver nitrate or oxytetracycline into eyes of newborn infants. Am J Dis Child 95:609–611, 1968

11. Watts SG, Gleich MW: Penicillin-silver nitrate prophylaxis against gonorrheal ophthalmia of the newborn. JAMA 143:635–637, 1958

12. Yasunaga S, Kean EH: Effect of three ophthalmic solutions on chemical conjunctivitis in the neonate. Am J Dis Child 131:159–161, 1977

13. Thompson TR, Swanson RE, Wiesner PJ: Gonococcal ophthalmia neonatorum: Relationship of time of infection to relevant control measures. JAMA 228:186–188, 1974

14. Hammerslag MR, Chandler JW, Alexander ER, et al: Erythromycin ointment for ocular prophylaxis of neonatal chlamydial infection. JAMA 244:2291–2293, 1980

15. Rettig PJ, Patamasucon P, Siegel JD: Postnatal prophylaxis of chlamydial conjunctivitis. JAMA 246:2321–2322, 1981

16. Centers for Disease Control:Treatment:Sexually transmitted diseases—Treatment guidelines 1982. Morb Mortal Wkly Rep 31:358–608, 1982

17. Fairchild JP, Graber CD, Vogel EH Jr, et al: Flora of the umbilical stump: 2,479 cultures. J Pediatr 53:538–546, 1958

18. Wilson MG, Armstrong DH, Nelson RC, et al: Prolonged rupture of fetal membranes: Effect on the newborn infant. Am J Dis Child 107:138–146, 1964

19. Lipsitz PJ, Cornet JAM: Blood cultures from the umbilical vein in the newborn infant. Pediatrics 26:657–660, 1960

20. Nelson JD, Richardson J, Shelton S: The significance of bacteremia with exchange transfusions. J Pediatr 66:291–299, 1965

21. Anagnostakis D, Kamba A, Petrochilou V, et al: Risk of infection associated with umbilical vein catheterization: A prospective study in 75 newborn infants. J Pediatr 86:759–765, 1975

22. Andersen HJ, Holm SE: A bacteriological comparison between two methods of exchange transfusion. Acta Paediatr Scand 52:143–144, 1963

23. Egan EA II, Eitzman DV: Umbilical vessel catheterization. Am J Dis Child 121:213–218, 1971

24. Balagtas RC, Bell CE, Edwards LD, et al: Risk of local and systemic infections associated with umbilical vein catheterization: A prospective study in 86 newborn patients. Pediatrics 48:359–367, 1971

25. Bard H, Albert G, Teasdale F, et al: Prophylactic antibiotics in chronic umbilical artery catheterization in respiratory distress syndrome. Arch Dis Child 48:630–635, 1973

26. Kraus AN, Albert RF, Kannan MM: Contamination of umbilical catheters in the newborn infant. J Pediatr 77:965–969, 1970

27. Van Vliet PKJ, Gupta JM: Prophylactic antibiotics in umbilical artery catheterization in the newborn. Arch Dis Child 48:296–300, 1972

28. Pryles CV, Steg NL, Nair S, et al: A controlled study of the influence on the newborn of prolonged premature rupture of the amniotic membranes and/or infection in the mother. Pediatrics 31:608–622, 1963

29. Gunn GC, Mishell DR Jr, Morton DG: Premature rupture of the fetal membranes: A review. Am J Obstet Gynecol 106:469–483, 1970

30. Lebherz TB, Hellman LP, Madding R, et al: Double-blind study of premature rupture of the membranes: A report of 1,896 cases. Am J Obstet Gynecol 87:218–225, 1963

31. Shubeck F, Benson RC, Clark WW Jr, et al: Fetal hazard after rupture of the membranes. Obstet Gynecol 28:22–31, 1966

32. Light IJ, Sutherland JM, Cochran ML, et al: Ecologic relation between *Staphylococcus aureus* and *Pseudomonas* in a nursery population: Another example of bacterial interference. N Engl J Med 278:1243–1247, 1968

33. Light IJ, Atherton HD, Sutherland JM: Decreased colonization of newborn infants with *Staphylococcus aureus* 80/81: Cincinnati General Hospital, 1960–1972. J Infect Dis 131:281–285, 1975

34. Franciosi RA, Knostman JD, Zimmerman RA: Group B streptococcal neonatal and infant infections. J Pediatr 82:707–718, 1973

35. Steere AC, Aber RC, Warford LR, et al: Possible nosocomial transmission of group B streptococci in a newborn nursery. J Pediatr 87:784–787, 1975

36. Hall RT, Barnes W, Krishnan L, et al: Antibiotic treatment of parturient women colonized with group B streptococci. Am J Obstet Gynecol 124:630–634, 1976

37. Paredes A, Wong P, Yow MD: Failure of penicillin to eradicate the carrier state of group B streptococcus in infants. J Pediatr 89:191–193, 1976

38. Yow MD, Mason ED, Leeds LJ, et al: Ampicillin prevents intrapartum transmission of group B streptococcus. JAMA 241:1245–1247, 1979

39. Steigman AJ, Bottone EJ, Hanna BA: Intramuscular penicillin administration at birth: Prevention of early-onset group B streptococcal disease. Pediatrics 62:842–843, 1978

40. Siegel JD, McCracken GH Jr, Threlkeld N, et al: Single-dose penicillin prophylaxis against neonatal group B streptococcal infections: A controlled trial in 18,738 newborn infants. New Engl J Med 303:769–775, 1980

41. Siegel JD, McCracken GH Jr, Threlkeld N, et al: Single-dose penicillin prophylaxis of neonatal group B streptococcal disease: Conclusion of a 41 month controlled trial. Lancet 1:1426–1430, 1982

42. Pyati SP, Pildes RS, Jacobs NM, et al: Early penicillin in infants < 2000 gms

with early onset GBS: Is it effective? (abstract no. 1019) Pediatr Res 16:348A, 1982

43. Boyer KM, Gotoff SP, Gadzala CA, et al: Intrapartum ampicillin prophylaxis of group B streptococcal transmission based on prenatal colonization status. (abstract no. 312) Presented at the Twenty-first Interscience Conference on Antimicrobial Agents and Chemotherapy. Chicago, Nov 1981

44. Egan EA, Mantilla G, Nelson RM, et al: A prospective controlled trial of oral kanamycin in the prevention of neonatal necrotizing enterocolitis. J Pediatr 89:467–470, 1976

45. Nelson JD: Commentary. J Pediatr 89:471–472, 1976

46. Grylack LJ, Scanlon JW: Oral gentamicin therapy in the prevention of neonatal necrotizing enterocolitis: A controlled double-blind trial. Am J Dis Child 132:1192–1194, 1978

47. Boyle R, Nelson JS, Stonestreet BS, et al: Alterations in stool flora resulting from oral kanamycin prophylaxis of necrotizing enterocolitis. J Pediatr 93:857–861, 1978

48. Rowley MP, Dahlenburg GW: Gentamicin in prophylaxis of neonatal necrotizing enterocolitis. Lancet 2:532, 1978

49. Hansen TN, Ritter DA, Speer ME, et al: A randomized, controlled study of oral gentamicin in the treatment of neontal necrotizing enterocolitis. J Pediatr 97:836–839, 1980

50. Grylack L, Neugebauer D, Scanlon JW: Effects of oral antibiotics on stool flora and overall sensitivity patterns in an intensive care nursery. Pediatr Res 16:509–511, 1982

Appendix

Preferred Therapy for Specific Pathogens

Organisms	Drugs of Choice	Alternatives
Acinetobacter species	Ticarcillin + amikacin	TMP-SMX*, aminoglycoside
Aspergillus species	Amphotericin B	—
Bacteroides fragilis	Chloramphenicol; metronidazole	Mezlocillin; ticarcillin
Bacteroides, other species	Penicillin G	Other beta-lactams
Bordetella pertussis	Erythromycin	Ampicillin
Campylobacter species	(?) Erythromycin	
Candida albicans	*Topical:* nystatin	*Topical:* clotrimazole
	Systemic: amphotericin B	*Systemic:* ketoconazole
Chlamydia trachomatis	*Topical:* tetracycline; erythromycin	*Topical:* sulfacetamide
	Systemic: erythromycin	*Systemic:* sulfa; ampicillin
Citrobacter species	Aminoglycoside	Moxalactam; cefotaxime; TMP-SMX
Clostridium species	Penicillin G	Other beta-lactams
Enterobacter species	Aminoglycoside	Moxalactam; cefotaxime; TMP-SMX
Haemophilus influenzae		
Beta-lactamase negative	Ampicillin	Moxalactam; cefotaxime
Beta-lactamase positive	Moxalactam; cefotaxime	Chloramphenicol
Herpes simplex	Vidarabine; acyclovir	*Topical:* idopuridine; acyclovir; vidarabine
Klebsiella species	Aminoglycoside	Moxalactam, cefotaxime; TMP-SMX
Listeria monocytogenes	Ampicillin + gentamicin	Ampicillin + another aminoglycoside

228

Organism	First choice	Alternative
Morganella morganii	Aminoglycoside	Moxalactam; cefotaxime; TMP-SMX
Mycobacterium tuberculosis	Isoniazid + rifampin + aminoglycoside	Isoniazid + rifampin
Neisseria gonorrheae		
Beta-lactamase negative	Penicillin G	Other beta-lactams
Beta-lactamase positive	Moxalactam; cefotaxime	TMP-SMX; cefoxitin
Neisseria meningitidis	Penicillin G	Other beta-lactams; chloramphenicol
Proteus mirabilis	Ampicillin	TMP-SMX; aminoglycoside; cephalosporin
Proteus vulgaris	Aminoglycoside	Moxalactam; cefotaxime; TMP-SMX
Providencia species	Aminoglycoside	TMP-SMX; moxalactam; cefotaxime
Pseudomonas aeruginosa	Ticarcillin (mezlocillin) aminoglycoside	—
Pseudomonas cepacia	TMP-SMX	—
Salmonella species	Ampicillin	TMP-SMX; chloramphenicol
Serratia marcescens	Aminoglycoside	TMP-SMX; moxalactam; cefotaxime
Shigella species	TMP-SMX	Ampicillin (if susceptible)
Staphylococcus aureus		
Beta-lactamase negative	Penicillin G	Other beta-lactams
Beta-lactamase positive	Penicillinase-resistant penicillin	Vancomycin
Staphyloccus epidermidis	Penicillinase-resistant penicillin	Vancomycin
Streptococcus species		
Enterococcus	Ampicillin + aminoglycoside	Vancomycin + aminoglycoside
Other species	Penicillin G	Other beta-lactams (except moxalactam); (vancomycin for penicillin-reesistant pneumococci)
Toxoplasma gondii	Spiramycin (outside U.S.A.)	Sulfa + pyrimethamine
Treponema pallidum	Penicillin G	—
Varicella-Zoster	Vidarabine	—

*Trimethoprim-sulfamethoxazole

Index

230

a
b
3 c
4 d
5 e
6 f
7 g
8 h
9 i
8 0 j